CW01189835

Life

STUDENT'S BOOK | ADVANCED

NATIONAL GEOGRAPHIC
LEARNING

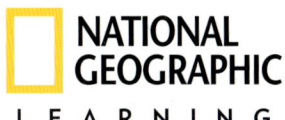

PAUL DUMMETT
JOHN HUGHES
HELEN STEPHENSON

Australia • Brazil • Mexico • Singapore • United Kingdom • United States

Contents

Unit	Grammar	Vocabulary	Real life (functions)	Pronunciation
1 Lessons for life pages 9–20	time phrases the continuous aspect	personality and identity wordbuilding: binomial pairs word focus: *life*	getting to know people	linking in word pairs merged words in everyday phrases
VIDEO: Arctic wisdom **page 18** ▶ REVIEW **page 20**				
2 More than a job pages 21–32	perfect forms passive forms	wordbuilding: phrasal verb *get* idioms: safety word focus: *foot/feet* personal qualities	presenting yourself	word stress
VIDEO: Climbing Yosemite **page 30** ▶ REVIEW **page 32**				
3 Design for life pages 33–44	qualifiers intensifying adverbs	describing towns adverb + adjective collocations word focus: *ground*	expressing opinions	*quite, fairly* and *pretty* stress in intensifying adverbs linking vowel sounds (intrusion)
VIDEO: A story of solutions **page 42** ▶ REVIEW **page 44**				
4 Innovation pages 45–56	future probability past modals	wordbuilding: *-able* phrasal verb *come* word focus: *give*	making a short pitch speaking skill: making key points	weak forms in past modals word stress
VIDEO: This man risked it all **page 54** ▶ REVIEW **page 56**				
5 The magic of travel pages 57–68	emphatic structures avoiding repetition	repeated word pairs wordbuilding: synonyms word focus: *matter*	telling an anecdote speaking skill: linking events	*do, does* and *did* stress in short responses long sounds
VIDEO: On the road: Andrew McCarthy **page 66** ▶ REVIEW **page 68**				
6 Body matters pages 69–80	phrasal verbs verb patterns	wordbuilding: compound words injuries idioms: health word focus: *face*	discussing proposals speaking skill: proposing and conceding a point	stress in two-syllable verbs toning down negative statements
VIDEO: The art of parkour **page 78** ▶ REVIEW **page 80**				

Listening	Reading	Critical thinking	Speaking	Writing
two speakers talk about important lessons in life a talk by a sociologist about understanding what makes people who they are	an article about the lessons we learn from the past an article about the language of Shakespeare	purpose	your favourite saying situations in your life call my bluff	taking notes writing skill: using abbreviations
a talk about the livelihood of Kazakh nomads an interview with a firefighter	an article about the Moken people of Myanmar an article about rock climbing in Yosemite	analysing language	more than a job safety features your comfort zone	a covering letter or email writing skill: fixed expressions
a description of a photograph an interview with an architect about small homes	an article about two towns with individual characters an article about the architect Zaha Hadid	summarizing	your home town a bit of luxury how spaces affect you	an opinion essay writing skill: discourse markers
a news report about bionic body parts an interview about the inspiration for inventions	an article about the future of bendable technology an article about a social entrepreneur	finding counter arguments	future solutions how people managed in the past a social business	a proposal writing skill: making recommendations
an extract from a talk by a travel writer a radio interview about holidays to unknown places	a travel blog about different approaches to travelling an article about travel in graphic novels	evaluating sources	how you travel a mystery tour knowing places	a review writing skill: using descriptive words
a conversation between two friends about health and exercise an interview with an ultrarunner about sports injuries	an article about different exercise regimes an article about beauty	author influence	exercise trends describing an injury does beauty sell?	a formal report writing skill: avoiding repetition

Unit	Grammar	Vocabulary	Real life (functions)	Pronunciation
7 Digital media pages 81–92	passive reporting verbs nominalization	wordbuilding: verb prefix *out* idioms: business buzz words word focus: *break*	making a podcast speaking skill: hedging language	new words
VIDEO: Talking dictionaries page 90 ▶ REVIEW page 92				
8 The music in us pages 93–104	the adverb *just* purpose and result	themes of songs idioms: music word focus: *hit*	your favourite music speaking skill: responding to questions	expressions with *just* intonation to express uncertainty
VIDEO: A biopic page 102 ▶ REVIEW page 104				
9 Window on the past pages 105–116	linking words present and perfect participles	wordbuilding: verb + preposition crime and punishment word focus: *board*	checking, confirming and clarifying	silent letters
VIDEO: Collecting the past page 114 ▶ REVIEW page 116				
10 Social living pages 117–128	adverbs and adverbial phrases negative adverbials and inversion	being a good member of society having fun word focus: *free*	making conversation speaking skill: showing interest	sentence stress intonation and elision
VIDEO: Initiation with ants page 126 ▶ REVIEW page 128				
11 Reason and emotion pages 129–140	unreal past forms conditionals and inversion	feelings wordbuilding: heteronyms word focus: *beyond*	recognizing feelings	heteronyms adjectives ending in *-ed*
VIDEO: Madeline the robot tamer page 138 ▶ REVIEW page 140				
12 Mother nature pages 141–152	approximation and vague language *would*	wordbuilding: adverb + adjective collocations idioms: adjective collocations word focus: *move*	a debate speaking skill: interrupting	intonation in interruptions
VIDEO: Three years and 6,000 miles on a horse page 150 ▶ REVIEW page 152				

COMMUNICATION ACTIVITIES page 153 ▶ GRAMMAR SUMMARY page 156 ▶ AUDIOSCRIPTS page 180

Listening	Reading	Critical thinking	Speaking	Writing
a talk by a journalist about digital technology an interview about social media marketing	a study of global facts about selfies an article about a day at a hackers' conference	identifying personal opinion	the impact of digital media brands attitudes to security	a news report writing skill: cautious language
an interview with a busker a talk by a neuroscientist about music therapy	an interview with a musician about cultural influences a review of a documentary about Bob Marley	identifying key points	themes of songs how to relax a charity concert	a description writing skill: parallel structures
a talk about the significance of historical objects a story about an unusual crime	an article about what personal letters reveal about our past a story about hidden treasure	unanswered questions	an important past event a case of fraud historical irony	describing a past event writing skill: sequencing events
an extract from a radio programme about ethnic communities a podcast about the importance of play	an article about ant society an article about the Hadza of Tanzania	reading between the lines	being a good member of society social games feeling free	a discursive essay writing skill: referring to evidence
a short talk by a photographer about photographing people a lecture about irrational thinking	an article about understanding emotions an article about artificial intelligence in the future	analysing structure	modern life mind games technology and occupations	an email message writing skill: avoiding misunderstandings
three people describe the landscape where they live an extract from a radio interview about the Japanese poet Basho	an article about the importance of geo-literacy an article about how wildlife are moving into our cities	different perspectives	natural and man-made features events in nature the animal and human worlds	a letter to a newspaper writing skill: persuasive language

Life around the world – in 12 videos

Unit 11 Madeline the robot tamer

Discover how one project is bringing humans and robots closer together.

Unit 1 Arctic wisdom

Learn how generations pass on their accumulated wisdom in Iqaluit, Canada.

Canada

France

Spain

USA

Unit 2 Climbing Yosemite

Find out how Jimmy Chin made a career out of mountaineer photography.

Jamaica

Unit 3 A story of solutions

Find out about how an architecture company made an impact on a small town in the USA.

Unit 5 On the road: Andrew McCarthy

Brazil

Learn how a travel experience changed the life of travel writer Andrew McCarthy.

Unit 8 A biopic

Learn about the inspiration behind the making of the biopic *Marley*.

Unit 10 Initiation with ants

Find out about an unusual ceremony in the Amazonian jungle in Brazil.

Unit 6 The art of parkour

Learn about the history of free running.

Unit 7 Talking dictionaries

Learn about a project which is helping to preserve dying languages.

Unit 12 Three years and 6,000 miles on a horse

Find out about the impact of an unusual journey on horseback.

Russia

Mongolia

Palestine

China

Uganda

Unit 9 Collecting the past

Find out how China's cultural heritage is being preserved by shopping.

Unit 4 This man risked it all

Learn how Sanga Moses took a risk to set up a social enterprise in Uganda.

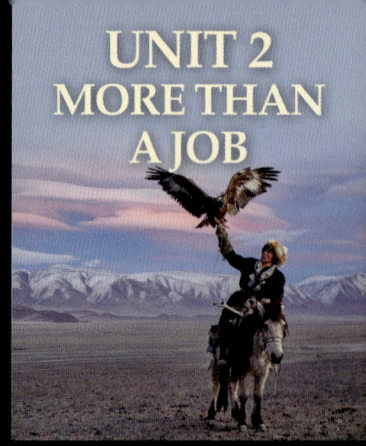
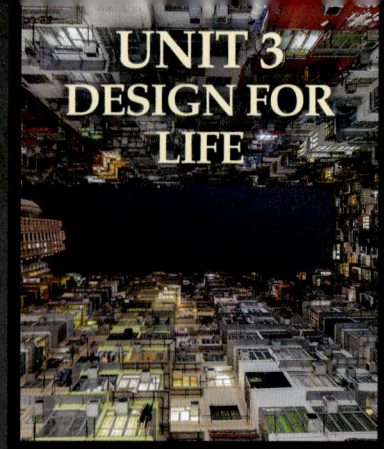

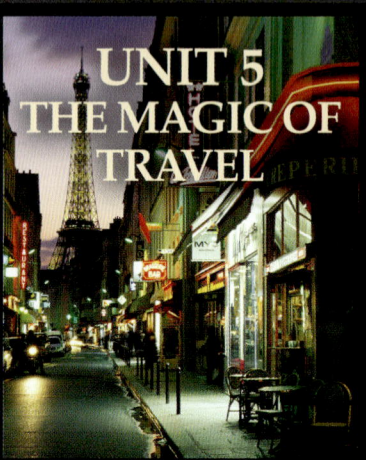

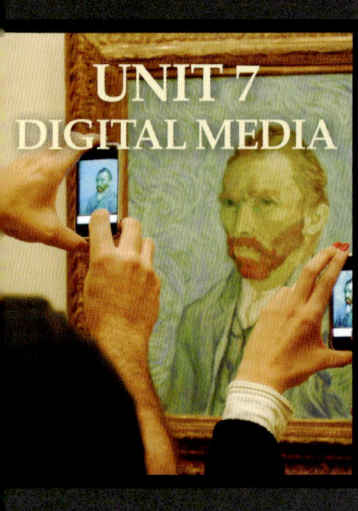

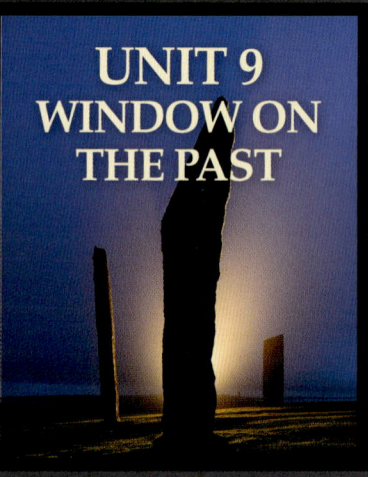
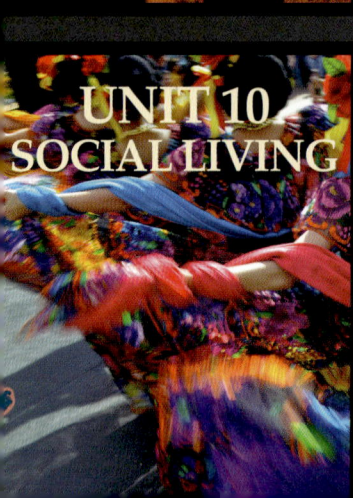

Unit 1 Lessons for life

A Tuareg tribesman at twilight, Libya

FEATURES

10 Learning from the past
The lessons we learn from the past

12 What makes us who we are?
Understanding what makes people who they are

14 Immortal words
The language of Shakespeare

18 Arctic wisdom
A video about how Inuit elders pass on their knowledge

1 Work in pairs. Look at the photo and these Tuareg proverbs. What do the proverbs tell you about the Tuareg attitude to life?

"Better to walk without knowing where than to sit doing nothing."

"In life, it is always possible to reach agreement in the end."

"Acquiring things you do not need will kill you."

2 ▶1 Listen to two people talking about important lessons they have learned in life. Answer the questions.

1 What advice does each speaker now try to follow?
2 What experience led them to learn this lesson?
3 Which lesson do you think a Tuareg person would agree with? Why?

3 ▶1 Complete the phrases the speakers use to describe the life lessons they have learned. Then listen again and check.

1 The most _____ lesson I've learned was …
2 That's become a sort of _____ principle for me …
3 A good rule of _____ is …
4 But it's a lot easier _____ than done …
5 I always make a _____ of not getting …

4 Think of an occasion when you learned an important lesson or found a good way of doing something (e.g. about people, friends, family, money, work, health, risk, fun). Describe what happened. What did you do? What have you learned from it?

my life ▶ YOUR FAVOURITE SAYING ▶ SITUATIONS IN YOUR LIFE ▶ CALL MY BLUFF ▶ GETTING TO KNOW PEOPLE ▶ TAKING NOTES

9

reading **lessons in life** • grammar **time phrases** • speaking **your favourite saying**

1a Learning from the past

Reading

1 Work in pairs. Read the quotation. Do you think this is good advice? Is it easy to follow? Discuss with your partner.

"Learn from the mistakes of others. You can't live long enough to make them all yourself."

Eleanor Roosevelt, Diplomat

2 Read the article. Match the person (1–2) with the type of lesson they taught (a–c). There is one extra type of lesson.

1 Confucius
2 Nelson Mandela

a a lesson that is difficult to follow
b a lesson that has been misinterpreted
c a lesson that has been forgotten

3 Read the article again. According to the article, are the sentences true (T) or false (F)?

1 Sometimes people don't want to follow the lessons of the past.
2 A lot of Chinese people feel that their society is not interested in the past.
3 China's rapid development has begun to slow down.
4 Mandela was not opposed to violence in principle.
5 Nelson Mandela wanted the two sides in South Africa to forget what had happened in the past.
6 The writer suggests that most people are too selfish.

4 Find words or expressions in the article with these meanings.

1 show the right direction (para 1)
2 period of significant growth (para 2)
3 do something as a result of information or advice (para 3)
4 work hard towards a goal (para 4)
5 copy someone's behaviour (para 4)

LEARNING FROM THE PAST

▶ 2

Why do we never seem to learn from the past? The mistakes or correct actions of others should point the way for us in the future. But either we forget these lessons or we fail to follow them or, in some cases, we deliberately choose to ignore them. Of all the lessons that we have to learn, perhaps the most difficult is how not to be selfish or think only of ourselves.

In China, the government is trying to remind people of the lessons given by Confucius, the ancient philosopher. Because of China's economic boom in recent years, the government has become worried that people are becoming more selfish and individualistic. Many Chinese have been saying for some time that the traditional values in society of harmony, respect and hard work have been lost. Accordingly, a few years ago the government focused attention again on the teachings of Confucius.

Prior to the 1990s, Confucianism had not been fashionable, but in a country which is currently developing at a dizzying speed, his teachings offer a sense of stability and order. Nowadays, people often talk about Confucius' idea of a 'harmonious society', even if they do not always act on it.

Sometimes it is difficult to learn lessons because the standards of the 'teacher' are so high. This is certainly the case with Nelson Mandela, who tried to spread the message of reconciliation to two sides in South Africa who hated and distrusted each other deeply. Mandela had always been committed to peace, and while he was living in prison, he decided that the only way to unite his divided country was if the two sides could talk about what had happened in the past and begin to rebuild some measure of trust. All those who strive for peace know that in the long term they will have to begin a dialogue with their enemy. Yet few are able to follow the example set by Mandela, because it requires such a high degree of unselfishness. It seems that heeding this warning – not to be selfish – is perhaps the hardest lesson of all for people to learn.

'Consideration for others is the basis of a good life, a good society.'
Confucius

'If you want to make peace with your enemy, you have to work with your enemy.'
Nelson Mandela

dizzying (adj) /ˈdɪziɪŋ/ very fast and confusing
reconciliation (n) /ˌrek(ə)nsɪlɪˈeɪʃ(ə)n/ making peace and re-establishing relations

Grammar time phrases

> **TIME PHRASES**
>
> Certain time phrases are commonly (but not always) used with certain tenses.
>
> **Present simple:** *often, never, every week, generally*
> **Present continuous:** *now, at the moment, this week*
> **Past simple:** *two days ago, last week, at the time, when*
> **Past continuous:** *at the time*
> **Present perfect simple:** *just, recently, so far, over the last two years, how long, for, since (2010), already, yet, ever, never*
> **Present perfect continuous:** *how long, for, just, recently, since*
> **Past perfect simple and continuous:** *already, before that, up to then*
> **will, going to and present continuous for future:** *next week, in three days / in three days' time, soon, on Friday*
>
> For further information and practice, see page 156.

5 Look at the grammar box and the time phrases (1–8) below. Then follow the steps (a–b).

1 in recent years
2 for some time
3 a few years ago
4 prior to the 1990s
5 currently
6 nowadays
7 while
8 in the long term

a Find the verbs that are used in the article with each of the time phrases and identify the tenses.
b Match the time phrases (1–8) with the tense in the grammar box.

6 Complete the sentences with these time phrases.

| at the moment   at the time   before that |
| ever   fifty years ago   for years |
| in the coming years   nowadays   often |
| over the last 25 years |

a ¹_____ military service was compulsory in the UK. But ² _____ young people don't have to go into the army. I think this will change ³ _____ because there is a feeling that young people need more discipline.
b ⁴ _____ , people have definitely become more greedy. I've been saying ⁵ _____ that it is not right for anyone to earn a hundred times the average salary.
c I'm having an interesting debate with my father ⁶ _____ . He says that young people don't ⁷ _____ show respect to their elders anymore. But I don't think you can just demand respect; you have to earn it.
d When I was forty, I decided to stop working so hard. ⁸ _____ , I was working sixty hours a week. It was the best decision that I have ⁹ _____ made. ¹⁰ _____ , I had had no time to enjoy life.

7 Complete the conversations with the correct form of the verbs. Use the time phrases to help you decide which form to use.

1 A: How long _____ (you / learn) Japanese? You speak it really well.
   B: Thanks! I _____ (start) having lessons two years ago. But I _____ (learn) a few words on a trip to Japan before that.
2 C: _____ (you / try) out the new gym yet? I _____ (go) last night. It's great.
   D: No. Every week I _____ (tell) myself I'm going to go, but I never _____ (seem) to make it. I'm sure I _____ (get) there in the end, though.
3 E: What _____ (you / work) on currently?
   F: Well, for the last two weeks I _____ (do) some work at the university computing department.
   E: Oh, that explains it. I _____ (see) you outside the university building the other day.

8 Complete the sentences by writing facts about yourself. Write one sentence which is not true. Then work in pairs. Compare sentences with your partner and try to guess the false sentence.

1 My work? Currently, I …
   Currently, I'm looking for a new job.
2 I like seeing new places. A few years ago, I …
3 In my free time, I usually …
4 I have never … , but I've always wanted to.
5 I didn't … last weekend, because I had already …
6 I met my best friend when I … . I … at the time.
7 I … for several years.
8 I don't have the time or money at the moment, but sooner or later I …

9 Complete the advice about life using these words. Then compare answers with your partner. Which piece of advice do you like most? Why?

| ever   for   in   never   now   while |

1 Life is what happens _____ you are making other plans.
2 Value your friends. If you ignore them _____ a long time, they will start to ignore you.
3 When you're feeling stressed, ask yourself this question: _____ five years, will the problem still seem so important?
4 No one has _____ become poor by giving.
5 Get out more. A whole world of amazing experiences is waiting for you right _____ .
6 You should _____ take yourself too seriously.

Speaking my life

10 Work in groups. Each write down two of your favourite (or least favourite!) sayings about life. Then discuss your choices.

my life ▸ YOUR FAVOURITE SAYING ▸ SITUATIONS IN YOUR LIFE ▸ CALL MY BLUFF ▸ GETTING TO KNOW PEOPLE
▸ TAKING NOTES

vocabulary and listening personality and identity • wordbuilding binomial pairs •
pronunciation linking in word pairs • grammar the continuous aspect • speaking situations in your life

1b What makes us who we are?

A Paris painter next to his self-portrait

Vocabulary and listening
personality and identity

1 Work in pairs. Look at the photo and caption. Discuss the questions.

1 Why is the painter putting his hands up?
2 What impression of the painter do you get from his self-portrait?

2 Look at the expressions to describe people. Answer the questions.

> a control freak   a dreamer
> a driven person   a family person
> a free spirit   a joker
> the life and soul of the party
> an outgoing type

1 What do you think each expression means?
2 Which expressions do you think are positive, negative or neutral?
3 Give an example of someone you know who fits each description.

3 Look at these factors which can give people information about you. Which do you think are the most significant? Number them in order (1–8) of importance.

a   your friends   e   your life experiences
b   your work   f   your interests/hobbies
c   your age   g   your background
d   your character   h   your beliefs and values

4 ▶ 3 Listen to a sociologist describing how we define ourselves. Tick (✓) the factors in Exercise 3 that he mentions. Which is the most important, according to him?

5 ▶ 3 Listen to the talk again. Choose the correct option to complete the sentences.

1 The speaker thinks the question 'What do you do?' can sound *aggressive / judgmental* as a conversation starter.
2 Sally has been defined by her background because she didn't grow up in *the city / a normal family*.
3 Sarah has dedicated her life to helping people who *are ill / live in poor countries*.
4 The most important thing for John about his work is the *challenge / security*.
5 Jack hasn't been in a relationship since he was *34 / 25*.
6 Anne wants school children to eat *better / more vegetarian* food.

Wordbuilding binomial pairs

> **WORDBUILDING binomial pairs**
>
> Certain pairs of words in English are irreversible, i.e. they always appear in the same order.
> *rock and roll* (never ~~*roll and rock*~~), *law and order*
>
> For further practice, see Workbook page 7 and 11.

6 Look at the wordbuilding box. Choose the correct form of these irreversible word pairs (a–b).

a He picks up *pieces and bits / bits and pieces* of work *as and when / when and as* he can.
b It seems that what defines people *first and foremost / foremost and first* is experience.

7 Complete the word pairs using these words. Discuss what you think each phrase means.

| fro | games | large | pains | quiet | sound |
| sweet | then | wide | | | |

1 I need **peace and** _____ to concentrate.
2 They all came back from their canoeing trip **safe and** _____ . No one was injured, but most of them had a few **aches and** _____ .
3 Try not to give a long talk. **By and** _____ , it's better to keep it **short and** _____ .
4 People come from **far and** _____ to see Stonehenge. There are busloads of tourists coming **to and** _____ all day.
5 You think my job is all **fun and** _____ , but actually **now and** _____ we do some serious work too!

8 Pronunciation linking in word pairs

▶ 4 Listen to the word pairs in Exercise 7. Notice a) how the words are linked and b) the pronunciation of *and* in the word pairs. Then practise reading the sentences.

Grammar the continuous aspect

> **THE CONTINUOUS ASPECT**
>
> **Present continuous**
> 1 … you feel as if people **are always judging** you …
> 2 *It's* now **becoming** a national movement.
>
> **Present perfect continuous**
> 3 He **has been saying** that since he was 35.
>
> **Past continuous**
> 4 When his children were born, he **was working** as a carpet salesman.
>
> **Past perfect continuous**
> 5 At one point, he **had been intending** to leave the company …
>
> **Future continuous**
> 6 In a few years, he **won't be moving** about anymore.
>
> For further information and practice, see page 156.

9 Look at the grammar box. Which verb form in bold describes something which:

a is a current trend?
b we expect to be happening (now or) in the future?
c started in the past and is still continuing?
d is the background to another more important event in the past?
e was in progress up to a point in the past?
f happens regularly and is irritating?

10 Work in pairs. What is the difference in meaning, if any, between these verb forms?

1 What *do you do / are you doing*?
2 My husband *is always phoning / always phones* me at work.
3 *I've been reading / I've read* the book you gave me.
4 When I left school, I *was working / worked* at a restaurant at weekends.
5 This time next week, *I'll be sitting / I'll sit* on a beach in the Bahamas.
6 He *had been working / had worked* as a nurse before he became a paramedic.
7 She *was living / had been living / lived* in Germany before she moved to this country.
8 California is eight hours behind us. Anne-Marie *will be going / usually goes* to bed now.

11 Complete the sentences using the appropriate continuous form of the verbs.

1 Marlon's a fantastic football player, isn't he? I _____ (watch) him playing the other day. I expect in a few years he _____ (play) professionally. Apparently, some clubs _____ (already / watch) him.
2 Katja is such a great friend. Last week I _____ (feel) really fed up about work and she gave me some chocolates that she _____ (save) for a special occasion.
3 Marta _____ (get) very eccentric. She keeps budgerigars and recently she's started letting them out of their cages; so they _____ (fly) all over the house. I _____ (sit) in her kitchen the other day and one flew down and landed on the table.

Speaking my life

12 Think of examples of the following things. Then work in pairs and take turns to tell each other your ideas and ask follow-up questions.

- a habit of other people that irritates you
- two things that you imagine people you know will be doing right now
- a situation that you hope is temporary
- something you haven't finished but keep meaning to
- something you had been intending to do but then changed your mind

reading the language of Shakespeare • critical thinking purpose • word focus *life* • speaking call my bluff

1c Immortal words

Reading

1 Work in pairs. Discuss the questions.

1 Who are the most famous writers in your country's history? What did they write?
2 What Shakespeare plays or characters can you name? What do you know about them?

2 Read the article. According to the author, why are Shakespeare's plays still so popular today?

3 Read the article again and answer the questions.

1 What adjective describes what England was like in Shakespeare's time? (para 1)
2 What new element did Shakespeare bring to play writing, according to Bloom?
3 Why does Hamlet find it difficult to make a decision?
4 In *Romeo and Juliet*, what is the nurse's attitude to relationships?
5 Which adverb means that Shakespeare was good at expressing ideas in just a few words? (para 4)
6 What verb tells you that Shakespeare created new words and expressions? (para 4)

4 Look at the expressions in italics in paragraph 4. Use them to replace the words in bold below.

1 I need a new jacket. This one **is past its best.**
2 I'm 24. I have money and a university degree. **I can do anything I want to.**
3 He said that one of the shops in town would have the right battery, but it turned out to be **a search for something that couldn't be found.**
4 What the critics say is **not significant**. What matters is whether the public like the film.
5 Everyone says it's **an obvious result** that Johanna will win, but I'm not so certain.
6 There's no point telling her he's no good. **You can't see the faults in the person you love.**
7 The teacher got us to play a game to **help people relax at the start.**
8 After six different jobs, I'm with my first company again. I've **arrived back at the starting point.**

Critical thinking purpose

5 Which option(s) (a–d) describes the author's main purpose for writing this article? Underline the sentences in the article that tell you this.

a to review Harold Bloom's book
b to explain why Shakespeare is popular today
c to examine if Shakespeare's reputation is justified
d to examine Shakespeare's contribution to modern-day English

6 Did the author state her purpose at any point? In which of these writing types do you think it is important for an author to begin by stating the reason for writing?

- a description
- a job application
- a business report
- a personal letter

7 Do you think the author achieved her purpose? Why? / Why not?

Word focus *life*

8 Look at the article again. Find words or expressions with the word *life* that mean:

1 realistic (para 2)
2 for all one's life (para 2)
3 with a 'big' personality (para 3)

9 Work in pairs. Look at the expressions with *life* in bold. Discuss what they mean.

1 I sold my old Citroen 2CV car last year for £300. Now I've just read that they've become really valuable! That's **the story of my life.**
2 Work stress is just **a fact of life** these days – you have to learn to deal with it.
3 There were people at the conference from **all walks of life** – writers, students, business people.
4 My son was worried about going to university, but now he's **having the time of his life.**
5 Thanks for driving me to the station – it was a real **life-saver**. I'd have missed my train.

10 Work in groups. Each think of a personal example for two of the expressions in Exercises 8 and 9.

Not doing well in exams has been the story of my life!

Speaking my life

11 Work in two groups of three. Play the game *Call my bluff* using words coined by Shakespeare.

Group A: Turn to page 153.

Group B: Turn to page 154.

- For each word, rewrite the true definition in your own words, then write two false definitions. Write example sentences for each definition.
- Group A reads the three definitions of the first word. Group B must guess which is the true definition.
- Group B then reads the definitions of their first word for Group A to guess the true one.
- Then repeat this procedure with the other words.

12 Think of an aspect of your life. Choose a word related to this, and find the English word. Then play *Call my bluff* with that word.

14

Unit 1 **Lessons for life**

▶ 5

The sixteenth-century dramatist Ben Jonson generously called his rival, Shakespeare, a writer 'not of an age, but for all time'. And so it has proved to be, because Shakespeare's plays are still the most translated and most performed of any playwright's in the world. But if you ask people the reason for Shakespeare's continued popularity, you get different answers. Some say he was a great storyteller, others that the magic lies in the beauty of his poetry. Some say it is simply because he left us a huge volume of work, which was written during a vibrant time in English history, particularly in the theatre.

A more interesting answer that I came across recently is one put forward by the critic Harold Bloom in his book *Shakespeare: The Invention of the Human*. Bloom argues that Shakespeare gave us something that the world had not seen in literature before – characters with personalities, and particularly weaknesses, that we could relate to. These lifelike characters and the observations that Shakespeare made about the human condition are really what Jonson was referring to when he talked about Shakespeare's universal appeal. For Bloom, a lifelong fan of the poet, English speakers have Shakespeare to thank for much of their current language, cultural references and their understanding of human psychology.

While some might disagree with Bloom's assertion about the invention of 'personality' in literature – many earlier storytellers like Homer and Petrarch could claim this – there is no doubt that Shakespeare's characters resonate with people very strongly. We sympathize with poor Hamlet because we all know that frustrating situation where our hearts tell us one thing must be true and our heads another. We laugh at the larger-than-life nurse in *Romeo and Juliet* because of the amusing way she offers advice to Juliet about relationships, putting practical considerations before romance; she is a person that we too have met. The name Lady Macbeth has become synonymous with cold, over-ambitious women; while the character of Iago still serves as a warning about the dangers of jealousy and how it leads to the manipulation of others.

Of course the language plays a big part too. The observations about people and life are made more memorable by the way in which they are phrased, both succinctly and poetically. Shakespeare has been dead for 400 years, but certain words and sayings of his still exist in the English language today. Whether you are 'fashionable' or 'faint-hearted', thank Shakespeare, who probably coined the terms. Iago promises to 'wear his heart on his sleeve', a phrase still commonly used for people who do not try to hide their true feelings. In fact, it is amazing just how great Shakespeare's influence on everyday modern language has been. Take, for example, these commonly used phrases: *a foregone conclusion, come full circle, has seen better days, break the ice, neither here nor there, the world is my oyster, a wild goose chase, love is blind.*

Bloom's title *The Invention of the Human* may seem a bit strong. 'The enduring humanity of Shakespeare', on the other hand, would not be an exaggeration.

---

enduring (adj) /ɪnˈdjʊərɪŋ/ lasting a long time
faint-hearted (adj) /ˌfeɪnt ˈhɑː(r)tɪd/ lacking courage to act
resonate with (v) /ˈrezəneɪt/ create a feeling that something is familiar or relevant

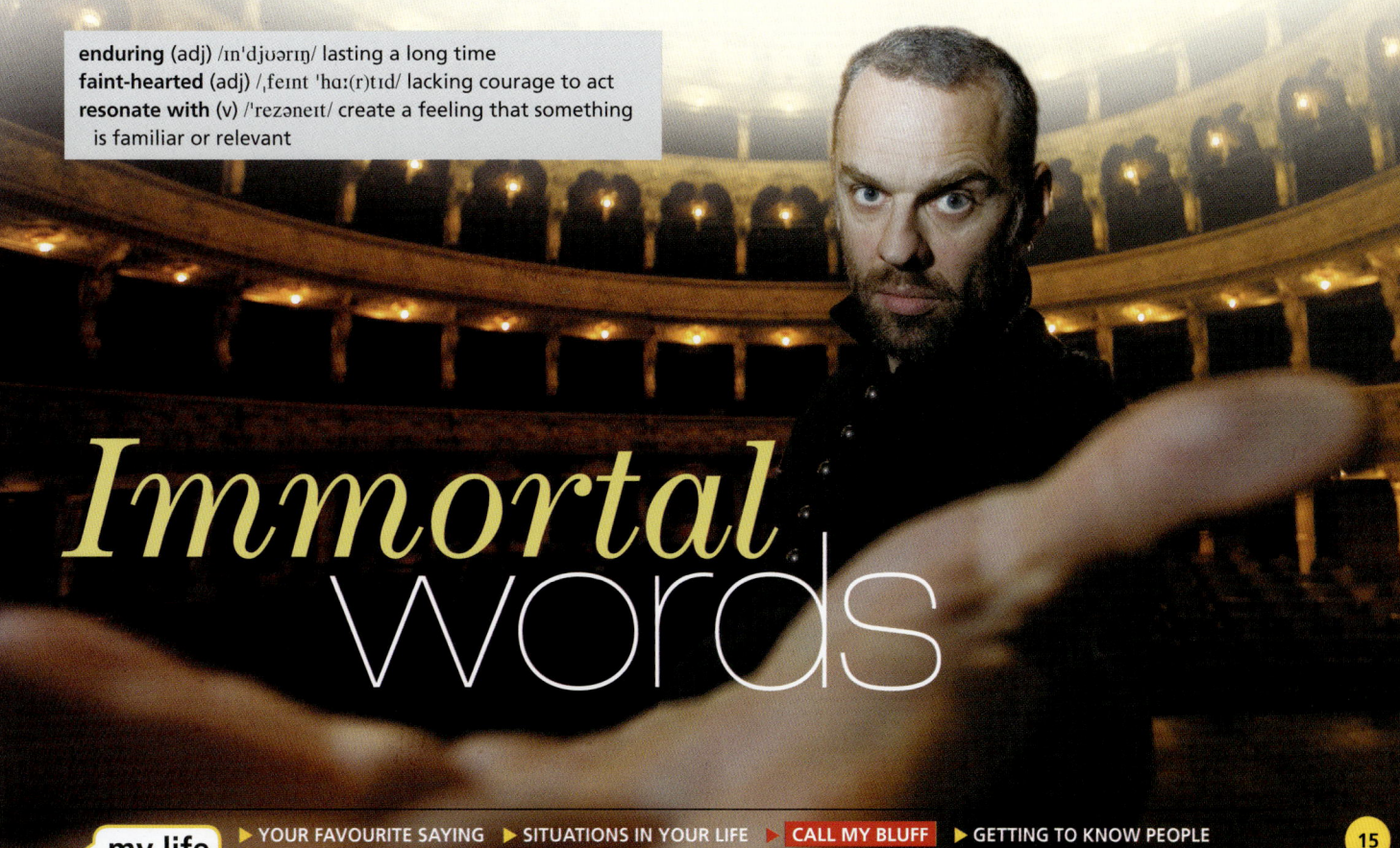

Immortal words

my life ▶ YOUR FAVOURITE SAYING ▶ SITUATIONS IN YOUR LIFE ▶ **CALL MY BLUFF** ▶ GETTING TO KNOW PEOPLE
▶ TAKING NOTES

real life **getting to know people** • pronunciation **merged words in everyday phrases**

1d How did you get into that?

Real life getting to know people

1 Work in pairs. Discuss the questions.

1 What kind of subjects do you generally like to talk about – sport, entertainment, the news, family and friends, work, something else?
2 What do you find are good conversation topics for getting to know other people?

2 Write three tips for a blog about 'getting to know people'. Then share your ideas with the class.

3 ▶6 Look at the conversation openers for getting to know people. Then listen to six short conversations. Tick (✓) the conversation opener they use in each conversation.

> ▶ **GETTING TO KNOW PEOPLE**
>
> Hi, I don't think we've met. I'm …
> Hi. Is it your first day at college too?
> Hey, I like your jacket.
> Whereabouts are you from?
> So, what do you do?
> What did you think of the show?
> This is a long queue, isn't it?
> Have you seen that film everyone's talking about?
> I'm supposed to have given up sweet things, but I can't stop eating this cake.

4 ▶6 Listen to the conversations again. Make notes on the follow-up questions that each person starting the conversation asked. Then compare answers with your partner.

5 Pronunciation merged words in everyday phrases

a ▶7 Listen to these questions and notice how the underlined words merge together when said quickly.

1 I <u>don't think</u> we've met.
2 Is it <u>your first day</u> too?
3 <u>What do you</u> do?
4 What did you <u>think of the</u> show?
5 <u>What kind of films</u> do you like?

b ▶8 Listen to these questions and write in the missing words.

1 _____ eat here?
2 _____ living in New York?
3 _____ apartment have you got?
4 _____ the new building?
5 _____ coffee or something?

6 Work in pairs. Act out two of the conversations for getting to know people you heard in Exercise 3. Use the same conversation openers and follow-up questions. Answer as naturally as possible.

7 Work with a new partner. Act out two more conversations. Follow these steps.

- Choose two of the conversation openers in the box that you did not hear in Exercise 3.
- Think of follow-up questions you might ask.
- Act out the conversations.

my life ▶ YOUR FAVOURITE SAYING ▶ SITUATIONS IN YOUR LIFE ▶ CALL MY BLUFF ▶ **GETTING TO KNOW PEOPLE** ▶ TAKING NOTES

writing taking notes • writing skill using abbreviations   Unit 1 Lessons for life

1e Your first day

Writing taking notes

1 Do you write notes sometimes on things you read or listen to? In what situations do you write notes? What do the notes consist of? What do you do with them?

2 ▶9 Look at the notes taken by a student at a university orientation day. Then listen to an extract from the talk and complete the information where the student put *???* in points 1 and 2.

Talk by Principal to new students   ???

1 Course reg 10 a.m. – 3 p.m. Mon in main uni hall – compulsory.

2 Overseas students. i.e. all except UK and ???, must take docs to Admissions office – incl. education certificates, student visas + bank account details – by end of next week.

3 Uni has 'buddy' system (a 2nd year student) to help OS sts know where things are and what to do.

4 Most courses approx. 9-12 contact hrs p.w.; plan study time carefully. Lots of places to work, e.g. faculty library, main library, IT centre.

5 If worried about study or sthg else, see student counsellor. NB each group has native speaker counsellor.

6 Extra academic writing skills tuition available for 1st year sts – details in student booklet (times, level, etc.).

---

3 Work in pairs. What other information did the speaker give that isn't in notes 1 and 2? Discuss with your partner.

4 ▶9 Listen again and check your answers. Why do you think this information wasn't included?

5 Writing skill using abbreviations

a Work in pairs. How many different abbreviations can you find in the notes? Try to guess what each one means.

b Compare your answers in Exercise 5a with another pair. Did you guess the same meanings? Which abbreviations have the following meanings?

Shortened words   Latin abbreviations
a including   e for example
b roughly   f that is to say
c please note
d and so on

c We use abbreviations in semi-formal writing and when writing in note form, but not in more formal contexts. In which of the following could abbreviations be used?

1 an academic essay
2 your notes on a book you have read
3 a letter of complaint
4 an internal email to a close colleague

d Look at this email message and rewrite it in note form. Exchange notes with your partner, cover the original email and try to reconstruct it from the notes.

> Please note that the meeting with Ellis & Company will be tomorrow, Tuesday 12th May at 3 o'clock. Please can you let me know approximately how many people from your department will be attending and if you need further information. Thanks.

6 ▶10 Listen to a talk from a university tutor about reading for your university course and take notes. Remember to include only the relevant points and to use abbreviations where necessary.

7 Exchange notes with your partner. Use these questions to check your notes.

- Do the notes include the same relevant points?
- Have they left out unnecessary information?
- Do they use abbreviations correctly?

---

my life ▸ YOUR FAVOURITE SAYING ▸ SITUATIONS IN YOUR LIFE ▸ CALL MY BLUFF ▸ GETTING TO KNOW PEOPLE
▸ TAKING NOTES

17

1f Arctic wisdom

An Inuit man ice fishing, Nunavut Territory, Canada

Before you watch

1 Look at the photo and the map of where the Inuit people live. Discuss with your partner what you think this place is like. Talk about:

- Population (many/few, old/young, etc.)
- Weather
- Communications (transport, internet, speaking/writing, etc.)
- Way of life (traditional/modern/changing, stressful/relaxed, etc.)

2 Key vocabulary

a Read the sentences. The words in bold are used in the video. Guess the meaning of the words.

1 They have asked the government to **fund** the building of a new community centre.
2 The **elders** of the tribe meet once a week to discuss any problems in the community.
3 He has low **self-esteem** because as a child he was always criticized for not being clever enough.
4 Thank you for all your comments on my essay. They have been **invaluable**.
5 A **disproportionate** number of the university's students are from wealthy backgrounds.

b Match the words in bold in Exercise 2a with these definitions.

a extremely useful
b too large or small in comparison to something else
c older members of a group
d finance, provide the money for
e how good you feel about yourself

While you watch

3 ▶ 1.1 Watch the video and check your ideas from Exercise 1. What is your overall impression of the place?

4 ▶ 1.1 Watch the first part of the video (0.00 to 2.24) again which features an interview with the Mayor of Iqaluit. Answer the questions.

1 What has happened to the elders in a short time?
2 What is important about the elders?
3 What phrase is still relevant and is often used in Iqaluit?
4 How did these people's parents live?
5 How were traditions passed down between generations?

5 ▶ 1.1 Watch the second part of the video (2.25 to 3.39) and complete the summary.

In the past, elders were ¹_____ for the others in the community. Each one was an ²_____ on a particular area, helping the community to ³_____: on the weather, on the environment, on different kinds of ⁴_____. Inuits were happy with the ⁵_____. The woman's mother told her daughter that she would see many ⁶_____, but she said, 'Never ⁷_____ who you are.'

6 Watch the third part of the video (3.40 to the end) and answer the questions.

1 What has happened to the Iqaluit population in recent times? Why?
2 Name two things the woman mentions when talking about the key to a happy life.
3 Why does she have a communication problem with the younger generation?
4 What is significant about the number 23?
5 What was the main characteristic of the culture of the Iqaluit in the past?
6 What does the narrator say is the key to these people's future?

After you watch

7 Vocabulary in context

a ▶ 1.2 Watch the clips from the video. Complete the collocations. Then discuss your answers.

b Complete the sentences in your own words. Then compare your sentences with a partner.

1 I always seek advice when …
2 The last time I experienced a communication barrier was when …
3 The key to living a happy life is …

8 Work in pairs. Discuss the questions.

1 Is the advice and wisdom of elders highly respected in your society?
2 Is this as it should be? Why? / Why not?

9 Think of a story that one of your grandparents (or an older person in your community) told you and retell the story to your partner. Do the stories have a lesson that is still relevant today? Why? / Why not?

---

infant mortality (n) /ˈɪnfənt mɔː(r)ˈtæləti/ the number of children that die before they are two years old
nomadic (adj) /nəʊˈmædɪk/ with no fixed home, wandering from place to place

UNIT 1 REVIEW AND MEMORY BOOSTER

Grammar

1 Read the article. What is a 'griot'? What lesson did the writer take away from his visit to Timbuktu?

2 Choose the correct options to complete the article.

Some years ago I ¹ *visited / have visited* Timbuktu in Mali. Generally, people ² *are thinking / think* of Timbuktu as a desert town somewhere at the end of the world. But once upon a time, Timbuktu ³ *was / has been* a thriving city and key trading post, a place in Africa with a long and rich history.
In the marketplace you get a sense of this: women in brightly coloured clothes selling produce of all kinds. But my attention was drawn to a very old man who ⁴ *had sat / was sitting* in a corner. For a while, people ⁵ *had gathered / had been gathering* around him, so I joined them. He was a griot, or traditional storyteller.
Griots ⁶ *have been singing / sang* about kings and magicians, wars and journeys for generations. This is how Malians ⁷ *learned / have learned* about their history. He poured me a glass of tea and then I ⁸ *listened / was listening* to him tell the story of King Mansa and the golden age of Timbuktu, a story he ⁹ *told / had told* countless times before. At the end, the griot quoted old Mali saying: 'To succeed you need three things – a brazier, time and friends.' The brazier is to heat water for tea. Time and friends are what you need to share stories. It's advice that ¹⁰ *will stay / will be staying* with me in future years.

3 ›› MB Find six time phrases in the article. Which tenses are used with each time phrase? Then choose four of the phrases and make your own sentences with them.

I CAN	
use the correct tense with specific time phrases	☐
use the continuous aspect to describe actions in progress	☐

Vocabulary

4 Complete the expressions.
1 a lifel_____ painting
2 people from all w_____ of life
3 to have the t_____ of your life
4 a lifel_____ passion
5 it's the s_____ of my life
6 just a f_____ of life

5 ›› MB Work in pairs. Which of these phrases best describes these people: your best friend, your mother, your sister or brother? Give reasons.

> a control freak   a dreamer   a driven person
> a family person   a free spirit   a joker
> the life and soul of the party
> an outgoing person

6 ›› MB Correct the underlined words to complete these phrases about life lessons. Then give an example from your own experience that illustrates each phrase.

1 Trying to remain positive is a lot easier <u>spoken</u> than done.
2 A good rule of <u>finger</u> is: if you want something done properly, do it yourself.
3 It's a good idea to put a little money aside <u>then</u> and when you can.
4 My <u>leading</u> principle in life is: by and <u>whole</u>, it's better to ignore what others say about you.

I CAN	
describe different types of personality	☐
use idioms and expressions about life	☐

Real life

7 Work in pairs. Complete the conversation starters.
1 Hi, I don't think we _____ . I'm _____ .
2 Hi. Is it your first _____ too?
3 Hey, I like _____ .
4 So, whereabouts _____ ?
5 So, _____ you do?
6 What did you think _____ ?
7 This is a long queue, _____ ?
8 Have you seen that film everyone _____ ?

8 ›› MB Choose four of the conversation starters from Exercise 7. Act out four short conversations, using follow-up questions and answers.

I CAN	
start a conversation with someone I don't know	☐
ask follow-up questions to get to know someone better	☐

Unit 2 More than a job

A golden eagle with a Kazakh hunter, Mongolia

FEATURES

22 Living off the sea
The last nomads of the sea

24 Smokejumpers
A firefighter who risks her life to save others

26 Daring, defiant and free
Rock climbing unaided

30 Climbing Yosemite
A video about the mountaineering photographer Jimmy Chin

1 ▶11 Work in pairs. Look at the photo and caption. What do you think this man is doing? Then listen to an anthropologist talking about these people and check your ideas.

2 ▶11 Listen to the speaker again and answer the questions.

1 What is the livelihood of the nomads in western Mongolia?
2 How are many Kazakhs making a living these days?
3 What is their more traditional way of life?
4 What task requires great patience?
5 What does the hunter share with his eagle?
6 What sort of activity do people think eagle hunting is these days?

3 Look at the phrases in bold. Discuss the difference in meaning between the phrases in each pair.

1 it's **my occupation** and it's **my vocation**
2 **a trade** and **a profession**
3 it's **a living** and it's **my livelihood**
4 **a job** and **a task**
5 **work** and **a job** *(grammatical difference)*

4 Work in groups. Can you think of (at least) two examples of each of the following things?

a people who depend on animals for their livelihood
b a traditional occupation which is now dying out
c a task that requires great patience

my life ▶ MORE THAN A JOB ▶ SAFETY FEATURES ▶ YOUR COMFORT ZONE ▶ PRESENTING YOURSELF ▶ A COVERING LETTER OR EMAIL

reading the Moken people • wordbuilding phrasal verb *get* • grammar perfect forms • speaking more than a job

2a Living off the sea

Reading

1 Work in pairs. Look at the facts about the sea and try to complete the missing numbers. Then check your answers on page 190. Did any of the numbers surprise you?

SEA FACTS

1 ___% of the Earth's surface is covered by water.
2 About ___% of the world's population live in coastal regions.
3 ___% of the world's goods are transported by sea.
4 ___% of the world's animals live in the sea.
5 The average consumption of fish per person per year is ___ kg.
6 Fish is the main source of protein for ___ people.
7 The average time someone can hold their breath underwater is ___.

2 Read the article about the Moken people. Answer the questions.

1 Are there more or fewer people living off the sea now than in the past?
2 How do the Moken 'live off' the sea?
3 What special qualities do the Moken possess?
4 What does the future hold for the Moken people?

Wordbuilding phrasal verb *get*

▶ **WORDBUILDING phrasal verb *get***

Get is one of many common verbs (e.g. *take, come, go*) which change their meaning when combined with a particle (e.g. *by, on, with, across*) to make a phrasal verb.
get by (on/with), get on with, get round to

For further practice, see Workbook page 12.

▶ 12

Humans have been living off the land for thousands of years, developing the skills to hunt animals and harvest edible plants. But they have been living off the sea for probably just as long. However, in recent years, with the industrialization of fishing, the number of people who depend on the sea for their livelihood has declined. Yet in one corner of the world, true 'sea people' can still be found.

The Moken people, who migrated from China 4,000 years ago, live among the islands dotted across the Andaman Sea off the coast of Myanmar. Their homes are small hand-built boats called 'kabang' on which they live, eat and sleep for eight months of the year. The Moken came to public attention in 2004, when many of them escaped the tsunami that devastated coastal settlements around the Indian Ocean. Because of their intimate knowledge of the sea, they had felt the tsunami coming long before others realized the danger.

The Moken use nets and spears to forage for food and get by on what they take from the sea and beaches each day – fish and molluscs to eat; shells and oysters to trade with Malay and Chinese merchants. To get these things, they have to dive underwater for up to six minutes at a time. Their extraordinary ability to do this has fascinated scientists. Anna Gislen of the University of Lund was particularly interested in how the Moken could see so well underwater. She discovered that Moken children, once they had entered the water, were able to quickly change both the size of their pupils and the shape of their eye lens so that their underwater vision was at least twice as good as European children of a similar age.

Although their way of life poses no threat to others, the Moken have been constantly pressured by the authorities to settle on the land. Ten years ago, 2,500 Moken still led a traditional seafaring life. Now that number stands at 1,000. In another ten years, this unique way of life and the Mokens' extraordinary skills will probably have disappeared from the sea completely.

LIVING off the Sea

22

3 Look at the wordbuilding box on page 22. Find the phrasal verb with *get* (line 20) in the article. Does it mean 'manage or survive' or 'eat or feed'?

4 Look at these other phrasal verbs with *get*. Try to guess what they mean.

1 Sorry I haven't **got round to** fixing the tap yet.
2 I know you were disappointed not to win, but you've just got to **get over** it and move on.
3 I won't be free by 5.30. I have a meeting at 5 p.m. and I can't **get out of** it.
4 He just invents facts and no one contradicts him. I don't know how he **gets away with** it.
5 Thanks for sending me the details. I'll **get back to** you if I have any questions.

Grammar perfect forms

▶ **PERFECT FORMS**

Present perfect simple
1 *The number of people who depend on the sea for their livelihood* **has declined**.
2 *The Moken* **have been** *constantly* **pressured** *by the authorities to settle on the land.*

Present perfect continuous
3 *They* **have been living** *off the sea for just as long.*

Past perfect simple
4 *They* **had felt** *the tsunami coming long before others realized the danger.*

Future perfect simple
5 *In another ten years, these unique people* **will** *probably* **have disappeared** *from the sea completely.*

For further information and practice, see page 158.

5 Look at the grammar box. Which sentence(s) in the grammar box describe(s) an event or action:

1 that started in the past and is not finished?
2 that will be completed at a point in the future?
3 that is completed but might be repeated or continued and has a (strong) present connection?
4 completed before the main event in the past?

6 Work in pairs. Discuss the differences in meaning between the pairs of sentences.

1 a I've really enjoyed travelling around Laos.
   b I really enjoyed travelling around Laos.
2 a I've only met John once.
   b I only met John once.
3 a The meeting started when we arrived.
   b The meeting had started when we arrived.
4 a The votes will all be counted on the Thursday after the election.
   b The votes will all have been counted by the Thursday after the election.
5 a No one has taught him how to hold his breath underwater.
   b No one had taught him how to hold his breath underwater.

7 Choose the correct options to complete the text.

Before 2004, few people in the West [1] *heard / had heard* of the Moken people. But since then, their way of life and their situation [2] *have attracted / had attracted* a lot of interest. People are amazed, for example, that Moken children [3] *learn / had learned* to swim before they can walk, and that they [4] *became / have become* experts at reading the ways of the sea. This knowledge, which their ancestors [5] *acquired / have acquired* and then [6] *passed / have passed* down to them, is now in danger of being lost as more and more Moken [7] *are forced / had been forced* to settle on the land.

Sadly, this is not the first time that people [8] *try / have tried* to interfere in the Moken's way of life and it probably [9] *won't be / won't have been* the last. The Moken [10] *just want / have just wanted* to be left alone. The ones I met [11] *were / have been* proud of their simple way of life. But I suspect in ten or twenty years' time their situation [12] *will change / will have changed*.

8 ▶ 13 Complete the description. Use the correct perfect or non-perfect form of the verbs in brackets. Then listen and check.

My grandfather was a forestry commissioner, which meant he [1] _____ (be) responsible for managing forests. I think he [2] _____ (intend) originally to be a biologist, but then he [3] _____ (get) a job looking after forests in Wales. He [4] _____ (retire) now, but he's still fascinated by trees and plants. I guess his job was a way of life for him because it [5] _____ (occupy) all his time and he [6] _____ (spend) so much of his life living in or around forests. Over the years, I [7] _____ (often / think) about working outdoors too, but I don't think I [8] _____ (follow) in his footsteps.

Speaking my life

9 Work in groups. Look at these jobs and decide which are a way of life (i.e. much more than a job) for the people who do them. Give reasons.

Have they chosen to work in an unusual environment? Is this a job that previous generations in their family had done?

banker   coal miner   graphic designer
IT consultant   farmer   firefighter
fisherman/woman   lorry driver
physiotherapist   teacher

10 Think of another job (from the past, present or future) that is a way of life. Describe the job and your reasons for adding this job to the list. Is your job or studies a way of life for you?

listening smokejumpers • idioms safety • grammar passive forms • speaking safety features

2b Smokejumpers

Listening

1 Work in pairs. Look at these verbs. Which verbs collocate with *fire* and which collocate with *a fire*? Try to put each collocation in a sentence.

| be on | catch | contain | fight | light |
| put out | set ... to | set on | start | |

be on fire: We could see smoke in the distance but we couldn't see what was on fire.

2 Look at the photos and answer the questions.
  1 What kind of fire is shown in the photo on page 25? How does this kind of fire start? How can they be stopped?
  2 What qualities are needed to be a firefighter? Is it a job you could do?

3 ▶14 Listen to an interview with smokejumper, Kerry Franklin. Are the sentences true (T) or false (F)?
  1 Smokejumpers are sent into places that are difficult to reach.
  2 Their job is to evaluate a fire, not to fight it.
  3 Being a woman in this profession isn't easy.

4 ▶14 Listen to the interview again and answer the questions.
  1 What are the consequences if a smokejumper is a) too heavy? b) too light?
  2 What is Kerry's view of her own personal safety?
  3 When are smokejumpers sent to fight a fire?
  4 How do they usually try to contain a bad fire?
  5 How do you become a smokejumper?

Idioms safety

5 Look at this idiom Kerry used about safety in her job. What does it mean? Then complete the idioms about safety in the text below using these words.

"… in this job you can't **wrap people in cotton wool**."

| be | become | cut | do | err | follow |

The first rule of safety is always to ¹_____ **things by the book**. Don't try to make up your own rules or to improvise or to ²_____ **corners**. You'll find that if you ³_____ **the correct procedure** each time, soon it will ⁴_____ **second nature to you** – you won't even think about it. If you're in any doubt about how something should be done, always try to ⁵_____ **on the side of caution**. It's **better to** ⁶_____ **safe than sorry**.

6 Think of something you regularly do or have done that involves risk. What do/did you do to keep safe? Use idioms from Exercise 5 in your description.

Grammar passive forms

▶ **PASSIVE FORMS**

Tenses
1 *Smokejumpers are firefighters with parachutes who **are dropped** into inaccessible areas …*
2 *Kerry Franklin explained her career choice when she **was interviewed** by this programme.*
3 *That's **been known** to happen.*
4 *We **get dropped** in with tools.*

Modal verbs
5 *If … there's a strong wind, you **might be carried** a long way …*
6 *You **can get injured** when you hit the ground.*

Infinitives and gerunds
7 *This information has **to be relayed** back to base …*
8 *First, the fire needs **to be assessed** …*
9 *The job involves **being trained** to a certain standard …*

For further information and practice, see page 158.

24

Unit 2 More than a job

7 Look at the grammar box on page 24. Answer the questions.

1 What tenses are the passive verb forms in bold in sentences 1–3?
2 How is the passive infinitive formed (sentences 7 and 8)? And the passive gerund (sentence 9)?
3 What verb is used (informally) in place of *are* and *be* in sentences 4 and 6?

8 Rewrite the sentences using passive forms of the underlined phrases.

1 You always need to treat fire with caution.
2 He burned his hands badly while he was trying to put a fire out.
3 I did the training course three times before they accepted me.
4 I was very grateful to the fire service for giving me the opportunity.
5 People or natural causes, like lightning, can start forest fires.
6 Smokejumpers sometimes make their smokejumper suits themselves.
7 We haven't seen forest fires in our region since 1996.
8 Above all, firefighters need to be calm. It's easy for the situation to overwhelm you.

9 Complete the sentences with passive forms. Use these verbs.

| arrest | catch | do | explain | force |
| pay | | | | |

1 It doesn't need _____ – it's obvious how to do it.
2 It wasn't my choice to be here. I _____ to come.
3 I _____ at the end of every month. Usually I'm broke for a week before that.
4 If you _____ speeding in your car, you risk _____ .
5 It's too late. What _____ cannot be undone.

10 Look at sentences 1–5 in the grammar box again. Find these sentences in the audioscript on page 181 (track 14). Then match each sentence with these uses (a–c) of the passive.

a The agent (person doing the action) is obvious, unknown or unimportant.
b We are following a series of actions that happen to the same subject.
c We want to give emphasis to the agent by putting it at the end of the sentence.

11 Choose the most appropriate form (active or passive) to complete the text. Sometimes both forms are possible.

If you are thinking of a career in firefighting, there are a few facts you should know. It is a highly respected profession; in most countries ¹ *people rank it / it is ranked* in the top ten respected jobs. The money is also good. ² *We need to compensate firefighters / Firefighters need to be compensated* well for the risks ³ *they take / that are taken by them*. But it is not all adventure. Firefighters spend sixty per cent of their time waiting ⁴ *for someone to call them / to be called* into action. Moreover, eighty per cent of the events ⁵ *they attend / that are attended by them* are not even fires. Most are medical emergencies: for example, ⁶ *freeing someone / someone being freed* from a crashed car. Others are things like building inspections to make sure that ⁷ *people are following fire regulations / fire regulations are being followed*. And the hours are long, with some firefighters working shifts of up to 24 hours without ⁸ *anyone giving them / being given* a break.

Speaking my life

12 Work in pairs. List two safety and security features for the following things. Say how each feature works and what its purpose is. Use passive forms.

- my mobile phone
- a car
- my home or office block

My mobile phone is protected by a password. Some phones use fingerprint recognition so the phone can only be unlocked by the owner. I guess that's probably safer.

13 Work in groups. Look at the idea for car safety. Then think of your own 'new' safety feature for one of the items in Exercise 12. Follow the steps below.

I think a lot of accidents **could be prevented** if people always drove with two hands on the wheel. My idea is that if people didn't have two hands on the wheel, an alarm would go off. That way, people **would be discouraged** from using their phones or eating while driving.

- Decide what a good feature would be.
- Write a short description of it and how it would work.
- Describe your feature to another group.
- In class, vote on the best idea.

my life ▸ MORE THAN A JOB ▸ SAFETY FEATURES ▸ YOUR COMFORT ZONE ▸ PRESENTING YOURSELF
▸ A COVERING LETTER OR EMAIL

25

reading climbing Yosemite • critical thinking analysing language • word focus *foot/feet* • speaking your comfort zone

2c Daring, defiant and free

Reading

1 Look at the photo and answer the questions.

1 How do you think the man got to this place?
2 How do you think he is going to get out of there?
3 How do you think the photo was taken?

2 Read the article and find the answers to the questions in Exercise 1.

3 Read the article again and answer the questions.

1 What are the three things you need for free-soloing?
2 How did Honnold feel after climbing for two hours and 45 minutes?
3 Why did Honnold carry on after his moment of panic on the rock face?
4 What was the effect of this climb on Honnold's reputation?
5 What is Jimmy Chin's greatest passion?
6 When he is on an assignment as a mountaineer-photographer, what does he believe is his first job?

4 Find words and expressions in the article with the following meanings.

1 an adjective meaning 'almost vertical' (para 1)
2 a noun meaning 'the top of a mountain' (para 1)
3 an adjective meaning 'oily' (para 1)
4 an adverb meaning 'perfectly' (para 2)
5 an adjective meaning 'very surprised' (para 3)
6 an adjective meaning 'very skilled and capable' (para 4)
7 a phrase meaning 'made a very strong impression on' (para 4)
8 a verb meaning 'thought about the past' (para 4)

Critical thinking analysing language

5 Find three examples of each of the following language techniques (a–d) which the author uses to make the description more dramatic.

a short sentences (nine words or fewer)
b use of the historic present (present tense to describe past events)
c words with a strong meaning (e.g. *sheer*, line 3)
d use of direct speech

6 Work in pairs. Rewrite these sentences to include the features (a–d) in Exercise 5. Then compare your more dramatic version with another pair.

Chin watched as the climber above him held onto the rock by one hand, hesitating at first to take the picture. He wondered if it would be right to take the picture in case the man then fell and hurt himself, but then he decided that he had to, because it was his job.

Word focus *foot/feet*

7 Work in pairs. Find two words or expressions in the article with the word *foot* in them and discuss what they mean.

8 Read the sentences. Look at the other expressions with *foot* or *feet* in bold. Discuss what each expression means.

1 It's all a bit new: the college, the accommodation, the people. But I'm sure I'll **find my feet** in a few weeks.
2 When she told them at the interview that money wasn't important to her, she really **shot herself in the foot**.
3 You **put your foot in it** when you asked Jim about his job – he was made redundant two weeks ago.
4 She **followed in her mother's footsteps** and became a dentist.
5 Well, I like dancing, but I'm not sure anyone else likes my dancing. I'**ve got two left feet**.
6 We're friends now, but we **got off on the wrong foot** when we first met.

9 Work in pairs. Ask each other these questions.

1 In what kind of organization/sector is it difficult to get your foot in the door?
2 When was the last time you put your foot in it?
3 When have you got off on the wrong foot?

Speaking my life

10 Work in pairs. Climbers like to live at the limits of their comfort zone. Do the quiz on page 153 to find out what your comfort zone is.

11 Look at the answers to the quiz on page 190 to find out what your comfort zone is. Discuss if you agree with the answers.

26

DARING, DEFIANT & FREE

▶ 15

It's a bright Saturday morning in September and a young man is standing on a small ledge high up on the north-west face of Half Dome, a sheer 650-metre wall of granite in the heart of Yosemite Valley in California. He's alone, far off the ground and without aids. Most climbers take two days to climb the face, using ropes and carrying up to 20 kilos of equipment and bivouacking for the night half-way up. Not Honnold. He is attempting the route free-solo, which means climbing with only a chalk bag and his rock shoes, and is trying to reach the top in less than three hours. But less than 30 metres from the summit, something potentially disastrous happens. He loses the smallest amount of confidence. 'What am I doing here?' he says to himself, staring at a greasy bump on the rock face. 'My foot will never stay on that.'

For two hours and 45 minutes, Honnold has been in the zone, flawlessly performing one precise athletic move after another, and not once has he hesitated. In free-soloing, confidence is everything. All you have is belief in your own ability. If Honnold merely believes his fingertips can't hold, he will fall to his death. Now, with mental fatigue and a glass-like slab of rock above him, he's paralysed, out of his comfort zone. He hadn't felt like this two days before when he'd raced up the same route with a rope. For a few minutes, he stands there, staring out at the sky, unable to look up or down for fear of falling. Then suddenly, he's in motion again. He steps up, planting his shoe on the smooth stone. It sticks. He moves his hand to another hold, repeats the move, and within minutes, he's at the top.

'I rallied because there was nothing else I could do,' Honnold says later, with a boyish laugh. 'I stepped up and trusted that foothold and was freed of the prison where I'd stood silently for five minutes.' Word of his three-hour free-solo of Half Dome flashed around the world. Climbers were stunned, and the blog writers were buzzing. On that warm autumn day in 2008, a shy 23-year-old from the suburbs of Sacramento had just become a climbing legend.

That is the magic of Yosemite: it creates heroes. But for the climbers, they are just doing what they love and – if they're lucky – get paid for as a bonus. One such person is Jimmy Chin, who took this photograph. He is also an accomplished mountaineer; the difference between him and Honnold is that Chin always works closely with other climbers, taking photographs as he climbs. He was actually brought up in the flat countryside of southern Minnesota, but rock climbing has been his passion since Glacier National Park first 'blew his mind' on a family vacation as a boy. Photography came later, when an outdoor clothing company bought one of the photos he had taken on an expedition. As a photographer, it isn't easy to get your foot in the door with a good client, so Chin, encouraged by their interest, bought his own camera. He hasn't looked back.

Combining a natural gift for photographic composition with his mountaineering skills, Chin has become one of the leading specialists in what has been called 'participatory photography'. He is able to carry a camera where few dare to go, at the same time remaining a reliable member of the climbing team. For Chin, that is always the priority.

bivouac (v) /ˈbɪvʊˌæk/ to make a temporary camp without a tent
chalk (n) /tʃɔːk/ soft white stone (formed from limestone)
ledge (n) /ledʒ/ a narrow horizontal surface projecting from a wall
slab (n) /slæb/ a large thick flat piece of stone

my life ▶ MORE THAN A JOB ▶ SAFETY FEATURES ▶ YOUR COMFORT ZONE ▶ PRESENTING YOURSELF
▶ A COVERING LETTER OR EMAIL

vocabulary personal qualities • pronunciation word stress • real life presenting yourself

2d Tell me a bit about yourself

Vocabulary personal qualities

1 Look at these words and expressions people use to describe themselves at interviews. Which of the words and expressions match the situations (a–d)? Sometimes there is more than one answer.

| conscientious   enthusiastic   a fast learner |
| flexible   focused   motivated |
| reliable   resourceful   well-organized |

a It was too late to post all the invitations, so I researched each person's email address and emailed them instead.
b I regularly stayed late to finish the job. Sometimes you have to do that.
c I didn't miss a single day at work all last year.
d I had to do all sorts of jobs as Head of Social Events: booking venues, dealing with entertainers, greeting new students, making food sometimes.

2 Pronunciation word stress

a ▶16 Mark where you think the stress falls on each of the words in Exercise 1. Then listen and check.

b Work in pairs. Practise saying the words with the correct stress.

Real life presenting yourself

3 Read the advice about a common interview question. What are some examples of things you probably shouldn't talk about when asked this question?

> Almost every interview will either begin with or include the question 'Can you tell me a bit about yourself?' While it's important not to give a scripted answer, it *is* important to think about how you'll answer this. The interviewer doesn't want your whole life story. What they really want to know is: your relevant background, what has brought you to this point in your career and your hopes and goals for the future.

4 Work in pairs. Make a list of five more questions that are often asked at an interview. Use these words to help you. Then compare your questions with another pair.

| goals   this job/position   strengths |
| in five years   weaknesses |

5 ▶17 Listen to Katy presenting herself to a careers advisor. Note down the questions that the careers advisor asks. What kind of work is Katy looking for and why is she suited to this?

6 ▶17 Look at the expressions for presenting yourself. Complete the expressions with a suitable preposition. Then listen to the interview again and check your answers.

▶ **PRESENTING YOURSELF**

Background
I graduated [1] _____ there last June …
I've been looking [2] _____ a job [3] _____ journalism …
Goals
My ambition is to …
The media is not an easy sector to break [4] _____ …
That's what I'm working [5] _____ .
I'd be (perfectly) happy to start [6] _____ the bottom and then work my way [7] _____ .
I wouldn't mind -ing …
Qualities
I'm good [8] _____ -ing …
Once I start something, I follow it [9] _____ .
When it comes [10] _____ -ing … , I …
I have some experience [11] _____ -ing …
I have a tendency [12] _____ …*

* for discussing weaknesses only

7 Work in pairs. Take turns to act out the roles of either a career advisor and an interviewee OR an employer and a job applicant. Follow these steps:
- decide what type of interview it is
- interviewer: make some notes on the questions you want to ask
- interviewee: make some notes on the answers you are going to give
- act out a short (e.g. five-minute) interview.
- begin the interview with the question 'Tell me a bit about yourself.'

writing a covering letter or email • writing skill fixed expressions   Unit 2 More than a job

2e A letter of application

Writing a covering letter or email

1 Read the letter of application. Find and underline the following key elements of a covering letter. Then compare answers with your partner.

1 the job applied for
2 where and when it was advertised
3 the candidate's current situation
4 why the writer is a good candidate
5 thanks for reading the letter
6 how and when the candidate can be contacted

2 Look at the statements about a covering letter. Using the letter as a model, say if the statements are true (T) or false (F). Explain your answers.

> 1 Keep it short. The letter should basically just refer the reader to your CV.
> 2 Show interest in and knowledge of the organization you are writing to.
> 3 Just mention your general suitability for the job. The letter should not respond to specific requirements the company has listed.
> 4 The letter should give a personal touch to your application.

3 Writing skill **fixed expressions**

The writer follows the conventions of letter writing by using certain fixed expressions. Find words and expressions in the letter with the following meanings.

a I am looking for
b I am sending
c a good person to consider
d I am free to come
e the things you say you need
f I am answering
g feel free to
h I liked the look of
i I hope you will reply
j my CV shows you that
k thanks for reading this

Dear Mr Fairburn

I am writing in response to your advertisement in last Tuesday's *Guardian* newspaper for a Trainee Marketing Assistant. Please find attached my CV. The job attracted me because it emphasizes opportunities for people who are keen to learn and also because of your company's reputation for innovative and high-quality travel books. I am currently doing some freelance travel writing.

As a recent graduate from university, I am well aware that I still have much to learn and it is exactly this kind of challenging environment that I am seeking. You will see from my CV that I am someone who believes in getting results. My two proudest achievements are raising over £15,000 for a local charity and organizing a highly successful student Arts Week.

Regarding the requirements you mention, I think I am a suitable candidate as:

• I have a degree in Business Studies with a specialization in marketing
• I am flexible about where in the south-east I work
• I have good organizational skills, acquired as head of the Student Social Committee

I am available for interview at any time. Thank you for taking time to consider this application and please do not hesitate to contact me at any time by phone or in writing if you have questions about any of the above.

I look forward to hearing from you.
Yours sincerely

Philip Morrissey

Philip Morrissey

4 Write a covering email to a company that you would like to work for. Make sure you include the key elements mentioned in Exercise 1.

5 Exchange emails with your partner. Look at their email as if you were the employer. Use these questions to check.

• Is it well organized and does it include all the key elements?
• Is it grammatically correct and without spelling mistakes?
• Does it use appropriate fixed expressions?
• Does it specify the key skills the organization needs?
• Is it interesting and does it have a personal touch?
• Does the application seem convincing?

my life ▶ MORE THAN A JOB ▶ SAFETY FEATURES ▶ YOUR COMFORT ZONE ▶ PRESENTING YOURSELF ▶ A COVERING LETTER OR EMAIL

29

2f Climbing Yosemite

Jimmy Chin climbs Half Dome, Yosemite, California, USA.

Before you watch

1 Look at the photo. Write down two words or expressions to describe what is happening. Then share your words with the class. What were the most common words?

2 Key vocabulary

a Read the sentences. The words in bold are used in the video. Guess the meaning of the words.

1 My work as a surgeon is very physical, but it's also very **cerebral**.
2 The acting in the film was so bad that it made me **cringe** at times.
3 We'll need to **shovel** all this sand into a big wheelbarrow and take it to the back of the house.
4 It's no good rushing an editing job. You have to be very patient and **methodical**.
5 On my first day at the company, they gave me a very simple **assignment** – to learn everyone's name in the office!

b Match the words in bold in Exercise 2a with these definitions.

a shrink back in embarrassment
b work or study task
c involving great thought and concentration
d going through something slowly and carefully (often in a certain order)
e move with a large spade

While you watch

3 **2.1** Watch the first part of the video (0.00 to 1.03). Note the adjectives Jimmy Chin used to describe his work. Did any of these adjectives surprise you? Were any of them the same ones you used in Exercise 1?

4 **2.1** Read these sentences about Jimmy Chin's career. Then watch the second part of the video (1.04 to the end). Are the sentences true (T) or false (F)?

1 Jimmy Chin's parents hoped he would follow a professional career.
2 Chin realized straightaway that climbing was something he wanted to do permanently.
3 Chin felt very at home in Yosemite.
4 Chin's real ambition was to be a photographer.
5 Being a photographer has allowed him to visit countries all over the world.

5 **2.1** Watch the second part of the video again (1.04 to the end) and complete the notes about Jimmy Chin's career. Use one word in each space.

1 In college he was part of the _____ team.
2 After college he went to the Bay area to find a job in the _____ realm.
3 Not finding a job, he decided to take a _____ off and ski full time.
4 Seven years later he was still living in the back of his _____ and doing various jobs, shovelling snow and waiting _____.
5 He spent most of his time in Yosemite, where he found his _____.
6 After some time in Yosemite, he decided he would like to visit the _____ ranges of the world.
7 He took a photo which a friend sold for $_____ and realized taking photos could help him continue what he was doing.
8 Yosemite is a special place for him because it helped to _____ his career.

6 Do you think Jimmy Chin made a good career choice? Why? / Why not? How do you think his career will develop?

After you watch

7 Vocabulary in context

a **2.2** Watch the clips from the video. Choose the correct meaning of the words and expressions.

b Complete the sentences in your own words. Then compare your sentences with a partner.

1 Before I go, I'll need to sort out a few odds and ends, like …
2 We left the house and headed out …
3 My parents freaked out when I said I wanted to …

8 Look at these things people do before starting out on a career. What are the benefits of each one, do you think?

- travelling
- doing military service
- doing various odd jobs (working in restaurants, shops, on building sites, etc.)
- building up a range of practical skills – driving, speaking languages, computer skills (e.g. Excel)
- doing some voluntary work in the community

Unit 2 More than a job

31

UNIT 2 REVIEW AND MEMORY BOOSTER

Grammar

1 Complete the article. Use the correct tense and form (active or passive) of the verbs.

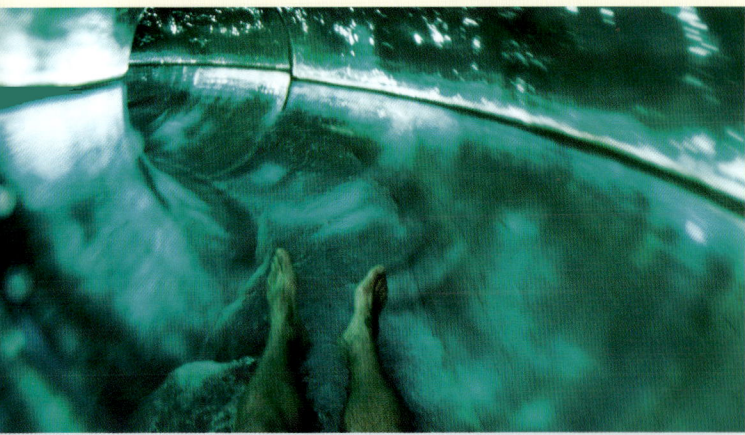

What would be your dream job? Tommy Lynch believes that he ¹ _____ (find) his. Two years ago, he ² _____ (employ) as a waiter in a restaurant, but more recently he ³ _____ (travel) around the world testing water slides at holiday resorts. That's because Tommy ⁴ _____ (give) the job by holiday operator First Choice of helping them to include the best water parks in their holiday brochures. So far, he ⁵ _____ (test) over fifty water slides and pools.
After the company ⁶ _____ (create) their own selection of 'Splash Resorts', they soon realized that they would need the quality of the facilities ⁷ _____ (check) regularly. A First Choice spokesperson said, 'We knew that to offer the best, we would have to appoint a full-time tester. Tommy ⁸ _____ (be) great.'
He was chosen from hundreds of applicants and ⁹ _____ (put) straight to work.
'I ¹⁰ _____ (have) the time of my life,' he says, 'but it's hard work. New resorts ¹¹ _____ (add) to the list all the time. So I spend a lot of my time travelling and doing paperwork. But if customers have had a great time on holiday, then all my work ¹² _____ (be) worthwhile!'

2 **»MB** Work in pairs. Find five passive forms in the article. Discuss the reason the passive has been used in each case. (Refer to the reasons (a–c) in Exercise 10 on page 25, if necessary.)

3 Answer the questions.
   1 Who created Tommy's job and why?
   2 What does the job involve?

I CAN	
use perfect forms to look back at actions at an earlier time	
use a variety of passive forms	

Vocabulary

4 **»MB** Choose the correct option to complete the questions about work. Then discuss the questions with your partner.
   1 What do you consider a reasonable monthly salary to get *along / by* on?
   2 In their careers, have any of your family followed in their parents' *footsteps / shoes*?
   3 What are the advantages and disadvantages of being in the teaching *trade / profession*?
   4 In a new work environment, how long does it take you to *find / set* your feet?
   5 Is getting *on / forward* in life and moving up the career ladder important to you?
   6 Would you rather do a challenging job or stay on the safe *road / side* and do something easy?

5 **»MB** What are these people talking about, do you think? Discuss with your partner.
   1 'You need to get over it and move on.'
   2 'Sorry, I haven't got round to it, but I will.'
   3 'I'd like to get out of it, but I can't.'

I CAN	
talk about jobs and careers	
use phrasal verbs with *get*	

Real life

6 Match the questions (1–4) with the beginnings (a–g) of the answers someone might give.
   1 So can you tell me a bit about your background?
   2 Where do you hope to be in five years' time?
   3 What are your strengths?
   4 And your weaknesses?

   a My ambition is to …
   b I graduated from …
   c I have a tendency to …
   d When it comes to … , I …
   e I'm working towards …
   f I'm conscientious …
   g I've recently been …

7 **»MB** Look at these adjectives. Can you think of a job for which each quality is especially important? Give reasons.

   conscientious   enthusiastic   flexible
   motivated   reliable   resourceful

8 **»MB** Work in pairs. Ask and answer the questions (1–4) in Exercise 6.

I CAN	
present myself at an interview	

Unit 3 Design for life

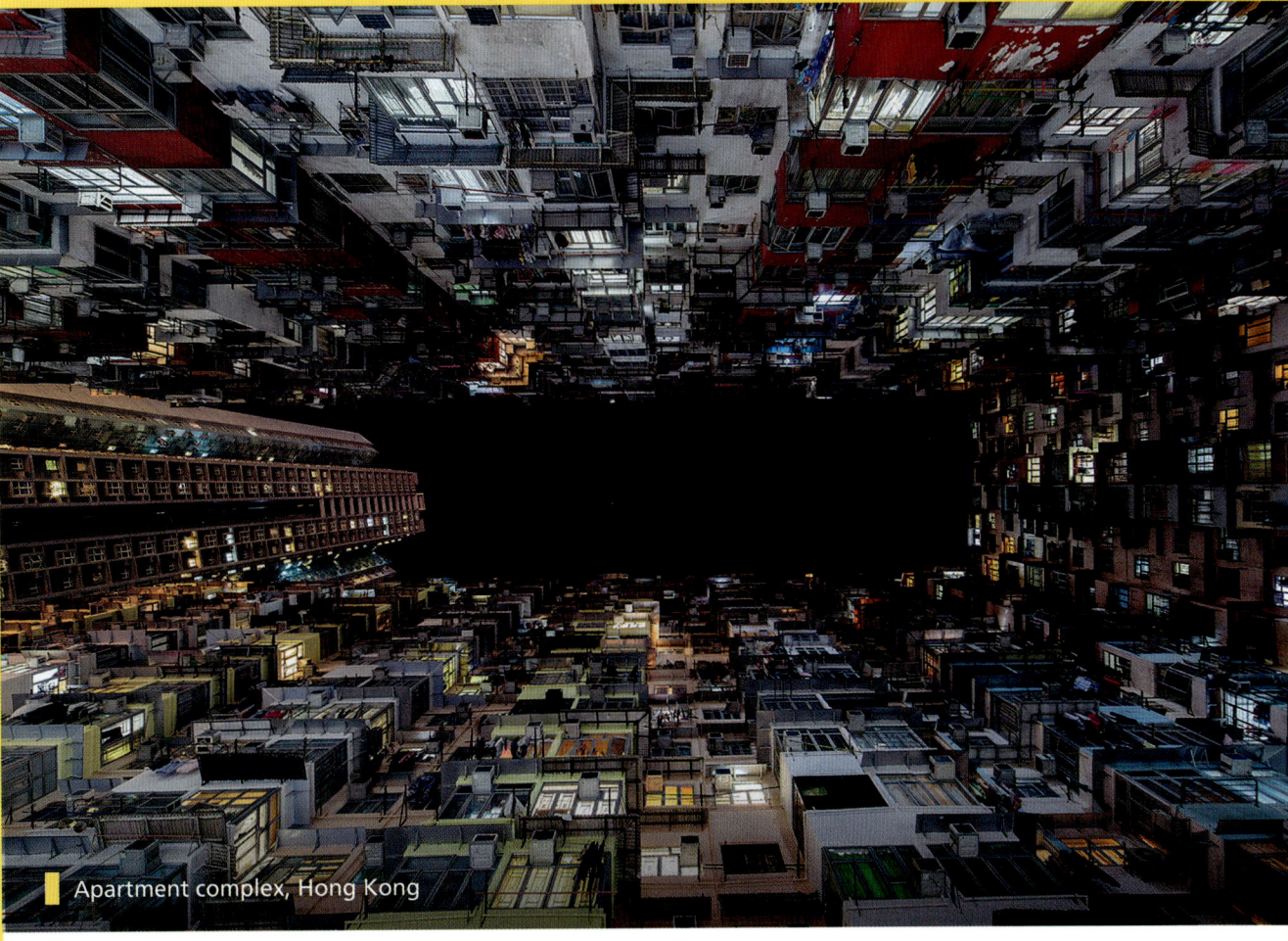

Apartment complex, Hong Kong

FEATURES

34 Towns with character
Two towns with individual characters

36 Compact living
A focus on small homes

38 The paper architect
The life and work of architect Zaha Hadid

42 A story of solutions
A video about the human impact of architecture

1 Look at the photo and caption. Discuss the questions.
  1 What do you think it's like to live in this place?
  2 How would you describe these buildings and what features can you see on them?

2 ▶18 Listen to someone discussing the photo. Compare your ideas from Exercise 1.

3 ▶18 Listen again. What adjectives does the speaker use to describe these things?
  1 apartments   3 buildings
  2 climate   4 the city

4 Look at these adjectives. Make adjective + noun collocations with these nouns: *apartment, building, street, area*. Which adjective can collocate with all four nouns?

> brick   built-up   deprived   first-floor   four-storey
> high-rise   imposing   main   narrow   one-way
> pedestrianized   residential   run-down   spacious   studio
> tree-lined   two-bedroom

5 Think of an area or neighbourhood you know. Describe this place and the buildings in it, saying what you like or dislike about it.

my life ▶YOUR HOME TOWN ▶A BIT OF LUXURY ▶HOW SPACES AFFECT YOU ▶EXPRESSING OPINIONS ▶AN OPINION ESSAY

33

vocabulary describing towns • reading the character of towns • grammar qualifiers •
pronunciation *quite*, *fairly* and *pretty* • speaking and writing your home town

3a Towns with character

Vocabulary describing towns

1 Work in pairs. Look at these different types of town and answer the questions.

| boom town   ghost town   historic town |
| holiday town/resort   industrial town   market town |
| port (town)   regional capital   shanty town |
| spa town   university town |

1 What are the characteristics of each type of town?
2 Can you give an example of three of these types of town from your own experience?

2 Look at these adjectives which describe towns. Make pairs of opposites or near opposites.

lively   modern and characterless   quaint   scruffy
self-contained   sleepy   sprawling   well-kept

Reading

3 Look at the photos of two towns with a special identity. Read the descriptions of each town that residents have written. Then match the statements (1–6) with the towns (Granada or Billund).

1 It is not a town that pretends to be something it isn't.
2 It is known for its period buildings.
3 It is very busy with visitors from outside.
4 Its residents seem happy and comfortable.
5 It has a relaxed feel to it.
6 Its economy has grown in recent decades.

▶ 19

TOWNS WITH CHARACTER

Granada, Nicaragua

It might be cheating slightly to call Granada a town: it's officially a city, but not a big sprawling city like Managua. Granada's quite small and self-contained. It's also the oldest colonial town in Latin America (founded in 1524) with beautifully preserved, elegant architecture. In some historic towns you feel like you're in a museum, but Granada's not like that; it's not scruffy, but it's not particularly smart either and I quite like that. It just feels like a genuine working town, with farmers from the local countryside coming and going to sell their produce in the town's vibrant markets. Outside the commercial areas, life has quite a gentle rhythm and after dusk everything goes pretty quiet. That's changing a little now as tourism in Nicaragua increases and Granada becomes a magnet for visitors. But you can see why they come; it's such an incredibly photogenic place.

Billund, Denmark

I moved to Billund in east Jutland, Denmark about ten years ago. It's a rather ordinary kind of town – except in one respect. Almost everyone here has a connection with Lego. The town dates back to medieval times – it still has a few quaint streets with period buildings in the centre – but it boomed when the Lego factory started exporting its toys in the 1950s and 60s. Most residents either work in the factory or the Legoland theme park, or they have some other business like a hotel or café that caters for the endless stream of visitors to the park. We live in a house that was built by the company (not out of Lego, in case you wondered). Life's pretty good here, partly because it's such a family-friendly town – about thirty per cent of residents are couples with children – and partly because the company looks after its people. They charge us a fairly reasonable rent and they've built many amenities for the town – a church, a library, the local park. My children even wear Lego-branded clothes.

Grammar qualifiers

> **QUALIFIERS**
>
> **1 QUALIFIER + ADJECTIVE**
> *quite, pretty, fairly* (usually with positive ideas)
> Life's **pretty/quite/fairly** good here.
> Life has **quite** a gentle rhythm.
> They charge us **a fairly/pretty** reasonable rent.
>
> *rather*
> It's **a rather** ordinary kind of town.
> It's **rather an** ordinary kind of town.
> The town is **rather** ordinary.
>
> *not very, not particularly*
> It's **not particularly/very** smart either.
>
> **2 QUALIFIER + VERB**
> *quite, rather, not particularly* (with *like, enjoy, want*)
> I **quite/rather** like that.
> I didn't **particularly** like that.
>
> *slightly, a little, a bit*
> It might be cheating **slightly / a little / a bit** ...
> That's changing **slightly / a little / a bit** now.
>
> For further information and practice, see page 160.

4 Look at the grammar box. Answer the questions.
1. Do the qualifiers make the idea expressed:
   a. much stronger?   b. less strong?
2. What is the position of each qualifier when used with:
   a. an adjective?
   b. an article + adjective + noun?
   c. a verb?

5 Put the qualifier in the right place in the sentence.
1. I always feel excited when I move to a new town. (pretty)
2. Liverpool used to be a busy port in the last century. (fairly)
3. We wanted to visit Verona, but there wasn't time. (quite)
4. Industry in the town has declined in the last thirty years. (slightly)
5. After moving to the country, we regretted our decision. (a bit)
6. The museum isn't interesting, if you don't like local history. (particularly)

6 Complete the conversations using the qualifiers given.

1 | a little   particularly   pretty   quite |

A: Do you like where you live now?
B: I ¹_____ like it, but it's not a ²_____ lively place. Don't get me wrong: the people are ³_____ friendly and they've welcomed us very warmly. We've just had to adapt ⁴_____ after living in a big city like London.

2 | a bit   fairly   slightly |

C: We've just moved into a new housing estate.
D: What's it like?
C: To be honest, it's ⁵_____ modern and characterless. I'm ⁶_____ confident it'll get better with time as more people move in. But at the moment we're struggling ⁷_____ to enjoy it.

7 Pronunciation *quite*, *fairly* and *pretty*

a ▶20 Listen to the conversations. Does the stress fall on the qualifier or the verb/adjective?

1. A: Is it far?   B: It's quite a long way.
2. A: How do you feel?   B: Pretty confident.
3. A: How's the water?   B: It's pretty cold.
4. A: Is it urgent?   B: Yes, it's fairly important.
5. A: Is she famous?
   B: Yes, she's quite a well-known actor.
6. A: How was the show?   B: I quite enjoyed it.

b ▶20 Listen again. Which stress pattern means 'but not *very*'? Which stress pattern doesn't change the meaning of the verb or adjective very much?

c Work in pairs. Practise saying the phrases. Choose which pronunciation pattern you use and see if your partner can guess the meaning that you intend.

Speaking and writing — my life

8 Work in pairs. Answer the questionnaire about your home town. Use at least one qualifier in each answer.

*It's a **pretty** mixed town really. **Quite** a lot of students live there, but it also has an industrial part. Guides on the internet usually describe it as a university town, but that doesn't really give the whole story.*

1. How would you describe your home town? How does this compare to descriptions of it you have read?
2. What's your home town known for – a famous person, a historical event, its produce?
3. Has your home town changed a lot in the time you've known it? If so, how?
4. I've got a day in your home town. What can I do?
5. Where is the best place to get a nice, reasonably-priced meal in your home town?
6. If you could change one thing about your home town, what would it be?
7. Would you be happy to live in your home town all your life? Why? / Why not?

9 Write a short description of what makes your home town special (up to 140 words). Use the descriptions in the article on page 34 to help you.

listening small homes • grammar intensifying adverbs • pronunciation stress in intensifying adverbs • vocabulary adverb + adjective collocations • speaking a bit of luxury

3b Compact living

Listening

1 Work in pairs. Ask and answer the questions.

1 How many different rooms are there in your home?
2 Do any of the rooms have more than one function?
3 If you had more space, what would you use it for?

2 ▶21 Look at the photos. Then listen to an interview with an architect who specializes in compact designs. Answer the questions.

1 Where are these two homes?
2 Why is the architect inspired by them?

3 ▶21 Read the sentences. Then listen to the interview again and choose the best option to complete the sentences.

1 Jonas Wilfstrand specializes in designing *compact holiday homes / small homes in general*.
2 There's a demand for compact living spaces because they are *cheaper / more practical*.
3 Dolgan homes consist of *one room / a shared space and a bedroom*.
4 The Dolgan need to move house regularly because of *the weather / their animals*.
5 In the ten-square metre cabin in California there is little room for *belongings / domestic appliances*.
6 In Gary Chang's apartment you can *move / remove* the walls.

Grammar intensifying adverbs

4 Look at these adjectives. Match each gradable adjective (i.e. <u>not</u> with a strong meaning) with an ungradable adjective (i.e. with a strong meaning) that expresses a similar idea.

Gradable	Ungradable
1 cold	a tiny
2 surprising	b stunning
3 important	c delighted
4 small	d brilliant
5 original	e freezing
6 pleased	f amazing
7 clever	g essential
8 attractive	h unique

5 Work with a partner. Take turns to ask questions using a gradable adjective. The other student should answer using the equivalent ungradable adjective.

A: *Is your apartment cold?*
B: *Yes, it's absolutely freezing.*

6 Look at these common spoken phrases. Which underlined words mean 'very' and which mean 'completely'?

1 Yes, you're <u>absolutely</u> right.
2 That's <u>really</u> kind of you.
3 Thanks. I'd be <u>very</u> grateful.
4 I'm sorry. It's <u>totally</u> out of the question.
5 Yes, I'm <u>quite</u> certain.
6 That's a <u>completely</u> different matter.

A

B

36

Unit 3 Design for life

7 Pronunciation stress in intensifying adverbs

▶ 22 Work in pairs. Listen to the sentences in Exercise 6. Note where the stress falls. Then practise saying the sentences.

▶ **INTENSIFYING ADVERBS**

very, extremely, incredibly, really + gradable adjective
I'm **very** pleased to welcome …
They are **extremely** basic.

absolutely, really, utterly, quite + ungradable (extreme) adjective
Some of them are **really** stunning.
It's **absolutely** freezing there.

completely, entirely, totally, quite + ungradable (absolute*) adjective
Today we're looking at something **completely** different.

* 'absolute' means adjectives which do not have a comparative or superlative form

For further information and practice, see page 160.

8 Look at the grammar box. Turn to the audioscript of the interview on page 182 (track 21) and find:
   a five more examples of intensifying adverbs with gradable adjectives
   b two more examples of intensifying adverbs with ungradable (extreme) adjectives, e.g. *amazing, disgusting*
   c two more examples of intensifying adverbs with ungradable (absolute) adjectives, e.g. *right, true*

9 Choose the correct intensifier to complete the sentences.
   1 I prefer modern design because it's usually *absolutely / very* simple and neat. Having said that, my own house is *absolutely / incredibly* disorganized.
   2 The outside of the house is old but the interior is *completely / utterly* new. They've done a *completely / really* incredible job of renovating it.
   3 I saw an *absolutely / entirely* stunning penthouse flat for rent yesterday, but it's *utterly / extremely* expensive.
   4 She's a(n) *incredibly / quite* talented architect. I'd be *totally / very* surprised if she isn't famous one day.
   5 Cath is *very / quite* certain that there's a wasp nest under her roof. She's *entirely / utterly* miserable about it.
   6 The price of houses in London is *extremely / absolutely* ridiculous. Even a one-bedroom flat is *absolutely / completely* unaffordable.

10 Complete these sentences in your own words. Use intensifiers where there is a highlighted space.
   1 I would only eat … if I was .... desperate.
   2 I get .... irritated by people who …
   3 The last time I was .... tired was …
   4 It's .... wrong to let children …
   5 I think … are .... gorgeous.
   6 I'm .... certain that good health is …

Vocabulary adverb + adjective collocations

11 Look at this example of an adverb + adjective collocation from the interview. What does *strongly* mean here: 'very' or 'a little'?

"I've also been **strongly influenced** by the architect Gary Chang."

12 Look at these other adverb + adjective collocations. In most cases the adverb has the meaning of *very* or *absolutely*. Find the two collocations where this is NOT the case.

bitterly disappointed	mildly amusing
closely associated (with)	painfully slow
deadly serious	patently obvious
desperately unlucky	perfectly reasonable
hopelessly in love	vaguely familiar
ideally suited to	wildly optimistic

13 Work in pairs. Think of examples that fit the descriptions of these things (1–5) or use your own ideas. Then discuss your situations with another pair.
   1 something you learned where you found progress painfully slow
   2 an ambition one of your friends has that seems wildly optimistic
   3 a bad idea someone had, i.e. it was patently obvious that it wouldn't work
   4 a sporting competition where someone was desperately unlucky
   5 a job you are ideally suited to

Speaking my life

14 The architect in the interview designed 'a timber and glass vacation house with built-in sauna'. Work in pairs. Look at these luxury features of houses and say which three you would most like to have in your house and why. Try to use intensifying adverbs in your answer.

I'd absolutely love to have a home cinema, because there are so many films now with really amazing special effects that you can't appreciate on a small screen.

a conservatory	en suite bathrooms	a games room
a garage/workshop	a gym	a home cinema
a large kitchen	a library	a roof garden	a sauna
a walk-in wardrobe		

my life ▶ YOUR HOME TOWN ▶ **A BIT OF LUXURY** ▶ HOW SPACES AFFECT YOU ▶ EXPRESSING OPINIONS ▶ AN OPINION ESSAY

37

reading Zaha Hadid • critical thinking summarizing • word focus *ground* • speaking how spaces affect you

3c The paper architect

Reading

1 Look at the photos and answer the questions.
1 Do you like the designs? Why? / Why not?
2 Do you have a favourite modern building? What is it and what do you like about it? Have you been inside it?

2 Read the article about the architect Zaha Hadid. Choose the statement (a–c) that best summarizes her aims.

a to prove that women too can be successful architects
b to create original buildings that people like to be in
c to create buildings with unusual and complex forms

3 Read the article again and answer the questions.
1 Why was Hadid called 'the paper architect'?
2 What does it mean when it says Hadid became 'sought-after'?
3 What challenges did Hadid face when she entered the architecture profession in Britain?
4 How did Hadid begin when she wanted to create a new design?
5 Why were potential customers doubtful about Hadid's designs?
6 What was the most important thing for Hadid when designing a new building?
7 What is interesting about the inside of the Evelyn Grace Academy?
8 How does the author conclude that Hadid will be remembered?

Critical thinking summarizing

4 In order to check you have understood the main points of an article, it is useful to be able to summarize its message or arguments accurately. To help you summarize this article, underline adjectives or nouns that describe the following:

- Zaha Hadid's designs
- her character
- her buildings
- her position in the world of architecture
- the effect of her buildings on the user

5 Compare the words you underlined with your partner. Then together compose a short summary of Zaha Hadid's life and her contribution to architecture.

Word focus *ground*

6 Work in pairs. Look at the expression in bold from the article and discuss what you think it means. Then do the same for the other expressions in bold (1–5).

"But as with anyone who tries to **break new ground**, it was not easy to convince people to follow."

1 It's a very clever design, but as a business idea it will never **get off the ground** unless they get some money to develop it.
2 The council decided to close the swimming pool **on the grounds that** it wasn't making money.
3 It was a great meeting. We **covered a lot of ground** in the two hours.
4 Even though she's going to appear on TV, it's important that she **keeps her feet on the ground**, because it may lead to nothing.
5 No one seemed to think his plan would work, but to his credit, he **stood his ground**.

7 From your own experience, think of an example of each of the following.
1 someone who always keeps their feet on the ground
2 a time when you stood your ground (despite opposition)
3 a company which is always breaking new ground with its products

Speaking *my life*

8 Public buildings or spaces can sometimes have bad associations for people. Look at these places which people in a survey said they didn't like being in. How do you feel in each of them? Why?
1 a dentist's surgery
2 a lift
3 an airport departure lounge
4 a classroom or lecture hall
5 a large open plan office

9 Work in small groups. Choose one of the public spaces in Exercise 8. Discuss how the design of this space could be improved to make people feel more comfortable. Think about the following:

- shape and size of the space
- lighting
- arrangement of furniture
- other additions (music, plants, etc.)

38

THE PAPER ARCHITECT

▶ 23

For a long time, Iraqi-born Zaha Hadid was known as 'the paper architect'. That was because very few of her bold and daring designs, though frequently praised for their imagination and originality, ever left the page to become real buildings. Between 1978, when she graduated, and 1998, just four of her 27 projects were actually realized. However, following the successful completion of two art galleries in Cincinnati and Denmark and a commission for BMW in Leipzig in 2005, Hadid's buildings began to appear everywhere. Within ten years, she had become one of the most sought-after architects in the world. So why did Hadid's architecture take so long to be accepted?

Firstly, she was one of the few women in a profession dominated by men. Today in Britain less than fifteen per cent of practising architects are women. A lot more enter the profession, but over half leave, either because of slow career progress or because they become disillusioned with the conservatism of most British architectural design. But in Hadid's case, this seems to have been a motivator. From an early stage, she was determined to challenge the establishment with her own new ideas. But it was never going to be an easy fight.

Secondly, even during her student days, Hadid was interested in pushing boundaries and in creating buildings that were new and different. She felt that 21st-century developments in materials science and computer modelling tools provided an opportunity to experiment with more complex curved forms than architects had attempted in the past. She would initially sketch out her ideas in the form of an artist's drawing. But as with anyone who tries to break new ground, it was not easy to convince people to follow – to believe that these sketches could be translated into functional structures. However, once people began to see the results – in buildings such as the Guangzhou Opera House in China and the MAXXI art museum in Rome – they began not only to believe, but also to start shouting her name.

The idea of the architect as an artist was something Hadid herself rejected. She did not want people to think that she had designed a building just so that they could stare and admire its beauty from the outside. 'Architecture,' she said, 'is not a medium of personal expression for me. It facilitates everyday life.' In other words, her aim was to create buildings that were not just innovative, but practical too. The internal space and how people interacted with it were the keys for her.

For this reason, she was attracted particularly to public projects: for example, the Aquatics Centre for the 2012 Olympics and the Evelyn Grace Academy, a large secondary school in south London. For the latter, Hadid designed a building with lots of natural light and dramatic angles, so that pupils could view the activity of other students from different perspectives within the structure. Right in the middle of the site, between buildings, she placed a 100-metre running track to celebrate the school's emphasis on sports. The idea of offering the viewer multiple viewpoints inside a building is a common theme in Hadid's work. Internal spaces interconnect cleverly so that the visitor is surprised and charmed at every turn.

Zaha Hadid died of a heart attack in 2016 aged 65, leaving behind a groundbreaking body of work. She remained all her life something of an outsider; or, if not completely outside, then on the edges of the architectural establishment. Yet her impact on architecture was enormous: it will never be the same again.

real life expressing opinions • **pronunciation** linking vowel sounds (intrusion)

3d A lot to recommend it

Real life expressing opinions

1 Work in pairs. Think about a public work of art in your town or area. Describe it to your partner, saying what you like or dislike about it.

2 Look at the photo and the caption and discuss the questions.

1. Do you like these public works of art? Why? / Why not?
2. What benefits do you think they might bring to the city (for both locals and visitors)?

3 ▶ 24 Listen to two people discussing a proposal for a public work of art in a city. Answer the questions.

1. What piece of work is being proposed?
2. Are the speakers in favour of or against it?

4 Work in pairs. Read the short text below. Then discuss which way of expressing opinions you most commonly encounter. How much does this depend on the person you are talking to?

> Different people express their opinions in different ways. Some people disagree briefly and bluntly, e.g. 'I don't agree,' or 'That's not correct.' Others disagree openly but politely, e.g. 'I'm afraid I don't share your opinion.' In some cultures, it is considered rude to disagree openly and people express disagreement by keeping silent or even by saying the opposite, e.g. 'Yes, I agree.'

5 ▶ 24 Listen to the discussion again. Complete the arguments that each speaker gives in favour of or against the idea.

1. Speaker A: I think it's _____ .
2. Speaker B: Personally, I'd rather have something _____ .
3. Speaker B: I'm also not convinced that it will _____ .
4. Speaker A: I reckon people … will really like the fact that it _____ .
5. Speaker B: I'm all in favour of something that's relevant …, but I'm afraid it just seems _____ .
6. Speaker A: Well, for me, it's very important that it's _____ .

The Crown Fountain and the 'Bean' in Millennium Park, Chicago

6 Look at the expressions for expressing opinions. Say which expressions are used to agree, disagree politely, disagree or give an opinion.

> ▶ **EXPRESSING OPINIONS**
>
> I think … / I reckon …
> I have to say, …
> Personally, I …
> For me, … / If you ask me, …
> It seems a bit … to me.
> It's pretty obvious that … / It's fairly clear that …
> I'm (all) in favour of …
> I'm against …
> I agree completely. / Absolutely.
> I disagree. / I don't agree.
> I don't think you should underestimate …
> I can see that, but …
> I'm not (entirely) convinced that …

7 Pronunciation linking vowel sounds (intrusion)

a ▶ 25 Listen to these phrases. Which consonant sounds (/w/ or /j/) are used to link the vowel sounds in each of these sentences (1–6)?

1. Have you seen the artwork?
2. It's more likely to attract people.
3. If you ask me, …
4. I disagree about the cost of it.
5. I expect you're right.
6. I'm not so interested in architecture.

b Work in pairs. Practise saying the sentences in Exercise 7a, linking the vowel sounds with /w/ and /j/.

8 Work in pairs or small groups. Look at the two proposals for a public work of art on page 154. Ask each other for your opinion of each proposal. Use expressions to agree or disagree.

What do you think of the LED screen idea? Personally, I think …

---

40 **my life** ▶ YOUR HOME TOWN ▶ A BIT OF LUXURY ▶ HOW SPACES AFFECT YOU ▶ **EXPRESSING OPINIONS** ▶ AN OPINION ESSAY

writing an opinion essay • writing skill discourse markers

Unit 3 Design for life

3e Old and new

Writing an opinion essay

1 Look at the photo of two buildings. Do these two buildings go well together? Why? / Why not?

2 Read the essay question and the essay. Answer the questions.

   1 What is the writer's opinion?
   2 What arguments does he give to support this?
   3 What points against his own argument does he mention?

3 Look at the four key elements of an opinion essay. Find each element in the essay. What is the correct order?

   a deal with opposing arguments
   b give your opinion and present the arguments supporting it
   c make your conclusion
   d analyse the question and set out your starting point

4 **Writing skill** discourse markers

a The writer uses certain phrases to present his ideas. Look at the underlined discourse markers in the essay and match the discourse markers with the function (1–5).

   1 introduce an opinion (1 adverbial phrase, 2 verb phrases)
   2 qualify or make a concession to an opinion or argument (2 adverbial phrases)
   3 reinforce a point or argument (2 adverbial phrases)
   4 express the same point in another way (1 phrase)
   5 sum up the argument (1 adverbial phrase)

b Complete this text. Use discourse markers from Exercise 4a.

   ^{1}_____, modern buildings that try to imitate older architectural styles do not work. ^{2}_____, they sometimes look worse than an unimaginative modern design. Despite this, some architects and planners insist on building in a 'traditional' style. ^{3}_____, their intentions are good: they do not want to spoil the overall look of an area, but ^{4}_____ they are mistaken. It would be much better if architects and planners considered a range of new designs. ^{5}_____, they need to be more adventurous.

Should we allow modern buildings to be built next to older buildings in a historic area of a city?

In order to answer this question properly, first we need to ask whether people actually want to preserve the historic character of an area. Not all historic buildings are attractive, but they may contribute to an overall feeling that makes the area attractive to people. What should we do then if a new building is needed?

In my view, modern architecture can fit perfectly well with buildings from another period. Indeed, there are many examples in my own home town of Tours where radical modern designs sit comfortably next to old buildings. As long as the new building is pleasing and does not dominate its surroundings too much, it should enhance the attractiveness of the area. Having said that, there must also be a limit to the number of new buildings if people want to preserve the area's historic feel.

Admittedly, there are examples of modern buildings which have spoilt an area, but this is not an argument against putting new buildings among historic ones in principle. I suspect that the main reason for objections to such buildings is that people are conservative: in other words, they do not like change.

In conclusion, I believe that while we must respect the views of others, it is the duty of architects and planners to move things forward. After all, if we only reproduced what was there before, we would all still be living in caves.

5 Write an opinion essay about this question (200–250 words).

Should we create more socially mixed residential areas, where rich people live next to poorer people, instead of in separate communities?

6 Exchange essays with your partner. Use these questions to check your essays.

   • Is their opinion clear and have they presented both sides of the argument?
   • Have they followed the structure suggested in Exercise 3?
   • Have they used discourse markers correctly to present the ideas?

3f A story of solutions

The new fire station in Newbern, Alabama, USA

Unit 3 **Design for life**

Before you watch

1 Look at the photo. How does (or did) this building serve the community? Who works/worked there and what is their job like, do you think?

2 Look at this list of public buildings or buildings that serve the community. Add any others you can think of. Then answer the questions (1–2).

college	community centre	court house	fire station
hospital	museum	leisure/sports centre
post office	public library	theatre	town hall

1 Which buildings/amenities would you expect to find in a town of less than 500 people?
2 Which do you think are the most important buildings/amenities for residents?

While you watch

3 **3.1** Watch the first part of the video (0.00 to 0.14). Note down all the things you see. Compare notes with your partner. Then answer the questions.

1 What kind of town is Newbern?
2 Can you describe the buildings you saw in the town? What were they like?

4 **3.1** Watch the whole video. Give more details of what you saw by answering these questions.

1 What was the first fire engine you saw like?
2 What was the meeting about?
3 How would you describe the design of the new fire station?
4 What kind of fire did you see?
5 What did you see the architecture students doing?
6 Who did you see using the library?

5 **3.1** Watch the whole video again. Pause after each speaker and write in the words to complete the summary of each speaker's message. The first letter is given for you.

1 Sarah Curry: Having no local firehouse means houses b_____ d_____; so people can't get i_____ and they are h_____ .
2 Andrew Freear: Community groups focused on the o_____ and we helped with the b_____ .
3 Patrick Braxton: Our first call was to a grass fire and we took t_____-t_____ people with us.
4 Andrew Freear: Frances Sullivan came to us and said 'If you really want to help, build a l_____ .'
5 Kesha Jones: I don't know how you c_____ Newbern, but I'm very g_____ you came.
6 Sarah Curry: This works because everyone is working towards the s_____ g_____ as a team.
7 Frances Sullivan: Architecture is part of the s_____ , but it's the p_____ that really make the difference.

After you watch

6 **Vocabulary in context**

a **3.2** Watch the clips from the video. Choose the correct meaning of the words and phrases.

b Work in pairs. Complete these sentences in your own words. Then compare your sentences with a partner.

1 The sole reason that I learn English is …
2 … was a catalyst for …
3 The book, … , had a profound effect on me when I was younger.

7 Look at the viewer comments about the video. Which is closest to your impression after watching the film? Explain why.

AJ
I found this very uplifting. I agree with what the woman said at the end: it's people that make the difference. And you can see that these people really care about each other and their community.

HF
I love the simplicity of this architecture. It answers the need and nothing more.

TS
I came to this thinking that I was going to see some very innovative or radical new architectural designs. But actually, there weren't any. Disappointed.

YL
I can't really put my finger on why I like this. Perhaps it's just the way it's filmed.

8 What new building would your community most benefit from? Present your idea to the class and explain your reasons.

43

UNIT 3 REVIEW AND MEMORY BOOSTER

Grammar

1 Look at the photo. What do you think this building is for? Read the text and check your ideas.

2 Choose the correct options to complete the text.

I ¹ *really / completely* love the London Olympics Aquatics Centre. It's a great example of how to design a public building and actually it's ² *slightly / quite* rare for design and function to come together as successfully as this. It's both very practical and ³ *extremely / absolutely* pleasing to look at. Like many of Hadid's buildings, the outside has a ⁴ *quite / rather* organic feel to it. Some say it looks like a large turtle with its flippers outstretched. Hadid did not ⁵ *quite / particularly* want to add these 'flippers', but they were extra structures needed to accommodate the 15,000 spectators attending the Olympic swimming competitions. After the Olympics, 12,500 seats were ⁶ *completely / utterly* removed. If the exterior is ⁷ *a bit / pretty* remarkable, the interior is ⁸ *quite / entirely* spectacular. Bare concrete sweeps this way and that in beautiful curves and the diving boards seem to grow out of the floor. At floor level is the fifty-metre pool, which is ⁹ *totally / really* still and a deep, deep blue. The whole effect is ¹⁰ *entirely / incredibly* dramatic.

3 **>> MB** Work in pairs. Look at the adjectives which follow the modifiers or intensifiers in the text. Which are: a) gradable adjectives b) ungradable (extreme) adjectives and c) ungradable (absolute) adjectives?

I CAN	
use adverbs to modify or intensify meaning	☐

Vocabulary

4 Complete the phrases. Then put the phrases into three categories: a feature of a house, a feature of a town and an adverb + adjective collocation.

1 a two-b_____ flat
2 b_____ly disappointed
3 a b_____ wall
4 a b_____-up area
5 a s_____ing suburb
6 a ten-s_____ block of flats
7 an en-s_____ bathroom
8 w_____ly optimistic
9 a w_____-in wardrobe

5 Which of these adjectives would you use to describe these places from Unit 3?

characterless   compact   imposing   lively
modern   quaint   run-down   sleepy   smart
spacious

6 **>> MB** Work in pairs. Use the adjectives from Exercise 5 to describe a building, area or city that you know.

I CAN	
use adverb + adjective collocations	☐
describe buildings and places	☐

Real life

7 Match the sentence beginnings (1–7) with the endings (a–g).

1 Personally,
2 It seems a bit
3 It's pretty clear that
4 I'm all in favour
5 I can see that,
6 I agree with you
7 You shouldn't underestimate

a of public art works.
b the benefits.
c no one wants it.
d completely.
e I think it's a great idea.
f old-fashioned to me.
g but I still think it's too expensive.

8 **>> MB** Work in pairs. Give your opinions about an idea to create a small zoo in your local city where children can learn more about animals. Use the expressions in Exercise 7.

I CAN	
express my opinions	☐
agree and disagree politely	☐

Unit 4 Innovation

'Cyborg' woman with a bionic eye

FEATURES

46 Shrink it, bend it, fold it

The future of bendable technology

48 The mother of invention

What drives new discoveries

50 The shoe giver

The story of a successful social entrepreneur

54 This man risked it all

A video about a social enterprise in Uganda

1 Look at the photo and caption. What do you think 'cyborg' and 'bionic' mean? Is this science fiction or something real?

2 ▶ 26 Listen to a news report about bionic body parts. Answer the questions.

1 How badly damaged was the woman's sight before her operation?
2 What could she see after the operation?
3 Who are the ear buds designed for and what can they do?
4 What question does this new technology raise?

3 ▶ 26 Work in pairs. Try to replace the verbs in bold with the more scientific verbs used in the news report. Then listen to the news report again and check.

1 Surgeons **put** an electronic chip into her right eye.
2 It'll probably take months for Lewis to **teach** her brain to see again.
3 She can already **see** nearby objects …
4 They can **cut out** the background noise …
5 … or **make** surrounding sounds **louder** …

4 Discuss how bionic body parts (e.g. bionic legs, a bionic hand, a bionic eye, bionic skin) could be more 'effective' than biological body parts. What advantages or abilities could they have?

my life ▶ FUTURE SOLUTIONS ▶ HOW PEOPLE MANAGED IN THE PAST ▶ A SOCIAL BUSINESS ▶ MAKING A SHORT PITCH ▶ A PROPOSAL

reading bendable technology • wordbuilding -able • grammar future probability • speaking future solutions

4a Shrink it, bend it, fold it

Reading

1 Work in pairs. Answer the questions.

1 What everyday objects can you think of that you can shrink, bend or fold?
   You can shrink a jumper.
2 What other everyday things could it be useful to make smaller by shrinking, bending or folding?

2 Read the article. Make two lists of objects (a and b). Were these the same as your ideas in Exercise 1?

a objects we are already familiar with that can be shrunk, bent or folded
b objects we will see more of in the near future that can be shrunk, bent or folded

3 Read the article again and answer the questions.

1 How do 21st-century TVs and mobile phones compare with 20th-century ones?
2 Where will the next generation of solar cells be placed?
3 What is the author's prediction for bendable screens?
4 Who in future will be able to launch their own small satellite?
5 What are the benefits of the new specially coated 'super-pills'?

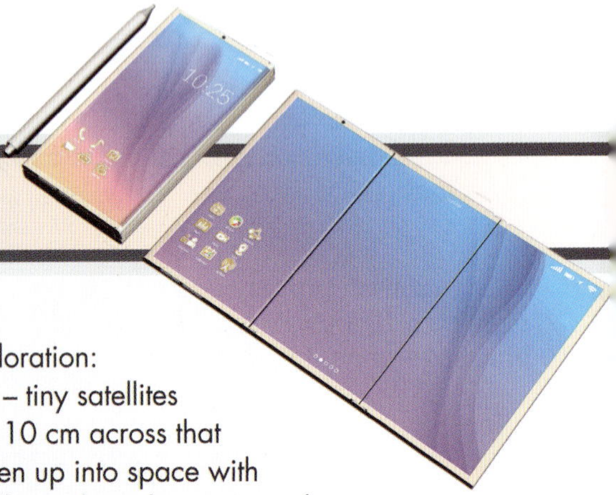

SHRINK IT, BEND IT, FOLD IT

▶ 27

There's always something rather satisfying about things that can be reduced in size and packed away: a folding bike you can take on the train; a raincoat you can roll up and pop into a carry bag; folding, unbreakable sunglasses you can put in your back pocket. Now advances in electronics and materials science are pushing the boundaries of what is possible, helping manufacturers to make increasingly smaller or thinner or more flexible devices: you only have to compare a 21st-century television or mobile phone with a 20th-century one to see that. What might the next ten years bring?

Energy: The idea of harnessing solar energy is nothing new, but we may well be about to see a revolution in the construction of solar cells which will allow them to be incorporated into an ultra-thin transparent film. So instead of expensive solar panels on roofs or in solar farms, in future they could form part of the windows on our buildings.

Communications: Using screens as thin as a sheet of paper, bendable technology is already here, but the chances are that it will become very widespread in the coming years: phones that wrap around your wrist, foldable computers that fit into your jacket pocket. Perhaps one day soon we will see TV screens that can be rolled up and carried with us.

Space exploration: 'Cubesats' – tiny satellites measuring 10 cm across that can be taken up into space with larger satellites – have become much more affordable: anyone can launch their own satellite now for as little as $3,000. This should increase our chances of making new discoveries in space.

Medicine: Doctors are already successfully repairing damaged eyesight with tiny electronic implants and removing blockages in arteries with small foldable stents. Progress in bionics is likely to continue at a fast pace, although it will almost certainly raise difficult ethical questions along the way. The other area in which materials science is making huge progress is in how drugs are delivered into the body. New types of coating around pills mean each pill needs to be taken just once and then the drug inside can be released over weeks and months, even years. It's likely that such 'super-pills' will in future be inserted directly into the area needing treatment, such as cancer cells, increasing the drug's effectiveness enormously.

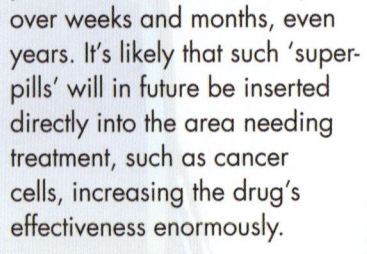

---

harness (v) /ˈhɑː(r)nɪs/ getting hold of and using
implant (n) /ˈɪmplɑːnt/ something that is put in your body during an operation
stent (n) /stent/ a small expanding tube used to replace damaged tubes in your body (e.g. in arteries)

Wordbuilding -able

> **WORDBUILDING** -able
>
> We can add the suffix -able to many verbs to form an adjective meaning something is possible. The prefixes un-, in- or non- can also be added to say that something is impossible.
> *foldable, removable, unbreakable, non-negotiable*
>
> For further practice, see Workbook page 29.

4 Look at the wordbuilding box. Then rewrite the sentences (1–6) using adjectives ending in -able. You will need to change other words in the sentence.

1 You can't **reuse** those cups: you're supposed to **dispose** of them.
   Those cups aren't reusable; they're disposable.
2 They said this camera could**n't** be **broken**. I hope they **refund** me the money.
3 Can I **wash** this jacket or does it have to go to the dry cleaners?
4 The car can be **repaired**. It's just a question of whether I can **afford** the repair.
5 I can't **excuse** his behaviour. All I asked was that I could **rely** on him.
6 You ca**n't imagine** how painful it was.

Grammar future probability

> **FUTURE PROBABILITY**
>
> **Modal verbs**
> *may (well) / could (well) / might (well), should*
> In future they **could** form part of the windows ...
> We **may well** be about to see a revolution in solar cells.
> It **should** increase our chances of making new discoveries ...
>
> **Adverbs**
> *perhaps, maybe, probably, almost certainly*
> It will **almost certainly** raise difficult ethical questions.
> **Perhaps** one day soon we will see TV screens that can be rolled up.
>
> **Adjective phrases**
> *It's possible/probable/(un)likely that; is likely to*
> It's **likely that** in future 'super-pills' will be inserted.
> Progress in bionics **is likely to** continue at a fast pace.
>
> **Noun phrases**
> *The likelihood is (that), The chances are (that), There's a good chance (that)*
> **The chances are** (that) it will become very widespread.
>
> For further information and practice, see page 162.

5 Look at the grammar box. Answer the questions.

1 How does *well* affect the meaning when it is used after *may, might* or *could*?
2 What are the usual positions of an adverb of probability?
3 Sentences with *(un)likely* have two possible grammatical forms. What are they? Transform each example in the grammar box using the other form.

6 Look at the expressions of probability again in the grammar box. Discuss which words or phrases mean the following:

1 something is possible (about 50% chance)
2 something is probable (about 70% chance)
3 something is not probable (about 20% chance)
4 something is very sure or almost certain (about 90% chance)

7 Look at the description of innovations. Rewrite the phrases in bold using the words in brackets.

> Smart textiles are already here but [1] **we will probably see** (chances) a lot more of them in the coming years. Some innovations will just be cosmetic but others [2] **are likely to have** (may well) practical uses. For example, scientists at Penn State University have created a self-repairing fabric. They believe that within the next ten years people [3] **will probably be wearing** (likely) clothes that mend themselves. [4] **It's possible this will mean** (could) the end of sewing as we know it. Meanwhile, researchers in China have made a fabric that generates electricity as you move. It [5] **is unlikely to produce** (probably) large amounts of power but [6] **it will probably be** (should) enough to recharge a phone.

8 Complete the conversation using one word in each space. There is sometimes more than one possible answer. Then discuss if you agree with the speakers' views.

A: Do you think that the problem of internet security [1] _____ get worse in the future?
B: Well, there [2] _____ be a technological solution, but I doubt it. I think what's more [3] _____ to happen is that we'll use the internet more and more and internet crime will almost [4] _____ increase.
A: I think you're right. Internet security may [5] _____ improve, but the criminals will [6] _____ get better at what they do too.

Speaking — my life

9 Work in pairs. Choose two of the challenges (or your own ideas) that people face in the 21st century. Discuss whether technology will be able to solve them, and if so, how. Use expressions of probability.

- Traffic congestion and pollution
- The growing shortage of water
- Curing illness and disease

I think technology will almost certainly be able to solve traffic congestion and pollution problems. There's a good chance that ...

my life ▸ **FUTURE SOLUTIONS** ▸ HOW PEOPLE MANAGED IN THE PAST ▸ A SOCIAL BUSINESS ▸ MAKING A SHORT PITCH
▸ A PROPOSAL

listening the inspiration for innovations • vocabulary phrasal verb *come* • grammar past modals • pronunciation weak forms in past modals • speaking how people managed in the past

4b The mother of invention

Listening

1 Work in pairs. Look at the saying below. Discuss what it means and if you think it is always true.

"Necessity is the mother of invention."

2 Look at the photo and the caption. What adjectives would you use to describe this invention? What do you think the inventor is trying to achieve?

3 ▶ 28 Listen to an interview about what inspires inventions. Choose the statement (a–c) that best summarizes the speaker's view.

  a Most inventions are an answer to an urgent need.
  b Most inventions are things that we didn't imagine we needed until we became used to them.
  c Most inventions come from companies who want to make a commercial profit.

4 ▶ 28 Listen to the interview again and choose the correct option to complete the sentences.

  1 People in their twenties probably can't imagine *doing research / following the news* without the internet.
  2 Martha Kay is *a business woman / an academic*.
  3 In the nineteenth century, British politicians said the telephone was *too expensive / of little use*.
  4 The presenter uses the telephone as an example of a case where a need *was filled / didn't exist before*.
  5 Most innovations make our lives *more satisfying / easier*.
  6 The presenter suggests that women in the 1960s liked *going out to shop / staying in the house*.
  7 The mobile phone and the personal computer are examples of innovations that were *very expensive at first / seen as unnecessary*.
  8 *Literary Digest* predicted that the motor car would *remain a luxury / go out of fashion*.

Charles Steinlauf's invention: a four-position bicycle which also contains a built-in sewing machine

Vocabulary phrasal verb *come*

5 Look at the sentences. Choose the correct meaning (a–c) of each phrasal verb. The first three sentences are from the interview.

  1 But how do such inventions **come about**?
    a succeed   b happen   c work
  2 Entrepreneurs often **come up with** ideas to make our lives a little more convenient.
    a think of   b ignore   c search for
  3 Over time, we **come to** rely on them.
    a start to   b try to   c have to
  4 A researcher **came across** the material for post-it notes when looking for a new kind of glue.
    a thought of   b found by chance   c stole
  5 Early experiments with flying didn't really **come off**.
    a succeed   b get noticed   c get taken seriously
  6 Perrelet was so respected that when other watchmakers **came up against** a problem, they would consult him.
    a solved   b encountered   c analysed

6 Work in pairs. Write three sentences using the phrasal verbs from Exercise 5. Then read your sentences to your partner omitting the verb and see if they can guess the missing verb.

48

Grammar past modals

> **PAST MODALS**
>
> 1 **had to (do)**
> They felt they **had to find** a way to communicate at a distance.
>
> 2 **needn't have (done) / didn't need to (do)**
> They **didn't need to have** phones.
> We have so many things around us that we **needn't have acquired**.
>
> 3 **must have, might/may/could have, can't have (done)**
> Life **must have been** very different before the invention of certain things.
> You **might** never **have considered** how people searched for information before the internet.
> It **can't have been** easy.
>
> 4 **should have / ought to have (done)**
> They probably **should have been** more open-minded.
>
> For further information and practice, see page 162.

7 Look at the grammar box. Match the past modal verb forms (1–4) with the uses (a–d).

  a to speculate on past events
  b to talk about an obligation
  c to say what was expected or advisable
  d to talk about a lack of necessity

8 Work in pairs. Complete the sentences with the correct past modal verb form.

1 | needn't have   didn't need to |

  a We use _____ to say something wasn't necessary but it was done anyway.
  b We use _____, to say something wasn't necessary whether it was done or not.

2 | may/might/could have   must have   can't have |

  a When we use _____, it means we are almost certain that something happened / was true.
  b When we use _____, it means we are almost certain it didn't happen / wasn't true.
  c When we use _____, it means we think it possibly happened / was true.

9 Choose the correct options to complete the conversation.
  A: I didn't hear you leave this morning. I ¹ *must / might* have been asleep.
  B: I left for work very early, actually. But I ² *didn't need to bother / needn't have bothered*. There was no traffic.
  A: I think it was a school holiday. That ³ *could / should* have been the reason. But you ⁴ *had to wake / should have woken* me. I got to work late in the end.
  B: Sorry. I was really focused on leaving in good time. I ⁵ *must have been / had to be* sure of getting to my meeting.

10 Complete the sentences. Use an appropriate past modal verb form with the words in brackets.

  1 Before cars were commonplace, it _____ (not / be) so easy to take your family for a weekend outing.
  2 In the 1940s, people _____ (not / own) a television, because radios provided news and entertainment.
  3 Before satellite navigation in cars, people _____ (depend) on printed maps.
  4 I never use this microwave oven. I _____ (buy) it.
  5 In the days before TV, it _____ (be) really exciting to go to the cinema!
  6 I'm not sure who invented the wristwatch. It _____ (be) a Swiss person.
  7 The inventor of 'cats eyes' in the road _____ (receive) more recognition. They've saved a huge number of lives.
  8 I think when Tim Berners-Lee invented the internet, he _____ (realize) that it would have negative as well as positive effects.

11 Pronunciation weak forms in past modals

  a ▶ 29 Circle the weak forms (words not stressed, including 'to') in these past modal verbs. Then listen and check.

  1 It should have worked, but it didn't.
  2 I had to wait half an hour.
  3 He must have forgotten.
  4 You needn't have worried.
  5 She may have left already.
  6 I didn't need to be there.

  b Practise saying the sentences in Exercise 11a.

Speaking my life

12 Work in groups. Use a range of past modals to speculate on the answers to these questions.

  How did people:
  • wake up on time before there were alarm clocks?
  • keep money safe before savings banks existed?
  • entertain themselves in the evenings before we had electricity in our homes?
  • deal with aches and pains without medicines?
  • contact each other in an emergency before the telephone existed?
  • clean their teeth without toothbrushes?
  • detect broken bones before x-rays existed?

13 Work in pairs. Think of two commonly used inventions: one that you couldn't live without and one that you find unnecessary. Discuss the inventions and the reasons you chose them.

I couldn't live without my electric kettle because I drink so much tea. I know in the past people used to boil water on the cooker, but it must have taken a long time.

my life ▶ FUTURE SOLUTIONS ▶ HOW PEOPLE MANAGED IN THE PAST ▶ A SOCIAL BUSINESS ▶ MAKING A SHORT PITCH
▶ A PROPOSAL

reading a social entrepreneur • critical thinking finding counter arguments • word focus *give* • speaking a social business

4c The shoe giver

Reading

1 Work in pairs and discuss the questions.
1 What are the main priorities of a business, in your opinion?
2 Can you think of ways that a business could make money and help society at the same time?

2 Read the article on page 51. Then summarize how TOMS makes money and does good at the same time.

3 Read the article again. Are the sentences true (T) or false (F)?
1 Blake Mycoskie's early career consisted of starting and then selling companies.
2 Mycoskie immediately saw the Argentinian children's shoe problem as another business challenge.
3 The main advantage of the one-for-one scheme is that Mycoskie doesn't have to keep asking people to donate money.
4 The author suggests that in business, energy and enthusiasm is a very important factor.
5 Mycoskie would like it if his customers became social entrepreneurs too.
6 Podoconiosis is a disease that concerns developed countries as much as developing countries.
7 Mycoskie thinks that any business could profit from making a similar one-for-one offer to its customers.
8 The author thinks that Mycoskie should be proud that he has a successful business, not just one that helps people.

Critical thinking finding counter arguments

4 The author presents a positive picture of TOMS, but there are suggestions that there are also arguments against the initiative. Find possible criticisms in the text in these areas.
a the price of the product
b the business model
c charitable giving

5 Work in pairs. Compare your answers from Exercise 4. Then write some questions for Blake Mycoskie that would challenge him on these points.

Word focus *give*

6 Work in pairs. Find these expressions with *give* in the article and discuss what they mean.
a give it a break (line 11)
b give it some thought (line 26–27)

7 Complete the expressions with *give* using these words. Discuss what each expression means.

| best | break | go | go ahead | thought | time |

1 It's difficult to be in a new environment, but **give it some** _____ and you'll feel more at home.
2 Don't worry if you don't win: just **give it your** _____ .
3 I wasn't actually expecting him to like our business proposal, but he **gave us the** _____ .
4 **Give him a** _____ . He's only been doing the job two months. He can't be expected to know everything.
5 There's no need to tell me your answer now. **Give it some** _____ and then let me know.
6 The only way to find out if you can mend it yourself is to **give it a** _____ .

8 Match these expressions with similar expressions from Exercise 7. Then make three sentences about your own experience using expressions with *give*.

| a chance | consideration | the green light | a try |
| a while | your all |

Speaking my life

9 Work in groups. Imagine these organizations come to you for financial help. Considering them both as businesses and as organizations with a social benefit, decide which you would help. Give reasons.

A This organization collects food near its sell-by date from supermarkets and uses volunteers to distribute it free to homeless people. The company needs money for transport and administration costs.

B This organization sells gardening and landscaping services to companies. The people it employs are all long-term unemployed people who get training, work experience and a little pocket money.

C This organization collects unwanted clothing. Clothes in good condition are washed and given to people in need. Clothes in poor condition are recycled and made into fashion clothing to be sold.

10 Do *you* know a company with a social purpose?

The shoe giver

Blake Mycoskie is a self-confessed serial entrepreneur. He set up his first business, EZ Laundry, a laundry service for students, when he was still at college. Having built up the company to serve seven colleges in the south-west of the USA, he sold his share to his business partner and moved on to a media advertising business in Nashville. This again he sold on to Clear Channel, one of the industry's leading companies.

Three more businesses later, still only 29 years old, and feeling a bit 'burned out' from work, Mycoskie decided to give it a break for a while and headed down to Argentina for some rest and relaxation. But rest isn't really part of an entrepreneur's make-up and it wasn't long before Mycoskie had hit on another idea, one that would come to define him as perhaps the world's best-known social entrepreneur.

On a visit to a village outside Buenos Aires, he was shocked to see that many of the children didn't have any shoes; or if they did, the shoes were ill-fitting and badly worn. Since shoes – particularly the local farmers' canvas shoe, the alpargata – are relatively cheap in Argentina, Mycoskie's first instinct was to set up a charity to donate shoes to the children. But after giving it some thought, he realized that this probably wouldn't work: the shoes would quickly wear out and if he asked people to donate repeatedly every time more shoes were needed, their sympathy for the cause might also wear out pretty quickly.

So he came up with the idea of 'TOMS: one-for-one shoes'. He would take the alpargata to America, manufacture it and sell it as a high-end fashion item at around US$50 a pair. Quite a lot for a canvas shoe you might say, but for each pair he sold, another pair would be donated to village children. That way he could guarantee a continuing supply and also run the project as a business rather than as a charity, which was something he had no experience of.

Mycoskie knew nothing about manufacturing, let alone shoe manufacturing, but he understood that he had to learn fast. At first, by his own admission, he made 'a poor job of making shoes', so he brought in help from people with experience in the industry and soon his product was getting high satisfaction ratings from customers. The vital element that Mycoskie added was his own passion. It is a passion he wants others to share. TOMS encourages customers to become more involved by volunteering to hand-deliver the shoes to the children in need. It's an intimate giving experience and Mycoskie hopes it might inspire volunteers to develop similar projects.

Ten years on and with revenues of $392 million a year, the business is thriving, supplying shoes not only to children in Argentina but also other parts of the world where foot diseases are a problem. In southern Ethiopia, where a high concentration of silicone in the soil causes podoconiosis, a disease that swells the feet, 300,000 people suffer simply because they have no shoes. The same type of soil exists in parts of France and Hawaii, but people there are unaffected.

But is the one-for-one model repeatable with other products? TOMS is a for-profit business, but for a long time it didn't show a profit. Mycoskie says it is not like a sales promotion you can just add to your existing business model; you have to build it in from the beginning. He now diverts a lot of his profits into other innovative social ventures. He is conscious that 'giving' alone is not the answer and that educating people to improve their own lives is the real key. Yet he still loves 'TOMS: one-for-one', calling it his 'greatest hit'. And why shouldn't he? It has made a difference to millions of poor children around the world and brought him great entrepreneurial satisfaction.

Changing a life begins with a single step

real life **making a short pitch** • speaking skill **making key points** • pronunciation **word stress**

4d An elevator pitch

Real life making a short pitch

1 Read the definition of an elevator pitch. Then work in pairs. What information do you think you should include? What don't you need to talk about?

> An elevator pitch is where you imagine you are in an elevator with someone you want to sell your new (business) idea to. You only have the time until the doors open again to convince this person.

2 ▶31 Listen to someone giving advice about making an elevator pitch. What three points does she make? Compare the three points she makes with your ideas from Exercise 1. Did you agree with what she said? Why? / Why not?

3 ▶32 Listen to a short pitch for a new phone app and complete the notes in the table.

Name of app	1
What is does	Links people who want to volunteer to ²
Problem it solves	People don't volunteer because they can't commit to a ³
Competition	Doodle and ⁴
Why it's different	Has a database of volunteers' ⁵ and ⁶
Developers' qualifications	Team of ⁷ with experience of ⁸
Needs	⁹ to bring it to market

4 Speaking skill making key points

▶32 Look at the expressions for making key points. Listen again and tick the rhetorical questions and sentence adverbs the speaker uses. Can you remember what the speaker said directly after each question?

> ▶ **MAKING KEY POINTS**
>
> **Rhetorical questions**
> What is it?
> How does it work?
> What does it do exactly?
> Why is it/that necessary?
> So what, you say?
> Won't that be expensive?
> How do we achieve this?
> What are we asking for?
> What's our ambition for …?
>
> **Sentence adverbs**
> Basically, …
> Essentially, …
> Clearly, …
> Obviously, …
> Of course, …
> Honestly, …
> To be honest, …
> Financially, ….
> Practically, …

5 Pronunciation word stress

a ▶33 Mark where you think the stress falls in each adverb or adverbial phrase in the box. Then listen and check.

b ▶33 Work in pairs. Practise saying the words with the same stress patterns. Then listen again and check.

6 Work in pairs or groups of three. Present your own elevator pitch for a new social enterprise. Follow these steps.

Student A: Turn to page 153 and read the notes.

Student B: Turn to page 154 and read the notes.

Student C: Turn to page 155 and read the notes.

- Prepare your pitch carefully. Use the expressions for making key points to help you (use no more than three rhetorical questions).
- Speak for no more than a minute.
- Write down the main message of each pitch and at the end compare your answers.
- Vote on who you think gave the most persuasive pitch.

writing a proposal • writing skill making recommendations   Unit 4 Innovation

4e Problem or solution?

Writing a proposal

1 Work in pairs. Read the proposal and answer the questions.

1 Does the author think the rise in the use of digital devices is a negative trend? How do you know?
2 Why does the author think the declining trend in book reading needs to be reversed?
3 Do you think the author's suggestions are good ones? Why? / Why not?

Introduction

This proposal suggests ways teachers can use technology to get children reading.

Current situation

It is a fact that children are now spending more time on digital devices, browsing on the internet, messaging friends, etc. It is also a fact that they are reading fewer books. This matters because reading books is known to help your ability to:

- focus and remember
- expand your vocabulary
- improve communication skills
- develop analytical thinking.

So how can we use students' enthusiasm for digital devices to encourage them to read more?

Possible solutions

First of all, we suggest that teachers actively encourage students to use the internet in class: either to research new subjects or to compare their conclusions with other people's. Secondly, we recommend using student blogs or learning diaries as a way of sharing ideas. Lastly, we think technology could help make reading a pleasure rather than a duty. One idea would be to put interesting short stories with visuals on screens in a quiet part of the classroom that students could read as a reward for finishing other work.

Recommendations

These are just a few examples of how technology could be an aid to reading. We strongly recommend teachers to explore similar ideas. Unless we begin to see technology as part of the solution, rather than part of the problem, we are unlikely to reverse the trend.

2 Look at how the proposal is organized. Answer the questions.

1 How is it divided into different sections? How are different points listed?
2 Underline the sentences in the proposal which do the following.
   a state the proposal's aim
   b state the problem that needs addressing
   c summarize the writer's opinion

3 Writing skill making recommendations

a Look at the forms used with the verbs *suggest* and *recommend*. Which forms are used in the proposal?

> 1 *recommend / suggest* (that) someone (should) do something
> 2 *recommend / suggest* something or doing something
> 3 *recommend* + someone to do something

b Complete these recommendations using appropriate verb forms.

1 I strongly recommend that _____ (people / follow) this advice.
2 We suggest that _____ (people / save) their money.
3 He recommends you _____ (wait) until after the summer.
4 We are not suggesting that _____ (teachers / always teach) this way.
5 I recommend that _____ (the company / look) into these options.

4 Write a proposal that each school child should be given a tablet computer at the age of five. Include the following points.

- different uses for these tablet computers
- the benefits they could bring
- why this is an opportunity not to be missed

5 Exchange proposals with your partner. Use these questions to check your proposals.

- Is your partner's proposal organized in the same way as the proposal in Exercise 1 (with sub-headings and bullet points)?
- Has your partner used the language to make recommendations correctly?
- Is it a persuasive proposal? Does your partner's proposal include any points you wish you'd included?

my life ▶ FUTURE SOLUTIONS ▶ HOW PEOPLE MANAGED IN THE PAST ▶ A SOCIAL BUSINESS ▶ MAKING A SHORT PITCH
▶ A PROPOSAL

4f This man risked it all

Women and children carrying firewood, Uganda

Before you watch

1 Look at the photo and caption. How do you think this activity affects:
   a the children's lives?   b the environment?

2 Key vocabulary

a Read the sentences. The words in bold are used in the video. Guess the meaning of the words.

1. I was **on the verge of** giving up my university course, but my parents persuaded me to carry on.
2. I don't know why I continued to believe him. It was as if I was **under a spell**.
3. We sell some products direct, but mostly, they are sold through high street **retailers**.
4. We supply over ten million **households** in the UK with gas and electricity.
5. The island has experienced terrible **deforestation** because the construction industry needs wood as a building material.

b Match the words in bold in Exercise 2a with these definitions.

   a shops that sell to individual customers
   b large-scale cutting down of trees
   c just about to
   d influenced by a powerful (often magical) force
   e homes

While you watch

3 ▶ 4.1 Watch the video and check your ideas from Exercise 1. What benefits did Sanga Moses' business bring to the community?

4 Describe the following things you saw in the video.
   - the tool used to cut wood
   - the buildings in the villages
   - the 'clean' cooking fuel he produced
   - the transport farmers were using

5 ▶ 4.1 Watch the first part of the video (0.00 to 1.50) again. Answer the questions.

1. What part of his sister's situation particularly inspired Sanga Moses to act?
2. What did his boss think about his decision to quit his job?
3. How many of the university students wanted to help him with his new business venture?
4. How did he raise the funds for his new business?
5. What was his girlfriend's reaction?

6 ▶ 4.1 Watch the second part of the video (1.51 to the end) again. Complete the facts and figures.

- Eco Fuel Africa turns farm [1] _____ into clean cooking fuel.
- The fuels burns cleaner and [2] _____, and is [3] _____ cheaper.
- Eco Fuel Africa has a network of 2,500 farmers and [4] _____ women retailers.
- It supplies [5] _____ households.
- Its ambition is to supply 16.6 million households in the next [6] _____ years.
- Eco Fuel Africa prevents [7] _____ and [8] _____ air pollution.
- It provides a living for farmers and [9] _____ and makes sure children get an [10] _____.

After you watch

7 ▶ 4.2 Watch the clips from the video. Choose the correct meaning of the words.

8 Complete the sentences in your own words. Then compare your sentences with a partner.

1. The news that … hit people hard.
2. It's important to have a good network of friends because …
3. I have an idea to … but I don't know if I should act on it.

9 Work in pairs. First summarize the benefits of Eco Fuel Africa's service and then discuss if you see any potential drawbacks of this system.

10 Sanga Moses described himself as an 'everyday community guy', meaning that he had identified a problem in his community and tried to solve it. What problem have you seen in your community and what could be done about it, do you think? Think about these areas or one of your own. Then prepare a short talk to describe the problem and possible solution.

- Crime/safety
- Transport
- Pollution
- Lack of shops
- Noise
- Lack of public/recreation space
- Jobs

husk (n) /hʌsk/ the outer shell of an edible seed, e.g. in wheat or coffee
sugar cane (n) /ˈʃʊɡə(r) keɪn/ a tall thick grass from which sugar is extracted

Unit 4 Innovation

UNIT 4 REVIEW AND MEMORY BOOSTER

Grammar

1 Read the article and complete it using these words. There are four extra words.

> can't   certainly   chances   had   likelihood
> likely   might   must   needn't   possible
> probably   unlikely

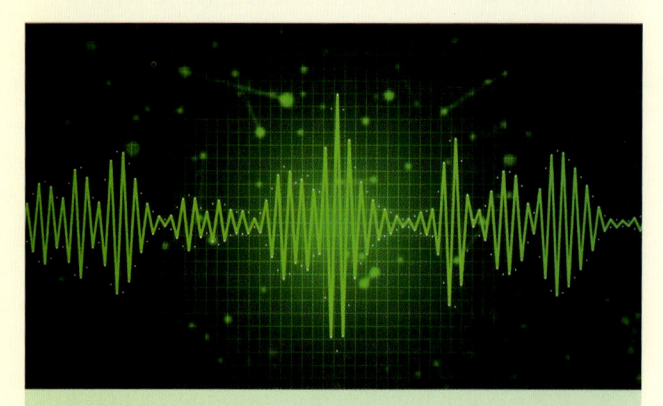

The problem of knowing what information to trust ¹_____ just have got harder. That's because a Canadian company has recently developed a computer program that can mimic people's voices. The program does not just copy words, it analyses speech patterns to create new sentences in the same voice. So, the person whose voice is being imitated ²_____ actually have said the words. The program is already very good at doing this and the ³_____ are that it will get better very quickly. Although the company developed the program for good reasons – for use in games and audio books – it is now worried that, in the wrong hands, the program is ⁴_____ to be used for identity theft. For example, it's ⁵_____ that someone could pretend to be a politician or a diplomat and use this ability to learn important secrets. The company felt it ⁶_____ to inform people about how powerful the technology is, because it thinks others ⁷_____ have developed similar programs. Their spokesperson said the development of these programs means that we will almost ⁸_____ not be able to trust audio evidence in future.

2 >> MB What is the probability (on a scale of 1–10) of these things happening, according to the article?

1 people using voice software to steal other people's identities
2 similar programmes already existing elsewhere
3 audio evidence no longer being useable

I CAN
talk about future probability
use past modals to express obligation or necessity

Vocabulary

3 Replace the underlined parts of each phrase with an adjective ending in -*able*. Some of the adjectives need to use the negative form.

1 A table that can be extended.
2 A coat that can't be washed.
3 A mistake that can be forgiven.
4 A car that can't be relied on.
5 A cover that can be removed.
6 A deposit that can't be refunded.
7 A bag that can be used again.
8 A cost that can't be avoided.

4 >> MB Look at the phrases (1–4). Think of a situation when you would use each of these phrases. Then compare answers with a partner. How similar were your situations?

1 'Give it some thought, anyway.'
2 'Give her a break.'
3 'Sure. I'll give it a go.'
4 'We came up against a lot of opposition.'

I CAN
use words with the *-able* ending
use expressions with *give* and phrasal verbs with *come*

Real life

5 Look at the statements from a short product pitch. Complete the rhetorical questions.

1 So, what _____? It's a vacuum cleaner that can clean any type of floor surface.
2 Why _____? Because there's no other machine that can perform all these functions.
3 How _____? At the base, there's a rotary brush which cleans as it sucks up the dirt.
4 Won't _____? Despite its sophistication, we're hoping to keep the cost down.
5 How _____? By making it in China, where manufacturing costs are much lower.

6 >> MB Think of a product that you use frequently. Then work in pairs. Take turns to present your product as if it was a new product. Use at least three rhetorical questions.

I CAN
give a short presentation for a new product
use rhetorical questions in a presentation

Unit 5 The magic of travel

A street at sunset in one of the world's most famous cities
© TOUR EIFFEL – Illuminations PIERRE BIDEAU

FEATURES

58 How we travel
Different approaches to travelling

60 Magical mystery tour
Trips to unknown places

62 The adventures of Hergé
Travel through the eyes of a comic book hero

66 On the road: Andrew McCarthy
A video about a memorable travel experience

1 Work in pairs. Look at the photo. Discuss what you know about this place (its character, its landmarks, its people, etc.).

2 ▶ 34 Look at the questions and discuss them with your partner. Then listen to a travel writer's opinion and compare your answers.
  1 What different factors (time of year, reason for travel, etc.) influence how we experience a place when we travel?
  2 What makes a good travel writer?

3 ▶ 34 Look at these adjectives. Which ones normally describe people (P), places (PL) or a time (T)? Then listen to the travel writer again and say what the speaker uses each adjective to describe. Did you use any of the same adjectives to describe Paris?

| romantic | cosy | officious | lazy | elegant | affable |
| wary | grand | lively |

4 Work in groups. Use adjectives to describe a place you have enjoyed visiting. Use words from Exercise 3 if helpful.

my life ▶ HOW YOU TRAVEL ▶ A MYSTERY TOUR ▶ KNOWING PLACES ▶ TELLING AN ANECDOTE ▶ A REVIEW

57

reading a travel blog • vocabulary repeated word pairs • grammar emphatic structures • pronunciation *do*, *does* and *did* • speaking how you travel

5a How we travel

Reading

1 Work in pairs. Discuss the questions about travel.
   1 Why do you think most people travel?
   2 Where and when do you travel? What is your reason for travelling?
   3 What do you enjoy / not enjoy about travelling?
   4 Do you think the concept of travel and holidays differs from culture to culture? If so, how?

2 Look at the blog post about how we travel. Answer the questions.
   1 How was the writer's experience of travel as a young boy typical of his culture?
   2 What is his father's attitude to travel? In what ways does the writer agree with him?
   3 What does the writer want from travel?
   4 Which of these attitudes (the writer's and his father's) is closest to your own?

3 Find words or expressions in the second paragraph of the blog with these meanings.
   1 without worries
   2 a fixed list of places to visit
   3 burning slowly with smoke but no flame
   4 very still and shiny
   5 bordered
   6 a steep valley

▶ 35

Going on holiday when I was a young boy meant going to spend the summer with my grandparents in my parents' home town in the north of India. For many Indians who live or work in a big city, that is still what travel is. For my father it was the same: escaping the heat of Kolkata to visit uncles and aunts in the cooler hills of Darjeeling. He is well off now and can afford to travel abroad to see the world, but instead he prefers to stay at home. On the few occasions he does travel, it's to visit my sister in Delhi or me in San Francisco, because he'd rather see us face to face than on a computer screen. But he doesn't behave like other tourists and visit the sights. What he enjoys is sitting and reading the newspaper with a good cup of coffee and wandering down to the local market to buy some food. Most people are pretending when they travel, he says, doing things they don't really want to do because they are on the traveller's checklist.

In some ways I understand his point of view. The thing we all value as travellers is that feeling of being carefree and open to experiences as they happen, just taking life day by day. But in other ways I disagree with him. Because it's exciting and unusual experiences that I want. Last month I had the trip of a lifetime in Chile. It was a guided trip with a strict itinerary, but it did fulfil my expectations of what travel should be, and more. We explored a volcanic cave under the smouldering Villarrica Volcano. We hiked through a forest of 1,000-year old monkey-puzzle trees and found ourselves looking down on the glassy Huinfuica Lagoon, flanked by majestic mountains. We stayed at a lodge in the Huilo Huilo Biological Reserve, a sustainable-tourism playground complete with walking trails, mountain-biking and kayaking. And we zip-wired across a 100-metre deep gorge called El Abismo.

I know what I like about travel; my father does too. It's just how we travel that's different.

How we TRAVEL

Vocabulary repeated word pairs

4 Work in pairs. Look at the expressions in bold (a–b) from the blog. Discuss what they mean. Then discuss the meanings of the other expressions in bold (1–6).

a He'd rather see us **face to face**.
b … just taking life **day by day.**

1 I saw Layla last night. She's just back from holiday. She went **on and on** about how terrible the hotel was.
2 A country's success in sport goes **hand in hand** with how much it invests in promoting it.
3 I couldn't predict the winner of the election. They've been **neck and neck** all the way.
4 We both recognized the problem, but we don't really **see eye to eye** on the solution.
5 They started their travel website in 2015 and it's just gone from **strength to strength.**
6 Writing is a process that you need to approach **step by step.**

5 Think of examples of the following things. Then work in small groups and compare your ideas.

- an experience that went on and on
- a subject you don't see eye to eye with your parents (or someone you know) about
- a person whose career has gone from strength to strength
- something that you (or someone else) are taking step by step (or day by day) to reach a goal

Grammar emphatic structures

> **▶ EMPHATIC STRUCTURES**
>
> **Cleft sentences**
> 1 **It's** relaxation **that** I want.
> 2 **What** I enjoy **is** sitting and reading the newspaper.
> 3 **The thing** we really value **is** being carefree.
>
> ***do, does, did*** **(in affirmative sentences)**
> 4 When I **do** travel now, I avoid the 'sights'.
> 5 I **did** take my laptop on my last holiday too.
>
> For further information and practice, see page 164.

6 Look at the grammar box. Notice the word order in the sentences. Rewrite the sentences (1–5) using a non-emphatic form.

1 *I want relaxation.*

7 Rewrite this sentence in four different ways. Use emphatic forms, starting with the words given.

'I love the unpredictability of travel.'

1 It's …
2 What …
3 The thing …
4 I …

8 Rewrite the parts of these sentences in italics using emphatic forms. Use the words given in brackets.

1 The destination is not important. *The journey matters.* (it)
2 I didn't miss my home town. *I missed my friends and family.* (what)
3 Colombia was full of surprises. *I read up a lot about it before I went,* but nothing really prepares you for it. (did)
4 When I went to Bali, *I was really struck by how relaxed the people were.* (what)
5 People always talk about how fascinating travel is. *But they never tell you how boring it can be too.* (the thing)
6 He's not normally a food lover, *but he likes to eat well when he's on holiday.* (does)
7 Our family holidays were hilarious. *I'll never forget the seven of us travelling through France in a tiny car.* (thing)
8 *I didn't mind the disruption*; it was the fact that they didn't apologize for it. (it)

9 Pronunciation *do, does* and *did*

a ▶ 36 Listen to these sentences and write in the missing emphatic auxiliaries. Note how the auxiliary verbs are stressed.

1 I _____ regret not stopping there.
2 She _____ travel a lot.
3 We _____ miss home sometimes.
4 I _____ spend a lot of time at the beach.

b Practise saying the sentences in Exercise 9a with the same stress.

Speaking my life

10 Work in small groups. Make a list of statements about how to travel (what's important, what you like, how you feel, etc.). Use emphatic structures in your ideas. Then compare your statements with your partner. Are your views similar or different? How?

- planning your journey
- things you always take with you
- avoiding stress when travelling (esp. flying)
- eating when travelling
- getting around from place to place
- holiday activities
- language and culture

*Try not to plan too much, because **it's** always the unexpected things **that** happen on a holiday that are the most memorable.*

wordbuilding synonyms • listening a mystery tour • grammar avoiding repetition • pronunciation stress in short responses • speaking a mystery tour

5b Magical mystery tour

Wordbuilding synonyms

> **WORDBUILDING synonyms**
>
> We often use synonyms in English as a way of avoiding repetition. It is important to remember that few words are exact synonyms. They often differ slightly in meaning or in the grammar that surrounds them:
> *holiday* and *break*, *succeed in* and *manage to*, *popular* and *well-liked*
>
> For further practice, see Workbook page 43.

1 Work in pairs. What synonyms or close synonyms can you think of for these words? How similar or different in meaning is each word you thought of?

> hotel   relax   travel around   trip

2 Look at these words which are used in the interview you are going to hear. Match the words (1–9) with the correct synonyms (a–i).

1	trip	a	swimming costume
2	spot	b	wonderful
3	head for	c	expectation
4	thrilling	d	journey
5	spoil	e	location
6	swimsuit	f	set off
7	start out	g	make your way to
8	anticipation	h	exhilarating
9	magical	i	ruin

Listening

3 ▶ 37 Listen to an interview about a 'mystery tour' that a reporter went on. Complete the information.

Company name	1 .... Adventures
Company based in	2 ....
Things to take	a 3 .... , a 4 .... , a dry bag
Length of trip	5 .... days
Type of cycling	6 ....
Destination	7 .... on the river
Night accommodation	slept in 8 ....
Return journey	By 9 ....
Cost of trip	10 ....

4 ▶ 37 Listen to the interview again and answer the questions.

1 Who started the fashion for mystery tours?
2 What kind of companies organize mystery tours nowadays?
3 How did Maggie describe her experience?
4 Why does the interviewer agree that it was better not to ask for too much pre-trip information?
5 What did the guide do as they travelled to their destination to add to the excitement?
6 How did Maggie feel about swimming to her 'accommodation' for the night?
7 How did she feel when she got back into London?
8 What lesson did the trip teach her?

Grammar avoiding repetition

> ▶ **AVOIDING REPETITION**
>
> **one, that, it, so**
> 1 *It was a magical experience … definitely* **one** *I'd recommend.*
> 2 *Did you know how far you would have to swim? Yes, I did ask* **that***.*
> 3 *[She] went on one of the trips and talked to me afterwards about* **it***.*
> 4 *Is that our island? I don't think* **so***.*
>
> **Ellipsis (omitting words)**
> 5 *I thought about asking … but then I decided not* **to***.*
> 6 *A few people were screaming and gasping – I know I* **was***.*
>
> **synonyms**
> 7 *a mystery tour* → *a journey to an unknown destination*
>
> For further information and practice, see page 164.

5 Look at the grammar box. Answer the questions.
1 What do the words in bold refer to in sentences 1–4?
2 Which of the words in bold in sentences 1–4 substitutes for:
  a a thing (i.e. a noun)?   b a phrase, clause or sentence?
3 What verbs have been omitted after the words in bold in sentences 5 and 6?

6 Look at the audioscript on page 183–184 (track 37). Answer the questions.
1 What synonym of 'idea' is used (para 1) and of 'track'?
2 What does 'that' refer to in the sentence 'And that gave us the chance …'?
3 What does 'it' refer to in the sentence '… but it was fine'?
4 What verb phrase has been omitted after 'had' in 'actually it had'?
5 What does 'one' refer to in the sentence 'it depends which one'?
6 What verb phrase has been omitted after 'to' in 'you really don't need to'?

7 Read the review of a Secret Adventures holiday. Rephrase the words in bold in the review to avoid repetition. Use appropriate forms from the grammar box, including synonyms where necessary.

> Four days in the freezing wilderness with no electricity. You might ask why you would do ¹ **four days in the freezing wilderness with no electricity**. Well, I just returned from an amazing holiday with Secret Adventures Arctic and it's the best ² **holiday** I've been on. ³ **Returning** to work after such ⁴ **an amazing** adventure is really hard. We spent four days in northern Sweden and each ⁵ **day** was magical. We rode on sleds pulled by dogs – we had to ⁶ **ride on sleds** because it's the only way to get around. We stayed in a simple log cabin, drank hot lingonberry juice and we went cross-country skiing. ⁷ **Cross-country skiing** was great fun too. Often it was dark and I thought I'd hate ⁸ **that it was dark**, but I ⁹ **didn't hate it**. The highlight was seeing the Northern lights. ¹⁰ **Seeing the Northern lights** is an experience everyone should have once in their lives – at least I think ¹¹ **they should have that experience**.

8 Put an appropriate word into each sentence to avoid repetition.
1 He said he wasn't going to take the car, but I think he _____, because I can't see it outside.
2 She said, 'Good things come to those who wait.' What do you think she meant by _____?
3 We need to set off early. So, shall we _____ at 7.30 a.m.?
4 I'm so tired that I might fall asleep during the film, but I'll try _____.
5 Sorry, this pen isn't working. Do you have _____ that I can borrow?
6 I had an amazing childhood. I'm going to write a book about _____ one day.

9 Pronunciation stress in short responses

a Work in pairs. We often use substitution in spoken exchanges. Complete the answers to each question using one word in each case.
1 A: You have to be careful not to get overcharged in the local markets.
   B: Yes, I know _____ .
2 A: Would you like to drive?
   B: No, I'd rather you _____ .
3 A: Did he take warm clothes with him?
   B: I hope _____ .
4 A: Do you mind travelling alone?
   B: No, I actually prefer _____ .
5 A: Are there many good guidebooks about this region?
   B: Yes, there are some excellent _____ .
6 A: Did she enjoy visiting Russia?
   B: Yes, she loved _____ .

b ▶ **38** Listen and check your answers. Underline the stressed words in each response. Then work with a partner and read the exchanges aloud using the same pronunciation patterns.

Speaking my life

10 Work in small groups. Design your own mystery tour. The tour should be a reasonable price, take participants to an unknown destination and involve activities that bring people together. Then present it to the class. When you present the tour, try to use at least three expressions for avoiding repetition.

reading the Graphic novel • critical thinking evaluating sources • word focus *matter* • speaking knowing places

5c The adventures of Hergé

Reading

1 Work in pairs. Look at the photo and discuss the questions.

1 What comics or cartoon books did you read when you were a child?
2 What did they contain that appealed to you: adventure, humour, interesting facts, life stories?
3 Do you still read any comics or graphic novels now?

2 Read the article. Are the sentences true (T) or false (F)?

1 Tintin is a writer who travels around the world in search of adventure.
2 The author Hergé loved to travel.
3 The artwork in *The Adventures of Tintin* is remarkable for its precise detail.

3 Read the article again. Choose the best option to complete the sentences.

1 The author *read / daydreamed* a lot about foreign lands as a child.
2 The author compares *Tintin* books to reading *thrillers / National Geographic*.
3 Hergé made multiple *drawings / models* of objects like cars and planes before putting them in his pictures.
4 Hergé's methods have been an inspiration to *other illustrators / movie makers*.
5 Visitors to Petra see the tall Treasury *at the last moment / from a long way off*.
6 The author thinks *Destination Moon* and *Explorers on the Moon* are Hergé's *best / most ambitious* books.

4 Find words in the article with the following meaning.

1 distant (para 1)
2 looked in amazement (para 1)
3 extremely careful (para 3)
4 truly and precisely (para 3)
5 very strange (often of a coincidence) (para 4)
6 talent (para 5)

Critical thinking evaluating sources

5 What sources (research, experts, first-hand experience) does the author mention to show that the following things were accurately represented by Hergé? NB For one item no real source is mentioned.

a the scientific expedition to the Arctic
b cars, planes, ships and bridges
c the Treasury at Petra
d sending a rocket to the Moon

6 Were you persuaded that Hergé represented things accurately for his readers? Do you think it's important that writers do this? Why? / Why not?

Word focus *matter*

7 Look at the expression in bold from the article. Choose the correct definition (a or b).

"[The books] were a kind of *National Geographic* for children – and adults, **for that matter**."

a of course (but you know that)
b also (now that I think of it)

8 Complete the expressions with *matter* using these words. Then discuss with your partner what you think about each statement.

| course | laughing | mind | principle | time |
| way | | | | |

1 With new technology, I think **it's only a matter of** .... before people are taking virtual holidays from their own living rooms.
2 Getting lost in a big city might seem like an adventure, but believe me, **it's no** .... **matter** when it happens to you.
3 I think you can put up with a lot of discomfort when you're travelling. It's just a question of .... **over matter**.
4 When I'm abroad, I use public transport **as a matter of** .... You discover much more that way.
5 **No matter which** .... **you look at it**, not speaking the language of the country you are visiting is a disadvantage.
6 I don't fly on planes **as a matter of** .... ; they create too much pollution.

Speaking my life

9 Work in small groups. Make a list of four places you all know about in one or other of the ways listed below (e.g. New York). Then compare what you know about these places. Do you have a similar view of each place? Would you like to go there? Why? / Why not?

• from visiting yourself
• from what friends or family have told you
• from what you have seen in the TV news or a documentary
• from what you have read in a magazine, book or online
• from photos you have seen

THE ADVENTURES OF HERGÉ

▶ 39

I spent a lot of my childhood travelling to far-off places and learning about their history and geography. I went to Peru and saw the Sacsayhuaman fortress of the Incas and the citadel of Machu Picchu. I visited the ancient rose-red city of Petra in Jordan and marvelled at the grand buildings carved out of the rock. I journeyed on a ship to the Arctic Ocean with a scientific expedition that was investigating a meteorite that had fallen to Earth. I even travelled to the Moon and learned what it was like to experience gravity six times weaker than I was used to.

I saw all these things not in person, of course, but through the eyes of the investigative journalist, Tintin, in the pages of the graphic novels of Hergé, the Belgian author and cartoonist. I was not the only one. In the days before full-colour television documentaries, Hergé's *Adventures of Tintin*, twenty-three books written between 1929 and 1976, were a kind of *National Geographic* for children – and adults, for that matter. These were not just great detective stories; they were learning adventures.

The amazing thing about the books is that their creator never travelled to these places either. They were all the result of painstaking research done from his studio. Hergé and his team of illustrators and researchers scoured libraries, museums and photographic archives to provide as accurate a representation, both in the drawings and the storylines, as they could. This included examining catalogues of cars and planes, and technical drawings of ships and bridges. Hergé made numerous sketches of these objects seen from different angles and sometimes created models of the characters and other items so as to be able to construct a particular scene and capture it more faithfully – a technique that has since been used by many film animators, such as Pixar.

Actually, I can personally attest to the incredible accuracy of Hergé's representations of foreign places because a few years ago, I visited Petra with my family. We rode on horses down the long narrow passage called *the Siq*, just as Tintin and his companion Captain Haddock do in *The Red Sea Sharks*. At the end, we came out from between the tall rock walls that frame the passage and caught our first sight of the magnificent forty-metre tall Treasury, sculpted from the pink sandstone. I was looking at a view straight from the pages of the book: the colours, the play of the sun on the walls, the dusty earth, the Bedouin guides with their keffiyehs wrapped around their mouths. It was uncanny.

Perhaps Hergé's greatest triumph is the two-part story *Destination Moon* and *Explorers on the Moon* which, considering the books were written in 1955, gave, according to commentators at the time, an extraordinarily realistic account of what would be involved in sending a manned rocket to the Moon. As well as the smaller drawings that carry the narrative, from time to time the reader turns the page to discover a stunning full-page image: a rocket on its launch-pad, complete with gantry, a mountainous moonscape, the Earth below as the rocket leaves the atmosphere. Few people in those days could imagine what it was like to be looking down at our planet from outer space. But that was Hergé's true gift: to understand and communicate what a place was like without ever having travelled there.

---

archives (npl) /ˈɑː(r)kaɪvz/ historic records or documents
citadel (n) /ˈsɪtəd(ə)l/ a fortress or castle, usually on a hill
gantry (n) /ˈɡæntri/ a bridge-like metal supporting structure
meteorite (n) /ˈmiːtiəraɪt/ a piece of rock or metal that falls from outer space
scour (v) /ˈskaʊə(r)/ to search intensively

5d To my amazement

Real life telling an anecdote

1 Look at the photo. Answer the questions.

1. Where do you think the photo was taken?
2. Can you name four things in the photo that you associate with a beach holiday?
3. Would you choose to go on a beach holiday somewhere like this? Why? / Why not?

2 ▶ 40 Listen to a travel story. Make notes about the main details of the story.

1. Issue that the story highlights
2. The speaker's background and setting for the story
3. Main events
4. The speaker's conclusion

3 Work in pairs. Retell the story to each other using your notes from Exercise 2.

4 ▶ 40 Look at the expressions for telling an anecdote. Tick (✓) the expressions the speaker uses in the travel story. Then listen again and write down what followed the expressions the speaker used.

> ▶ TELLING AN ANECDOTE
>
> It's a (well-known) fact that …
> We all know that …
> These days, …
>
> It's famous for …
> Consequently / Because of that …
>
> A few years ago, … / Last summer, …
> The following day/morning …
> As luck would have it, …
> By chance, I happened to …
> By coincidence, …
> To my amazement/surprise/horror/delight/relief, …

5 Speaking skill linking events

a Look at these expressions. Which are used to signal the time of an event (T) and which are used to indicate the speaker's feelings about an event (F)? Which expressions add a sense of drama?

a A few years ago, …
b As if by magic, …
c Worryingly, …
d A little while later, …
e To my relief, …
f Just at that moment …
g Amazingly, …
h By sheer luck, …
i The following week, …
j As soon as … , …

b Work in pairs. You are going to link events in a story. Start with the sentence below. Take turns to suggest a linking phrase to continue the next sentence in the story.

> *A few years ago*, I was travelling on my own in Australia.
> A: *By sheer luck*, …
> B: *By sheer luck*, I bumped into a friend in Sydney, whom I hadn't seen for years.

6 Pronunciation long sounds

▶ 41 Look at these expressions. How do you think the underlined vowel sounds are pronounced? Then listen and check. Which two are NOT long vowel sounds?

1. to my am<u>a</u>zement
2. to my rel<u>ie</u>f
3. to my surpr<u>i</u>se
4. to my h<u>o</u>rror
5. to my dism<u>a</u>y
6. to my del<u>igh</u>t
7. to my frustr<u>a</u>tion
8. to my emb<u>a</u>rrassment

7 Work in pairs You are going to develop a story. Follow these steps.

- Look at the main elements of the story.
- Discuss what extra details could be added and how you can link the ideas and events.
- When you have finished, work with a new partner and retell your stories.

1 Issue that the story highlights	When abroad, you can forget you are not at home and be surprised by something different
2 The speaker's background and setting for the story	Newly-wed couple, Theo and Eleni, on holiday in Cyprus; walking in the mountains
3 Main events	Long walk, stop at village café, look out at view, Theo feels Eleni's hand on his, looks down, not her hand but a huge insect
4 The speaker's conclusion	Eleni still laughs

8 Work in small groups. Tell a story of your own using the same structure as in Exercise 7.

writing a review • writing skill using descriptive words

Unit 5 The magic of travel

5e Book of the month

Writing a review

1 Work in pairs. Which of these ways of choosing a book to read or film to watch is most reliable or useful? Why? Discuss your answers.

a personal recommendation
b a book/film review in the press
c the blurb on the back cover or a film trailer
d choosing a book that has been made into a film or vice versa

2 Read the book review. What is the reviewer's opinion of the book? Explain why.

Book of the month

THE BRIDGE OF SAN LUIS REY
by Thornton Wilder

In 1714 a rope suspension bridge in Peru snaps and the five people on the bridge fall to their deaths. By chance Brother Juniper, a Franciscan monk, witnesses this tragedy. He is not only troubled by what he has seen but also troubled by why this should have happened. Why at this precise moment? Why these five people? Accordingly, he sets out to find out something about the lives of each person and so to make sense of the tragedy.

This short novel (only 124 pages long) is a beautiful reflection on the subject of destiny. It is not a true story, but some of the characters are based on real people. Written in elegant prose, each chapter describes the life of one of the five people on the bridge: from the aristocratic Marquesa de Montemayor, who longs to be back in her native Spain to the wise Uncle Pio, whose lifelong ambition to make a star of a young actress is in the end frustrated. Our interest is not kept alive by the mystery of their deaths, but by the compelling characters that Wilder has drawn so vividly: each eccentric in their own way, and each very human in their virtues and in their faults.

I cannot recommend this thought-provoking book highly enough.

3 Read the review again and answer the questions.

1 What type of book is it?
2 What is the main theme?
3 What tense is used to describe the plot?
4 What words describe the style of writing in the book?

4 Look at the different ways (a–e) to begin a book review. Which way does the reviewer use in the review in Exercise 2?

a give your opinion about the book directly
b talk about the writer's background
c describe the opening of the story
d give a short summary of the whole story
e discuss the topic of the book

5 Writing skill using descriptive words

a Underline the adjectives and adverbs in paragraphs 2 and 3 of the review. What does each describe? Which two are compound adjectives?

b Complete these compound adjectives.

| breaking | fetched | going | moving | packed |
| provoking | willed | written | | |

1 thought-_____ (book)
2 far-_____ (plot)
3 heavy-_____ (book)
4 well-_____ (book)
5 action-_____ (adventure)
6 heart-_____ (ending)
7 fast-_____ (plot)
8 strong-_____ (character)

c Match the compound adjectives from Exercise 5b with their opposites below.

convincing	easy-to-read	happy	indecisive
poorly written	slow-moving	uneventful	
uninspiring			

6 Write a review of a novel you have read or a film you have seen (approx 200 words). Follow this plan.

• Describe the setting and give a brief summary of the plot.
• Say what the theme of the book/film is.
• Describe the style of writing/filmmaking.
• Give your opinion or recommendation.

7 Exchange reviews with your partner. Use these questions to check your reviews.

• Is the review organized into clear paragraphs?
• Does it NOT reveal the whole story?
• Are you persuaded by the recommendation?

my life ▶ HOW YOU TRAVEL ▶ A MYSTERY TOUR ▶ KNOWING PLACES ▶ TELLING AN ANECDOTE
▶ A REVIEW

5f On the road: Andrew McCarthy

Walkers on the Camino de Santiago, Spain

Unit 5 The magic of travel

Before you watch

1 Look at the photo and answer the questions.

1. Where is this place?
2. What kind of trip do you think these travellers are on?

2 Key vocabulary

a Read the sentences. The colloquial expressions in bold are used in the video. Guess the meaning of the words.

1. I just **sort of went** … 'that's **kind of weird**'.
2. I read your book. It was **so cool**.
3. And he **was like**: 'You read my book?'
4. I called him **pretty much** every day.
5. … **truth be told**, I was a gold-card traveller.

b Match the words in bold in Exercise 2a with these definitions.

  a thought to myself   d said
  b almost   e really good
  c rather strange   f to be honest

While you watch

3 ▶ 5.1 You are going to watch an interview with travel writer Andrew McCarthy. Watch the video and answer the questions.

1. What was the trip that changed Andrew McCarthy's life?
2. In what way did it change him?

4 ▶ 5.1 Work in pairs. Watch the first part of the interview (0.00 to 2.09) again, where McCarthy describes how he became interested in this trip. Look at the words (a–e) and note why they are significant in the story. Then, with your partner, reconstruct the story.

  a a bookstore
  b a plane
  c the internet
  d Harper's magazine
  e home phone number

5 ▶ 5.1 Watch the second part of the interview (2.10 to 3.10) again and answer the questions.

1. What adjectives does McCarthy use to describe:
   a this travel experience?
   b his feelings while on the trip?
   c what the experience was not?
   d what he felt for the first time when travelling?
2. What was the reason for the trip that he didn't know at the time but now realizes?

6 ▶ 5.1 Watch the third part of the interview (3.11 to the end) again and answer the questions.

1. What makes McCarthy unsure about going again with his children?
2. How long was the trip?
3. Where did he stay?
4. Complete this description of himself: 'a _____ pilgrim'. What does he mean?
5. How did he justify not being this kind of traveller on this occasion?

7 Complete the summary of Andrew McCarthy's story using one word in each space.

About eighteen years ago, I was in a ¹_____ and I picked up a book by a guy who had ²_____ the Camino de Santiago in ³_____. It sat on my bookshelf for months and one day I ⁴_____ it when I was looking for something to read on the plane. And having read it, I decided I wanted to do that. There was no ⁵_____ to research places in those days so I called the ⁶_____ up and said, 'Hey, I read your book,' and I asked him questions about how to go about doing this trip.
I went to Spain for a month and I had a ⁷_____ experience. I felt ⁸_____ and frightened but then something happened that ⁹_____ my life. And for the first time I felt ¹⁰_____ in the world. I stayed in little pilgrim ¹¹_____ and to be truthful it wasn't very comfortable, so I sometimes stayed in *pensiones* instead and I justified it by saying that this is the way to meet the ¹²_____ .

After you watch

8 Vocabulary in context

a ▶ 5.2 Watch the clips from the video. Choose the correct meaning of the words and phrases.

b Complete these sentences in your own words. Then compare your sentences with a partner.

1. Often for lunch I just grab …
2. Sometimes I feel like I can't take … anymore
3. I didn't mind … . It was just one of those things.

9 Work in small groups. Discuss the questions.

1. What things do you think made Andrew McCarthy uncertain about travelling alone?
2. What do you think the event was that changed this (when he said 'then something happened and I had, sort of, one of those experiences that you have')?
3. Make a list of five things that make people nervous about travelling abroad. Which things make *you* nervous? What could you do to overcome this feeling?

67

UNIT 5 REVIEW AND MEMORY BOOSTER

Grammar

1 Read a travel writer's description of the Fiji islands in the South Pacific. Answer the questions.

1 In what ways is Fiji an exclusive destination? In what ways is it not?
2 Why does the writer suggest you might prefer to visit the main island?

Fiji is a collection of over a hundred islands in the South Pacific. Most are the image of what a perfect desert island should be like. So it's no surprise to find upmarket hotels catering for rich tourists and
5 honeymooners. I went there hoping to experience this paradise more simply and wondering if it was possible to do so on a limited budget.
I shouldn't have worried. The Fijian's experience of dealing with different types of tourists means they
10 have provided for this by offering less expensive youth hostel-style accommodation for backpackers like me in places like Yasawa. Here, hospitable locals will help you to feel part of their lives, inviting you to see their fishing villages – and even take you fishing
15 with them, if you want to.
But beautiful and relaxing though these islands are, the feeling of being a tourist remains. It's not an uncomfortable sensation, but if what you value is seeing the country's true way of life, then perhaps
20 you should visit the main island of Viti Levu. This is the cultural hub of Fiji, where most of the population live: it's here that you can experience real Fijian culture.

2 Look at the description again. What do these words refer to?

a most (line 2)   d Here (line 12)
b do so (line 7)   e want to (line 15)
c this (line 10)   f sensation (line 18)

3 >> MB Find two emphatic structures in the third paragraph (with 'what' and 'it'). Rewrite them as non-emphatic structures.

I CAN	
use substitution to avoid repetition	
recognize emphasis to statements	

Vocabulary

4 Make repeated word pairs using the words in brackets. Then rewrite the underlined words using the repeated word pairs. Sometimes you need to change the verb. Then use the word pairs in your own sentences.

1 We met for the first time yesterday. (face)
2 We don't really agree on many issues. (eye)
3 He talked a lot about his new car. (on)
4 I'm just taking things as they come. (day)
5 Hard work and success go together. (hand)

5 Complete the words using the synonyms in brackets to help you.

1 It was a mag_____ experience. (wonderful)
2 We found a co_____ restaurant. (warm and comfortable)
3 The coast has been rui_____. (spoiled)
4 It's a very scenic sp_____. (location)
5 The buildings are very gr_____. (large and impressive)
6 I was wa_____ of travelling alone. (cautious)
7 The doorman was offi_____. (self-important)
8 We hea_____ for the mountains. (went towards)

6 >> MB Use each of the words in Exercise 5 to describe a travel experience you have had.

I CAN	
use repeated word pairs	
describe places and journeys	

Real life

7 Match the words (1–8) with words (a–h) to make phrases for telling anecdotes.

1 It's a well-known fact   a ago …
2 Because   b luck ….
3 Well, a few years   c day …
4 By chance, I happened   d relief …
5 Just at that   e to …
6 So the following   f that …
7 By sheer   g of that …
8 To my   h moment …

8 >> MB Use the phrases in Exercise 7 to make a story about finding something you wanted to buy, thinking you had missed your opportunity and then finding you could get it after all. Tell the story to your partner.

I CAN	
use expressions for telling an anecdote	

Unit 6 Body matters

FEATURES

70 Exercise around the world

Different exercise regimes

72 No pain, no gain

How to avoid sports injuries

74 The enigma of beauty

What is beauty and why is it important to us?

78 The art of parkour

A video about the history of free running

1 Work in pairs. Write a short caption to accompany the photo.

2 ▶ 42 Listen to a woman discussing health and exercise with her friend, Rashmi, who is a doctor. What does Rashmi say about the following?

  1 intensive exercise versus gentle exercise
  2 the kinds of exercise that she does

3 ▶ 42 Look at the expressions to do with exercise and health. Four of the expressions need a preposition to complete them. Write in the prepositions. Then listen and check your answers.

  1 keep _____ shape
  2 take _____ exercise
  3 go _____ a walk/run/ride
  4 watch _____ your weight
  5 go _____ a diet
  6 stay _____ fit
  7 work _____ at the gym
  8 stretch _____ your legs
  9 keep _____ active

4 Work in groups. Ask each other questions about your fitness. Use the expressions in Exercise 3.

  A: *What do you do to stay fit?*
  B: *I walk a lot and I go swimming a couple of times a week.*
  C: *Don't you find swimming boring?*
  B: *Just doing lengths is a bit dull, but it keeps me in reasonable shape.*

my life ▶ EXERCISE TRENDS ▶ DESCRIBING AN INJURY ▶ DOES BEAUTY SELL? ▶ DISCUSSING PROPOSALS ▶ A FORMAL REPORT

reading exercise regimes • wordbuilding compound words • grammar phrasal verbs • speaking exercise trends

6a Exercise around the world

Reading

1 Look at the quotation by swimmer David Walters. What point was he making about exercise? Do you have any similar experiences?

> An hour of basketball feels like fifteen minutes. An hour on a treadmill feels like a weekend in traffic school.
>
> *David Walters, professional swimmer*

2 Read the sentences (1–6). Then quickly read the article. Match the sentences with the exercise routine it describes: Radio Taiso (RT), swogging (S) or yoga (Y).

1 It's a fashionable form of exercise.
2 It benefits the mind and the body.
3 It doesn't need a lot of effort or practice.
4 Your body feels as if it is under attack.
5 People have been doing this form of exercise for centuries.
6 It's an enjoyable way to exercise.

3 Work in pairs. Write a suitable heading for each paragraph. Then discuss whether any of these forms of exercise appeal to you. Give reasons.

Wordbuilding compound words

▶ **WORDBUILDING compound words**

We form certain nouns and adjectives using verb/noun/adjective + preposition. The combination can be a whole word or a hyphenated word.
breakdown, follow-up

For further practice, see Workbook page 51.

4 Look at the wordbuilding box. Find one similar compound adjective and compound noun in the article.

EXERCISE AROUND THE WORLD ▶ 43

Here are a few of our readers' experiences.

KEVIN

Not many people outside Japan have come across Radio Taiso. Each day at 6.30 in the morning you hear this tinkly piano sound coming from the radio and everywhere people start doing callisthenics – gentle warm-up exercises – to get ready for the day ahead. They're group exercises that everyone can join in with – at home, in the park. The group principle is a very Japanese thing. People say the idea was copied from US factories in the 1920s. It's fantastic, because it's good fun and it's not too strenuous: they're simple movements that anyone can do, old or young. Also, they get the brain working as well as the body.

JO

I do something called 'swogging': a mixture of swimming and jogging. The inspiration came from a book about people in the Caucasus mountains, who often live to well over a hundred and remain mentally and physically fit. The book puts this down to their practice of walking down steep slopes to swim in cold mountain streams – something they've been doing for generations. Then they dry off and climb back up the mountain. The idea of freezing cold water might put a lot of people off, but it's scientifically proven to help your circulation and boost your immune system, because it triggers your body's self-defence mechanisms. I do the same thing in North Wales where I live, but I jog two miles to a lake. It's very exhilarating, but I've a little way to go before I get to 100!

NICKY

I went on a group yoga retreat last year in Tamil Nadu. To an outside observer, yoga doesn't look demanding – just slow stretching and holding certain positions. Yoga practitioners came up with their own version of the saying 'Don't just sit there, do something' which is 'Don't just do something, sit there'. But actually, it's a very good workout. Like a lot of eastern exercise, it offers a more holistic approach to health by combining bodily fitness with mental well-being. The idea is to concentrate on your breathing to make movement easier and reduce tension. Although it started out in India, only a relatively small proportion of the population still practise yoga seriously. In the West, it's an increasingly trendy form of exercise, but Indian traditionalists say that the versions practised by many Westerners are far removed from the original form.

5 Complete the phrases with these compound words. Then try to put each word in a sentence.

backup	break-in	drive-through	far-off
stop-off			

1 a _____ of computer files
2 a _____ on the way to Australia
3 a house _____
4 a _____ land
5 a _____ restaurant

Grammar phrasal verbs

6 Look at these two verb + preposition(s) combinations (a–b) from the article. Which is a phrasal verb? Which isn't? Give reasons.

a come across   b coming from

> **PHRASAL VERBS**
>
> 1 Intransitive phrasal verbs
>   It *started out* in India.
>
> 2 Separable phrasal verbs
>   The idea of freezing cold water might *put* a lot of people *off*.
>   The idea of freezing cold water might *put off* a lot of people.
>   The idea of freezing cold water might *put* them *off*.
>
> 3 Inseparable phrasal verbs
>   Not many people have *come across* Radio Taiso.
>   Not many people have *come across* it.
>
> 4 Three-part phrasal verbs
>   Yoga practitioners *came up with* their own version.
>   Yoga practitioners *came up with* it.
>
> 5 Three-part phrasal verbs with two objects
>   The book *puts* this fact *down to* their practice of walking …
>   The book *puts* this *down to* their practice of walking …
>
> For further information and practice, see page 166.

7 Look at the grammar box. Notice the position of the noun and pronoun objects for each type of phrasal verb. When do we have to put the object between the verb and the preposition?

8 Read the sentences. Identify the words that make up the phrasal verbs in both options (a and b). Then say whether the position of the object(s) is correct or not. Sometimes both options are correct.

1 a When did you set up the company?
   b When did you set the company up?
2 a I'll catch you up with in a moment.
   b I'll catch up with you in a moment.
3 a I think you should definitely go for the job.
   b I think you should definitely go the job for.
4 a A lot of children look up to sport stars.
   b A lot of children look up sport stars to.
5 a I'd like to take up on you your offer.
   b I'd like to take you up on your offer.

9 Read the description of other exercise routines. What do the phrasal verbs in bold mean? Then put the objects of the phrasal verbs in the correct position.

Sickness as a child left Joseph Pilates, born in Germany in 1880, frail and weak. To ¹ **get over** (this), he developed exercises to build core muscle strength. Some of his early students then opened studios using his methods, ² **setting up** (them) in various cities. Pilates is now practised by millions all over the world.

The idea for Zumba *came about* by accident in the 1990s. Alberto Perez ³ **hit on** (it) when he was taking an aerobics class in his native Colombia. Having forgotten his usual music for the class, he ⁴ **fell back on** (some Salsa dance music) he had with him. Zumba, a routine combining aerobics with Latin dance moves, was born. Since then it has *taken off* and become an international exercise craze.

Most people think Tai Chi is a form of meditation. In fact, it's an old Chinese martial art based on the idea of ⁵ **getting out of** (dangerous situations) by turning an attacker's force against him. The most common form of Tai Chi today is a routine of slow movements. You often see people ⁶ **trying out** (them) in parks and public spaces.

10 Put the words in the correct order to make sentences using phrasal verbs.

1 I'm thinking / of / up / Pilates / taking
2 I hurt my back playing tennis. It took / it / me / over / ages / to get
3 At school we had to exercise twice a week. We / of / it / get / couldn't / out
4 The doctor / out / some tests / is going / to carry / on my knee
5 How / come / that idea / with / did you / up ?
6 She / hard work / puts / to / down / her success
7 Playing hockey / me / takes / back / my childhood / to

Speaking   my life

11 Work in pairs. Read the questionnaire and check you know the meanings of the phrasal verbs. Interview your partner using the questionnaire.

> ① How much time do you set aside for exercise each week?
> ② What kind of exercise do you go in for mainly?
> ③ Have you taken up any new forms of exercise in the last twelve months?
> ④ Do you keep up with trends in exercise routines?
> ⑤ Do you prefer to exercise alone or to join in with others?
> ⑥ What puts you off exercising more?

12 Compare your findings with another pair. What conclusions can you draw about attitudes to exercise?

vocabulary injuries • listening sports injuries • idioms health • grammar verb patterns • pronunciation stress in two-syllable verbs • speaking describing an injury

6b No pain, no gain

Ultrarunner on the 161 km
Ultra-Trail du Mont-Blanc
annual race, France

Vocabulary injuries

1 Match verbs and nouns from each box to make collocations about typical injuries. There is sometimes more than one possible answer. Then with a partner mime each injury to explain its meaning.

graze your knee

Verbs	
break	bruise
bump	chip
graze	lose
pull	sprain
strain	stub

Nouns	
your ankle	your arm
your back	your head
your knee	a muscle
your ribs	your toe
your tooth	your voice

2 Answer the questions. Use the collocations from Exercise 1.
  1 What injuries do you think the runner in the photo risks?
  2 Which injuries in general are:
     a the most common?
     b the most painful?

Listening

3 ▶44 Listen to an interview with ultrarunner Ben Newborn about sports injuries. Answer the questions.
  1 How does Ben define ultrarunning?
  2 What was his main concern about doing the Ultra-Trail du Mont Blanc?
  3 What mistake do many sports people make?
  4 How does Ben avoid getting sports injuries?

4 ▶44 Complete the descriptions of injuries and problems that Ben talks about. Then listen to the interview again and check your answers.
  1 He had to overcome _____ and the things that make you feel _____ .
  2 A lot of sports people try to ignore a small muscle _____ or _____ in a joint.
  3 Minor problems can develop into more _____ injuries.
  4 His exercises have prevented him from getting ankle _____ , lower _____ pain and runner's _____ .

Idioms health

5 Work in pairs. The ultrarunner used this idiom in the interview. What do you think it means?

"I'm not talking about when they're in a really bad way"

6 ▶45 Complete the idioms using these prepositions. Then listen and check your answers. Discuss the meanings of the idioms with your partner.

| down | in | off | on | out | under | up |

  1 A: I heard Sarah came off her bicycle. Is she *in* a bad way?
     B: Luckily she didn't break anything; she was pretty **shaken** _____ though.
  2 A: Is it true that Jack nearly cut his finger off?
     B: Yes, he practically **passed** _____ when he saw what he'd done … but he's _____ **the mend** now, I think.
  3 A: You look a bit _____ **colour**. Are you feeling _____ **the weather**?
     B: No, I'm not ill. I'm just **run** _____ from working too much.

Grammar verb patterns

> **VERB PATTERNS**
>
> **verb + *to* + infinitive**
> They **tend to take** some painkillers.
>
> **verb + object + *to* + infinitive**
> A race which **requires runners to run** 161 kilometres …
>
> **verb (+ object) + infinitive**
> … the things that can **make you feel** sick …
>
> **verb + -ing**
> It could **mean running** 100 kilometres in a single day …
>
> **verb + preposition + -ing**
> Didn't you **worry about doing** yourself real damage?
>
> **verb + object + preposition + -ing**
> … that shouldn't **discourage us from doing** exercise.
>
> For further information and practice, see page 166.

7 Look at the grammar box. Try to remember what verb patterns these verbs (1–10) take. Then check your answers in the audioscript on page 184 (track 44).

1	afford	6	prevent
2	avoid	7	succeed
3	carry on	8	try
4	involve	9	urge
5	let	10	warn

8 Pronunciation stress in two-syllable verbs

a Look at these verbs. Which syllable is stressed in each of these verbs?

afford	attempt	avoid	complain	convince
insist	involve	prevent	rely	succeed

b ▶ 46 Listen and check your answers. Then practise saying the words again.

9 Complete the sentences about sports injuries using the correct verb patterns. You need to add prepositions in some of the sentences.

1 These people often complain _____ (suffer) 'pink eye' from the chlorine in the water. They also tend _____ (be) susceptible to shoulder problems.
2 These people risk _____ (damage) the joints in their legs. But they can avoid _____ (get) long-term injuries by wearing the right shoes.
3 Since their sport relies so heavily _____ (use) the arm, these people tend _____ (have) problems with their elbow and wrist.
4 Because these people pull muscles so often, they are encouraged _____ (warm up) properly before a match to prevent such injuries _____ (occur).

5 Neck pain is common among these people. Because they insist _____ (bend) low over the handlebars, they are forced _____ (raise) their heads to see ahead.

10 Which of these sportspeople are being referred to in each sentence in Exercise 9? Discuss with your partner.

cyclists	footballers	runners	swimmers
tennis players			

11 Often verbs that express a similar idea are followed by the same verb pattern. Look at the sentences (1–8). Replace the verbs in bold with these verbs without changing the verb pattern.

appear	blame	convince	decide	expect
mean	postpone	stop		

1 We can't **prevent** people from having accidents.
2 The organizers were **criticized** for not having paid enough attention to track safety.
3 If the job **involves** straining my back in any way, I'm afraid I can't risk it.
4 I've **made up my mind** to get fit.
5 She **seemed** to pull a muscle as she stretched to reach the ball.
6 Don't **delay** going to the doctor. If you do, it'll take longer to recover from the injury.
7 I **hope** to be playing again in a few weeks.
8 The doctor **persuaded** him to take it easy for a while.

12 Complete this short description. Use the correct verb pattern of the verbs in brackets.

I remember ¹_____ (have) to play rugby at school when I was fourteen or fifteen. At that age, kids seem ²_____ (develop) at very different rates and so sometimes they'd ask you ³_____ (play) a match against people twice your size. One time I attempted ⁴_____ (tackle) a huge boy running with the ball. His knee struck me in the face, making me ⁵_____ (fall) back and I hit my head on the ground and passed out. The sports teacher never apologized ⁶_____ (for / put) me in that situation, so the next time he asked me ⁷_____ (play) for the team, I refused ⁸_____ (do) it!

Speaking *my life*

13 Work in pairs. Choose one of the following incidents and describe what happened. Try to use at least two verb patterns in your answer.

1 a time when you or a friend were injured doing a sport or in some other situation
2 a time when you or a friend narrowly escaped being injured

reading what is beauty? • critical thinking author influence • word focus *face* • speaking does beauty sell?

6c The enigma of beauty

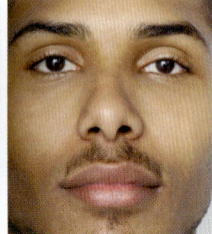

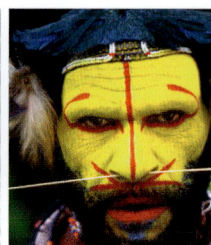

Reading

1 Work in groups. Look at the photos. Which faces do you find beautiful or handsome? Can you explain why? How many do you agree on? Discuss your findings.

2 Read the sentences. Do you think each one is true? Then read the article and find out the author's views.

1 There are no universally agreed characteristics of human beauty.
2 Perceptions of a person's beauty can be connected to their social position.
3 Your character can have an influence on whether people think you are beautiful or not.
4 The search for beauty is superficial and vain.

3 Read the article again. Find the phrases from the article. Choose the best meaning (a or b).

1 beauty is **in the eye of the beholder** (para 2)
   a subjective
   b related to how someone looks at you
2 a **glowing complexion** (para 2)
   a healthy skin   b smiling face
3 a **symbol of status** (para 4)
   a a sign of great wealth
   b a sign of a high social position
4 has **preoccupied** (para 4)
   a dominated the thoughts of   b worried
5 a **shallow quest** (para 5)
   a a pointless search   b a trivial search
6 **fussed over** (para 6)
   a made to feel special b made to feel comfortable

Critical thinking author influence

4 Look at these topics from the article. How did you personally feel about each one? Read the article again and discuss with a partner.

1 the experience of the women wanting to be models
2 the practice of extending your neck using copper coils
3 the way that our idea of an ideal body shape has changed
4 the fact that the author's grandmother still cared about her looks at 100 years old

5 What was the author's opinion about the topics (1–5) in Exercise 4? Did this influence your reaction to any of them? How?

Word focus *face*

6 Find two expressions with *face* in the article with these meanings:

a unhappy expressions (para 1)
b to be honest (para 6)

7 Work in pairs. Look at the expressions with *face* in these sentences and explain the meaning of each phrase.

1 He couldn't admit he was wrong. He didn't want to **lose face** in front of the boss.
2 She was disappointed not to be picked for the team, but she **put a brave face on** it.
3 I **took** her offer of help **at face value**. I don't think she had any hidden motive.
4 The actors had trouble **keeping a straight face** when Jon fell off the stage.
5 You should tell her that you scratched her car, because sooner or later you will have to **face the music**.
6 **On the face of it,** it seems like a good idea, but I wouldn't rush into making a decision.

8 Make two sentences of your own using expressions with *face* from Exercises 6 and 7.

Speaking my life

9 Work in pairs. You are going to design an advertising campaign. Read your role cards and prepare ideas. Then act out the meeting to agree on the advertisement you will run.

Student A: Turn to page 153.

Student B: Turn to page 155.

10 Discuss which view is closest to your own. Give reasons.

The ENIGMA of BEAUTY

Sheli Jeffry is searching for beauty. As a scout for Ford, one of the world's top model agencies, Jeffry scans up to 200 young women every Thursday afternoon. They queue up and one by one the line shrinks. Tears roll and there are long faces as the conclusion 'You're not what we're looking for right now' puts an end to the conversation – and to hope. Confronted with this, one poor hopeful, Rebecca from Rhode Island, asks: 'What are you looking for? Can you tell me exactly?' Jeffry simply replies, 'It's hard to say. I'll know it when I see it.'

Define beauty? Some say you might as well analyse a soap bubble; that beauty is only in the eye of the beholder. Yet it does seem that across different cultures we can agree on certain points. Psychologists have proven this by testing the attractiveness of different faces on children. Symmetry is one characteristic that wins general approval; averageness is another: we seem to prefer features that are not extreme. Things that suggest strength and good health – a glowing complexion and full lips in women, a strong jaw in men – are also universal qualities. Scientists say that this is the true definition of beauty, because ultimately we are influenced not by aesthetic but by biological considerations: the need to produce healthy children.

At the same time, we can also observe cultural differences in how beauty is defined. The women of the Padaung tribe in Myanmar put copper coils around their necks to extend them because in their culture, very long necks are considered beautiful. In cultures where people's skin is of a dark complexion, it is often seen as desirable to have a fair skin. Conversely, in the northern hemisphere among the naturally fair-skinned, people want a tanned skin.

Perceptions of beauty also change over time. Historically, in northern Europe, a tanned skin belonged to those who were forced to work outside – agricultural workers or other poorer members of society – and so a white skin was a symbol of status and beauty. But in the late 20th century, a tan reflected status of a different kind: those that could afford beach holidays in the Mediterranean or the Caribbean. Our idea of the perfect body shape is also different from 200 years ago. In almost all cultures a little fat was formerly seen as a positive trait, a sign of wealth and well-being. Nowadays, a very different image stares out at us from the pages of fashion magazines: that of a long-limbed, impossibly slim figure. Whatever the perception of ideal beauty may be, the search for it has preoccupied people of all cultures for centuries, from ancient Egypt to modern China.

Is it a shallow quest? We say that beauty is only skin deep; that personality and charm contribute more to attractiveness than superficial beauty. Certainly, as we grow older, the more generous our definition of beauty seems to become. Experience teaches us to look for the beauty within, rather than what is on the outside.

But let's face it, most of us still care how we look. Until she was a hundred years old, my grandmother had a regular appointment at the beauty salon down the street. A month before she died, I took her there in my car. I stayed and watched as she was greeted and fussed over by the hairdresser and manicurist. Afterwards, I drove her back to the nursing home. She admired her bright red nails every few minutes, patted her cloud of curls and radiated happiness. She is not alone in getting satisfaction from looking nice. It seems the quest for beauty goes deeper than vanity – maybe it fulfils a deep need in all of us.

real life discussing proposals • speaking skill proposing and conceding a point • pronunciation toning down negative statements

6d A bold initiative

Real life discussing proposals

1 Work in pairs. Read about the different methods governments around the world use to encourage their populations to keep fit and healthy. Answer the questions.

1 What do you think are the pros and cons of each method?
2 Which initiative would work best, do you think? Why?
3 Are there any similar initiatives in your country?

1 JAPAN: Broadcast a daily exercise routine on national radio each day.

2 WASHINGTON STATE, USA: Fast-food chains must publish the number of calories in each item on the menu.

3 QATAR: Get companies to install gyms at work so workers can exercise before or after work or during breaks.

4 UK: Run public health campaigns promoting exercise activities that are quick and easy to do.

5 SOUTH KOREA: Make good grades in Physical Education a qualification for university entrance.

6 PHILIPPINES: Promote sports like karate in school that combine exercise with self-defence skills.

2 ▶ 48 Listen to a discussion at a large insurance company about ideas to promote health and fitness among their employees. Answer the questions.

1 Why is promoting health and fitness among their employees important to the company?
2 What different ideas are proposed? Are any of them similar to the ideas in Exercise 1?
3 Which idea got approval from another member of the group? Which idea was rejected?

3 Speaking skill proposing and conceding a point

▶ 48 Look at the expressions for proposing and conceding a point. Then listen to the discussion again and say which phrases are used to propose and concede these points.

1 Spending money on a workplace gym – may not be a budget for this
2 Dance classes – people do these things in their free time
3 Group exercises in the morning – not an original idea
4 Give people incentives to do things on their own – don't know the details

▶ **PROPOSING and CONCEDING A POINT**

Proposing points
One possibility is / would be to …
Another alternative/idea is / might be …
You could …
It would be better to …
What about …?

Conceding points
Having said that, …
I realize/admit that …
Admittedly, …
I know that isn't really …
It's not (a) particularly … , I admit. / I'll grant you.
I haven't thought it through exactly, but …

4 Pronunciation toning down negative statements

a ▶ 49 Listen to these statements where an adverb is used to tone down (reduce the impact of) a negative statement. Underline the words most strongly stressed in each sentence.

1 It's not a particularly original idea.
2 It wouldn't be so easy to monitor …
3 I know that isn't really the intention …

b ▶ 50 Work in pairs. Practise saying these sentences where a negative sentiment has been toned down. Then listen and compare your pronunciation.

1 I know it's not a very practical solution.
2 It wouldn't be so simple to convince people.
3 I'm not entirely confident about the result.

5 Work in groups. Each person should think of another idea to promote the health and well-being of company employees. Then present and discuss your ideas. Concede any points against your proposal.

writing a formal report • writing skill avoiding repetition   Unit 6 Body matters

6e A controversial plan

Writing a formal report

1 Read the report about a public health issue and look at the questions. Underline the parts of the report that answer the questions.

1. What is the aim of the report?
2. What is the main finding?
3. What action is proposed?

2 Read the description of reports in general. Which of the features in bold appear in the report in Exercise 1?

> Formal reports present the **findings** of an investigation and make **recommendations** based on these findings. The reader should be able to scan a report quickly for key information, so **bullet points**, **subheadings**, and **short paragraphs** are all useful. Reports present **objective facts**, often using **passive verb forms**, but some internal reports can also offer more **subjective comments**.

INTRODUCTION
This report examines a proposal to make smokers pay higher health insurance premiums. Over 100 people of different ages and social backgrounds were interviewed about the proposal, which was based on a straightforward evaluation of risk: that if a person smokes, their chances of becoming ill increase.

RESULTS
30% of the interviewees objected to the proposal on the grounds that it was discriminatory. One common argument was that, according to this principle, higher premiums should also be paid by people who overeat.

18% of those questioned agreed that the habit of smoking was often beyond an individual's control. However, 55% took the opposite view: that smokers make a personal choice to smoke and therefore should pay for the consequences. With regard to assistance to quit smoking, 74% of respondents believed free help should be given to smokers.

RECOMMENDATION
Overall, interviewees were in favour of some change to insurance companies' current practice of treating smokers and non-smokers similarly. Accordingly, we recommend that a pilot scheme should be set up where smokers are given free help by their insurer to stop smoking over a six-month period. During this time, they will be offered various solutions to give up. If they succeed, they will be rewarded with a discount of 5% on their insurance premiums for as long as they remain non-smokers. Conversely, if they fail, their insurance premiums will rise by 20%.

3 Find formal phrases in the report that mean the following:

1. because (para 2)
2. if you follow (para 2)
3. so (para 3)
4. concerning (para 3)
5. in general (para 4)
6. in view of this (para 4)
7. on the other hand (para 4)

4 Writing skill avoiding repetition

a When writing reports, you often have to find ways of repeating the same idea using different words. Find these words (1–6) and then find the different ways that the writer used to describe these things.

1. the interviewees (two ways)
   those questioned
2. took the … view (that)
3. assistance
4. quit smoking (two ways)
5. insurance company
6. period

b Replace the words in bold in these sentences to avoid repetition.

1. This report examines the results of a survey on health, describing the main **results** and making some recommendations.
2. 260 members of staff were asked for their views on the proposal and they responded with a range of **views**.
3. 87% agreed that more exercise would be good for their physical health, while 54% said it would **be good for** their mental health.
4. We recommend that a fact-finding team should be set up. We also **recommend** that the leader of this **team** is someone from outside the company.

5 Write a short report on a survey of employees about how a company can help to improve employees' health. Use your own ideas or the ideas you discussed in Exercise 5 on page 76. Write 200–250 words.

6 Exchange reports with your partner. Use these questions to check your reports.

- Have they presented their aims, findings and recommendations?
- Does the report use formal language, including passive forms?
- Is the report divided into clear sections?
- Is the overall result a clear, concise and easy-to-read report?

my life ▶ EXERCISE TRENDS ▶ DESCRIBING AN INJURY ▶ DOES BEAUTY SELL? ▶ DISCUSSING PROPOSALS
▶ A FORMAL REPORT

77

6f The art of parkour

A parkour athlete, Vienna, Austria

Before you watch

1 Work in pairs. Look at the categories (a–e). Try to name a different sport for each category. Then compare your ideas with the rest of the class.

A sport that is:
a very dangerous
b creative
c very expensive
d urban / played in the street
e growing in popularity

2 Look at the photo and the caption on page 78. What does this sport involve? Which of the categories in Exercise 1 does it fall into, do you think?

3 Key vocabulary

a Read the sentences. The words in bold are used in the video. Guess the meaning of the words.

1 The documentary contains some **footage** of the two climbers reaching the summit.
2 He went into the army when he was eighteen. He had to – it was the official **draft** age.
3 I think some birds have made a nest on the **ledge** above my window.
4 He didn't jump from the bridge in the film. It was done by a **stuntman**.
5 We'd like to get more students involved in university decisions, but up to now they've shown complete **apathy**.

b Match the words in bold in Exercise 3a with these definitions.

a a narrow shelf or surface, usually made of stone or rock
b someone who does dangerous things in place of the actor in a film
c an official order to serve time in the armed forces
d lack of interest or concern
e (short) film of a particular event

While you watch

4 ▶ 6.1 Work in pairs. Answer the questions. Then watch the video and compare your answers.

1 What is parkour?
2 Who does parkour and why do they do it?
3 What kind of moves do parkour artists do?
4 Can you make a career out of parkour, do you think?

5 ▶ 6.1 Watch the first part of the video (0.00 to 0.50) again. Complete the facts about the footage of John Ciampa.

1 Date of film:
2 His job:
3 His age:
4 His abilities:

6 ▶ 6.1 Look at the questions. Then watch the second part of the video (0.51 to 1.26) again. Discuss the answers with your partner.

1 Where and when did the modern craze for parkour start?
2 What is a better description than 'sport' for parkour, according to the speaker?
3 What is the essence or fundamental principle of parkour?
4 Why has it been especially popular in places where opportunities are limited?

7 ▶ 6.1 Watch the last part of the video (from 1.27 to the end) again. Then complete this description.

These two young men from Khan Younis in Gaza both practise parkour. In this part of the world, for example, [1] _____ is over 40 per cent and 35 per cent live in poverty. But there is no sense of [2] _____ amongst the young: they are focused on staying [3] _____ and they like [4] _____ themselves.

Abed's mother feels [5] _____ of him, even though he has had injuries like a broken [6] _____. Injuries, like sprains, are common so it is important to learn how to [7] _____ without hurting yourself. Mohammed says it took time to [8] _____ people around him about the sport. But now they both feel a great sense of personal [9] _____ and hope that one day they might be asked to perform in a competition or a [10] _____.

After you watch

8 Vocabulary in context

a ▶ 6.2 Watch the clips from the video. Choose the correct meaning of the words and phrases.

b Complete these sentences in your own words. Then compare your sentences with a partner.

1 I don't think … will ever really catch on.
2 I have a friend who has an uncanny ability to …
3 Once I fell awkwardly when I was … and hurt my …

9 Work in groups. Discuss these questions and give reasons for your answers

1 Do you think parkour should become an official Olympic sport?
2 Do you think more sports should be just amateur sports, like parkour, and not professional sports?
3 Do you think street sports like parkour should be regulated (i.e. rules about where you are allowed to do it, what you are allowed to do, etc.)?
4 Would you like to try parkour yourself? Why? / Why not?

UNIT 6 REVIEW AND MEMORY BOOSTER

Grammar

1 Read the blog. Who in the world suffers from back pain? What can be done about it?

Back pain is an extremely common health problem, which affects eighty per cent of Americans at some time in their lives. It prevents people ¹ _____ (work), causes people ² _____ (become) depressed and affects general wellbeing.
You could be forgiven ³ _____ (think) that lower back pain is a result of our sedentary habits: working at computers, etc. But in fact, back pain is something that everyone around the world seems ⁴ _____ (suffer) from, whether they spend their days ⁵ _____ (sit) at a desk or ⁶ _____ (work) in the fields.

Scientists believe that back pain is an inevitable result of being bipedal – standing up on two feet. So, unless you ⁷ *go in for* regular posture training or are not susceptible to it, you will suffer from back pain at some point.
What to do about it is another question. You can ⁸ *look into* exercise classes such as yoga or Pilates, which help to build core muscle strength, but these are mainly preventive. Most treatment for chronic pain consists of taking painkillers, either synthetic or natural, as in Madagascar, where Baobab tree bark is used. Another possibility is manipulation, but it can be months before the practitioner can ⁹ *turn around* the situation. It seems that for the time being, we will just have to ¹⁰ *put up with* back pain.

2 Complete the first part of the blog by putting the verbs (1–6) in the correct form: infinitive, *to* + infinitive, *-ing* form or preposition + *-ing* form.

3 Look at the phrasal verbs (7–10) in the blog. Find the noun objects of each phrasal verb and replace these with a pronoun. Think carefully about the position of the pronoun.

4 >> MB Work in pairs. What kind of phrasal verbs are used in the blog: intransitive, separable, inseparable or three-part? Explain the difference.

I CAN
use correct verb patterns (verb + *-ing* or infinitive)
use different kinds of phrasal verbs

Vocabulary

5 Complete the sentences with the missing verbs. You have been given the first letter.

1 Shall we g_____ o_____ for a quick walk? I need to s_____ my legs.
2 How do you k_____ in such good shape? Do you t_____ a lot of exercise?
3 I think I p_____ a muscle when I was w_____ out at the gym.
4 I wasn't badly hurt. I just g_____ my knee and b_____ my ribs.
5 She only c_____ her tooth, but she was s_____ up by the experience.
6 I try to s_____ aside a couple of hours a week for exercise.

6 >> MB Work in pairs. When did you last do these things? Describe what happened.

a passed out
b felt off colour
c stubbed your toe
d lost your voice
e went on a diet
f sprained your ankle

I CAN
talk about exercise, health and injuries

Real life

7 Look at the proposal for workplace gyms. Complete the proposal with these words.

| admittedly | alternative | having | grant | out |
| particularly | possibility | through | | |

Workplace gyms are not a ¹_____ original idea, I'll ²_____ you, but I think they could be very popular with our employees. I haven't thought ³_____ all the details but the basic idea is to get people exercising during the working day. ⁴_____, it's not a cheap option, but, ⁵_____ said that, there are ways to lessen the cost. One ⁶_____ would be to make employees pay a small contribution. Another ⁷_____ would be to open it to the public. I'm just thinking aloud here - I haven't worked it ⁸_____ exactly.

8 >> MB Work in pairs. Look at these points. After each point make another point that concedes an argument against it.

1 It's always good to try out new food.
2 Team sports are great fun.
3 Walking is the best form of exercise.

I CAN
propose and concede points in a discussion

Unit 7 Digital media

Van Gogh's self-portrait at the Musée d'Orsay, Paris, France

FEATURES

82 Selfie world
A study of global facts about selfies

84 Creating a buzz
How companies use social media marketing

86 A hacker's life
A day at the DefCon annual conference

90 Talking dictionaries
A video about how digital media is preserving dying languages

1 Look at the photo. What are these people doing and why? Would you do the same? Why? / Why not?

2 ▶51 Work in pairs. Discuss the questions. Then listen to a journalist talking about digital technology and compare your answers. Do you agree with him?

1 How do digital media change the way we experience the world?
2 How do audiences use digital media at concerts, festivals and conferences?
3 Do you think digital media enhance our experiences or spoil them?

3 ▶51 What different digital media did the journalist mention? Listen again and check your answers.

4 Categorize the activities (a–c) according to how you use them. Then discuss your answers.

a things that you do yourself
b things you benefit from others doing
c things you never do

chat online   download music   post comments on forums
review products   tweet   upload photos
use professional networking sites   use social networking sites
write a blog

my life ▶ THE IMPACT OF DIGITAL MEDIA ▶ BRANDS ▶ ATTITUDES TO SECURITY ▶ MAKING A PODCAST
▶ A NEWS REPORT

reading global facts about selfies • wordbuilding verb prefix *out* • grammar passive reporting verbs • speaking the impact of digital media

7a Selfie world

Reading

1 Look at this caption that accompanied a 'selfie'. What are the names for the symbols used? What expression has the caption been adapted from?

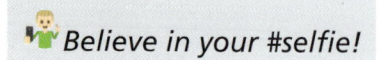

> *Believe in your #selfie!*

2 Work in pairs. What do you think is the best way to take a good selfie? Read the first paragraph of the article and compare your ideas.

3 Read the rest of the article. Try to find information about the following things:
1 how many selfies are taken each year
2 what kind of people take selfies
3 what is particular about selfies taken by people:
   a in London   b in São Paulo
4 how long it takes to take a selfie
5 the possible reasons that people take selfies

Wordbuilding verb prefix *out*

▶ **WORDBUILDING verb prefix *out***

When *out* is used as a prefix to a verb, it often means doing something 'more than' or 'better than'.
outweigh, outperform, outstay

For further practice, see Workbook page 59.

4 Look at the wordbuilding box. Complete the sentences with the correct form of these verbs. The first one is from the article.

| outclass | outgrow | outlive | outnumber |
| outsell | outweigh | | |

1 ... women selfie-takers _____ men.
2 My kids _____ their clothes very quickly.
3 The advantages _____ the disadvantages.
4 iPhones _____ Samsung phones again.
5 She completely _____ her opponent.
6 She _____ her husband by fifteen years.

Selfie world

▶ 52

The basic idea of a selfie is simple: flip the view on your phone so that you are looking at the image you are taking; hold the phone away from you – usually at a high angle to make your eyes look bigger and slightly right or left to show off your 'best' side; and then click.

Selfies have only been around since 2011, but it is said that in 2015 an incredible 24 billion such images were uploaded using Google's photo app. And that is only Google's app; it does not include Facebook, Instagram or Apple applications, which are believed to account for a far greater proportion of 'selfie' traffic.

Lev Manovich, professor at City University of New York and expert in digital media, was keen to get more data on this cultural phenomenon and so set up the project 'Selfiecity'. Taking six world cities as examples – London, New York, Bangkok, São Paulo, Berlin and Moscow – his study looked at who was posting these images and what the main characteristics of the images were. This is what it found.

First of all, it's a young person's game: the average selfie taker's age is around 24, although that age is thought to have risen slightly since the initial research was done. Secondly, women selfie-takers outnumber men, making up 55 per cent in Bangkok, 65 per cent in São Paulo and 82 per cent in Moscow. Further analysis showed that London selfies have the most poses 'straight to camera' – in other cities people take pictures from more of an angle – while Bangkok selfies are the most smiley (London and Moscow are the least). São Paulo boasts the most expressive selfies. But perhaps the most surprising thing is how long they take to produce.

People were reported to be spending on average seven minutes on each selfie. That is not just the time needed to take the picture; it also includes editing, deciding on a caption and perhaps adding a hashtag or emoji.

Manovich's study does not provide reasons for these global variations or for the phenomenon as a whole, but it has been observed by other researchers that in an age where online image matters, the selfie is now an indispensable tool.

Unit 7 Digital media

Grammar passive reporting verbs

> **PASSIVE REPORTING VERBS**
>
> *It + passive reporting verb + that*
> 1 *It <u>is said</u> that in 2015, 24 billion such images were uploaded.*
> 2 *It <u>has been observed</u> by other researchers that the selfie is now an indispensable tool.*
>
> *subject + passive reporting verb + to + infinitive*
> 3 *Other applications <u>are believed</u> to account for a far greater proportion of 'selfie' traffic.*
> 4 *That age <u>is thought</u> to have risen slightly since the initial research was done.*
> 5 *People <u>were reported</u> to be spending seven minutes on each selfie.*
>
> For further information and practice, see page 168.

5 Look at the grammar box. Answer the questions.
  1 What is the tense of each underlined passive reporting verb?
  2 Does the tense of the underlined passive reporting verb always match the time of the event which is reported?
  3 In which sentence(s) is the agent included? Why is it included here?
  4 Why do we often find this type of verb in news reports and in academic writing?

6 Rewrite the underlined words. Start with the words in brackets and use passive reporting verbs.
  1 <u>We don't really know</u> why women take more selfies than men. (It)
  2 <u>Many have said that</u> the social pressure on women to look good is an important factor. (It)
  3 <u>People also believe that</u> the proportion of men taking selfies is increasing. (The proportion)
  4 <u>People think that</u> another reason for the popularity of selfies is their democratic nature. (Another reason for the popularity of selfies)
  5 <u>Someone reported that</u> last year pictures of 'ordinary' people outnumbered those of celebrities by a million to one.
     (Last year, pictures of 'ordinary' people)
  6 <u>No one expects that</u> the selfie phenomenon will end soon. (The selfie phenomenon)
  7 <u>People think that</u> it will begin to decrease in the coming years. (It)
  8 At the same time, <u>people report that banks have started looking at</u> selfies as a possible replacement for passwords and PIN numbers. (At the same time, banks)

7 Complete the headlines from the radio news. Use the correct form of the passive reporting verbs.
  1 Two men _____ (report / be arrested) earlier today in connection with a robbery in the town centre.
  2 Builders _____ (say / work) around the clock to finish the new stadium in time for the official opening on 12th July.
  3 The Prime Minister _____ (expect / announce) big tax cuts in a speech later today.
  4 Three climbers, who _____ (fear / die), have turned up at their base camp six days after they went missing.
  5 A portrait, which _____ (claim / be) Picasso's last ever painting, will go on sale later today.
  6 It _____ (suggest) that a photo showing water on the surface of Mars is a fake.

8 Work in pairs. Write three sentences announcing a piece of news using passive reporting verbs. Use the words in the boxes to help you, if you like. Then read your sentences to another pair and question each other about further details of the story.

*Two walkers **are reported to have gone missing** during their round-the-world trip.*

People or things
a dog   two walkers   a famous celebrity   round-the-world trip   a fireman   the US president   a photo   an app $100 million   an old coin   three sisters   a four-year-old boy

Passive reporting verbs
believe   claim   expect   fear   know   report   say   suggest   suppose   think

Speaking my life

9 Work in small groups. Read the statements and discuss if you agree with them.
  1 Taking selfies is thought by many to be a sign of vanity.
  2 The obsession with self-image is feared to be causing an increase in insecurity among young people.
  3 It's said that overuse of digital media has given us 'grasshopper minds' (i.e. a very short attention span).
  4 The huge volume of information that we now have to process is believed to have made us more critical thinkers, not less.
  5 The fact that you can make comments anonymously and from a distance is often said to be the reason why a lot of online comments are angry and aggressive.

my life ▶ THE IMPACT OF DIGITAL MEDIA ▶ BRANDS ▶ ATTITUDES TO SECURITY ▶ MAKING A PODCAST
▶ A NEWS REPORT

listening social media marketing • idioms business buzz words • grammar nominalization • speaking brands

7b Creating a buzz

Listening

1 Work in pairs. Answer the questions. Then discuss your answers.

1 What kind of advertising do you take most notice of: TV, magazine, online, other?
2 Has any new company or product attracted your interest recently? How did they do this?

2 Look at the photo and answer the questions.

1 What are the children selling?
2 What benefits are they offering the buyer?
3 What advertising tools do they use to communicate these benefits?

> **worthy** (a) /ˈwɜːði/ admirable, deserving respect

3 ▶53 Listen to an interview with a social media marketing specialist, Sarah Palmer, and answer the questions.

According to Sarah:
1 What kind of customers can you get with successful social media marketing?
2 What two companies are good examples of this?

4 ▶53 Listen to the interview again. Are the statements true (T) or false (F), according to Sarah?

1 Good marketing means getting customers to share their enthusiasm about your company with others.
2 Customers aren't really interested in the story behind the products they are buying.
3 *National Geographic* uses competitions to involve visitors to their website.
4 *National Geographic* does not use special offers to sell its products.
5 It is difficult to involve the customer if you are selling a more everyday product.
6 The interactive tour of the teas of China on the tea company's website is a bit serious, but very informative.

Idioms business buzz words

5 A 'buzz word' is a word or expression that is fashionable at the moment. There are many examples in business. Work in pairs. Look at the words in bold from the interview and discuss what they mean.

1 We hear about companies being **customer-focused** all the time these days.
2 And if you can provide those things, and get them to **buy into** your story, …
3 Our research into social media marketing has given us some great examples of **best practice**.

6 Match the business buzz words (1–8) with the correct definition (a–h).

1 How much are we talking about? Give me a **ballpark figure**.
2 This is the area we need to concentrate on **going forward**.
3 Keep me **in the loop**. I'd be interested to know what happens.
4 You can understand it, surely? It**'s not rocket science**.
5 Great. I'm glad that we**'re on the same page**.
6 Finding out we weren't the only ones developing this product was a big **reality check**.
7 We're looking for really fresh ideas, so try to **think outside the box**.
8 It's **a win-win situation**.

a advantageous to both sides
b be imaginative
c moment to face the true facts
d rough estimate
e simple
f in the future
g understand each other
h up to date with events

Grammar nominalization

> **NOMINALIZATION**
>
> **Verb → noun nominalization**
> 1 a *If you can create a loyal following, it is a much more effective long-term strategy.*
>   b *The creation of a loyal following is a much more effective long-term strategy.*
> 2 a *If you engage your customers, it will boost sales.*
>   b *Customer engagement will boost sales.*
>
> **Adjective → noun nominalization**
> 3 a *It's pointless being focused on your customer if they …*
>   b *A focus on your customer is pointless if they …*
> 4 a *Good marketing is when you are able to turn your customers into fans.*
>   b *Good marketing is an ability to turn your customers into fans.*
>
> **Other types of nominalization**
> 5 a *That is mainly why they are so successful.*
>   b *That is the main reason for their success.*
>
> For further information and practice, see page 168.

7 Look at the grammar box. Compare the pairs of sentences (with and without nominalization). Then say if sentences (a–c) below are true (T) or false (F).

Nominalization allows us to:
a make an action into a noun.
b emphasize who is responsible for an action.
c express ideas more concisely and objectively.

8 Rewrite these phrases. Use nominalized forms of the underlined verbs and adjectives.

1 He intends to …
   His _____ is to …
2 After they announced the winner
   Following the _____ of the winner
3 No one knew they had discovered it
   No one knew of their _____
4 I respect that she wishes to be private
   I respect her _____ to be private
5 I appreciate that you are concerned
   I understand your _____
6 It's understandable that they are angry
   Their _____ is understandable

9 Complete the transformation of these sentences. Use nominalized forms of the underlined words.

1 How quickly a company responds to a complaint indicates clearly how interested they are in keeping their customers satisfied.
   A company's *speed* of _____ to a complaint is a clear _____ of their true _____ in customer _____.
2 When you interact with customers on social media it can be risky, because people will comment things that are negative as well as positive.
   _____ with customers on social media brings the _____ of receiving negative _____ as well as positive ones.

10 Rewrite the sentences, nominalizing the underlined words. You will need to make other changes too (e.g. prepositions).

1 If you want to be successful, you need to prepare well and work hard.
   _____ comes from _____ and _____.
2 People who lead well are able to say thank you to the people who work for them.
   _____ have _____ to thank _____.
3 If you are honest in business your business partners will respect you.
   _____ will earn you _____ your business partners.
4 When companies compete with each other, they are forced to reduce costs.
   _____ leads to a _____ costs.

11 We also use nominalization with passive verbs. Rewrite the underlined words using nominalized forms and the passive form of the verbs in brackets.

1 We paid by direct bank transfer. (make)
   Payment was made …
2 We have arranged for the guests to stay in local hotels. (make)
3 They will decide tomorrow. (take)
4 No one explained the long delay in delivery. (give)
5 You should complain in writing to the customer services department. (make)
6 They researched the new drug over a ten-year period. (carry out)
7 You can't photograph the inside of the building. (take)

Speaking my life

12 Answer the questions. Then work in pairs and compare your answers.

1 Make a list of six things you have bought recently (clothes, food, gadgets, household products, etc.). Which are brands that you are loyal to?
2 Explain why you are loyal to these brands. Is it because of:
   • their quality or image?
   • what others say about them?
   • their social media marketing?
   • other?

---

my life ▶ THE IMPACT OF DIGITAL MEDIA ▶ **BRANDS** ▶ ATTITUDES TO SECURITY ▶ MAKING A PODCAST ▶ A NEWS REPORT

7c A hacker's life

Reading

1 Work in pairs. How careful are you about your online security? Discuss what you do to keep your data safe and what more you could do.

2 Look at the two definitions of a 'hacker'. Which definition fits your idea of a hacker? Then read the article about a hackers' conference on page 87 and say what the author's view is.

> **hacker** (n) /ˈhækə/
> 1 an enthusiastic and skilful computer programmer or user
> 2 a person who uses computers to gain unauthorized access to data

3 Read the article again and answer the questions. Compare your answers with your partner.
  1 What do DefCon hackers do to help improve internet security?
  2 What are most hackers not?
  3 What do hackers look at apart from online security?
  4 What do they do with the information they find?
  5 What does the writer like about the people at DefCon?
  6 What phrase sums up what *Capture the Flag* is?
  7 What does the writer say about the majority of people who use the internet?
  8 What really motivates the hackers at DefCon?

4 Has your opinion of hackers changed after reading this article? How? Discuss with your partner.

5 Find collocations in the article that mean the following:
  a a very false description (para 2)
  b fix the gaps in something that could leak (para 3)
  c a lack of politeness (para 5)
  d with poor lighting (para 6)
  e a piece of furniture where documents are stored (para 7)
  f a person who is expert in (and obsessed with) computer technology (para 8)

Critical thinking identifying personal opinion

6 Work in pairs. Underline the adjectives and adverbs in the article that the writer uses to express his personal opinion about hackers and what they do for us.

> Every year **passionate** hackers meet ... (para 2)

7 Summarize the author's views about the following things.
  a hackers
  b the DefCon convention
  c the situation of most internet users

Word focus *break*

8 Work in pairs. Find an expression with *break* in paragraph 1 and discuss what it means. Then look at these expressions (1–6) and discuss what you think they mean.
  1 The manager called everyone together to **break the news** about the company closing.
  2 During the first lesson, the teacher got us to play a couple of games to **break the ice**.
  3 Once you get into playing computer games every night, it's very difficult to **break the habit**.
  4 You really should buy a new pair of shoes. It won't **break the bank**.
  5 It's a very big job but I think we've **broken the back of** it now.
  6 We didn't make a profit but I think at least we **broke even**.

9 Write a sentence using one of the expressions with *break*. Read it to your partner, omitting the phrase, and ask them to guess what the missing phrase is.

Speaking my life

10 Work in pairs. Look at the questionnaire on page 154 and ask each other the questions. Then evaluate each other's attitude to security on a scale of 1 to 5 (5 = very aware, 1 = unconcerned) and exposure to risk (5 = very safe, 1 = very exposed).

A HACKER'S LIFE

Hackers compete in *Capture the Flag*.

▶ 54

Have you ever locked yourself out of your home and had to break in? First, you get a sense of accomplishment in succeeding. But then comes the worrying realization that if you, an amateur, can break
5 into your own home, a professional could do it five times faster. So you look for the weak points in your security and fix them. Well, that's more or less how the DefCon hackers' conference works.

Every year passionate hackers meet at the DefCon
10 convention in Las Vegas to present their knowledge and capabilities. Mention the word 'hacker' and many of us picture a seventeen-year-old in their bedroom, illegally hacking into the US's defence secrets in the Pentagon. Or we just think 'criminals'. But that is actually a gross
15 misrepresentation of what most hackers do.

The experiments that take place at DefCon have an enormous impact on our daily lives. These are computer addicts who love the challenge of finding security gaps. They examine all kinds of systems, from the internet to
20 mobile communications to household door locks. And then they try to hack them. Their findings are dutifully passed on to the industries that design these systems so that they can plug the holes.

I saw a great example of this when I attended a
25 presentation on electronic door locks. The presenters showed us significant weaknesses in several brands of electro-mechanical locks. A bio-lock that uses a fingerprint scan for entry was easily defeated by a paper clip. Although all the manufacturers of the
30 insecure locks were then contacted by the hackers, not all of them responded.

DefCon is a vast mix of cultures as well as a culture in itself. People in dark clothes and ripped jeans talk to people in golf shirts and suit trousers. Social status here
35 is based on knowledge and accomplishment, not on clothing labels or what car you drive. It's refreshing.

There are government agents here, as well as video game enthusiasts. But no one asks where you work – that would be bad manners.

40 DefCon runs various competitions during the conference, the most famous of which is *Capture the Flag*. *Capture the Flag* is a cyber game of attack and defence between the best hackers that goes on 24 hours a day. In a dimly-lit conference hall, small groups of hackers sit five
45 metres from each other, intensely trying either to break into or to protect the system. There are huge video projections on the walls, pizza boxes and coffee cups are strewn everywhere. It's mesmerizing.

In another room, participants compete against the
50 clock: they have five minutes to free themselves from handcuffs, escape from their 'cell', get past a guard, retrieve their passport from a locked filing cabinet, leave through another locked door, and make their escape to freedom.

55 If you're someone who dismisses the DefCon attendees as a group of computer geeks, then you are probably also someone who has the same password for ninety per cent of your online transactions. Which means you are doomed. Because even if you think you're being
60 clever by using your grandmother's birth date backwards as a secure key, you're no match for the dedicated people that I met. There is no greater ignorance to be found online than that of an average internet user. I'm happy now to admit that I'm one of them.

65 But it isn't just criminals that we need to protect our data from. Big business is also trying to get more and more information about our personal online habits. Sadly, we have few tools to protect ourselves. But there is a group of people who are fanatical about online
70 freedom and safety and have the means to help us vulnerable users protect our privacy. Many of them can be found at DefCon.

my life • THE IMPACT OF DIGITAL MEDIA • BRANDS • ATTITUDES TO SECURITY • MAKING A PODCAST
        • A NEWS REPORT

87

real life making a podcast • pronunciation new words • speaking skill hedging language

7d A podcast

Real life making a podcast

1 Work in pairs. Discuss the questions.

1 How do you prefer to access news stories and reports? Which do you think is the most trustworthy source? Why?
   a print
   b internet
   c video
   d audio
2 What kind of news stories and reports interest you particularly? Explain why.

> arts and culture   business   politics
> science and environment
> sport   travel   other

2 ▶ 55 Look at the photo. Describe it and say what you think is happening. What kind of news report is this going to be? Listen to the podcast and check your answer.

3 ▶ 55 Listen to the news report again and answer the questions.

1 What did scientists already know about these blue lights in the waves?
2 What more do they know now?

4 Pronunciation new words

a With new words, try to look for clues to their pronunciation. For example:

- Is there a familiar prefix or suffix?
- Is a vowel followed by a single or a double consonant?
- Does the length or type of word tell you where the stress is likely to be?

Work in pairs and try to guess the pronunciation of these words from the podcast.

> glowing   phytoplankton   Martin Roddick
> bioluminescent   predators   emitted

b ▶ 56 Listen and check your answers to Exercise 4a.

5 Speaking skill hedging language

▶ 55 When we aren't absolutely certain of facts, we commonly use 'hedging' language. Listen to the podcast again and match the hedging expressions the speakers use with each fact (1–6).

1 glowing blue waves are one of the most spectacular sights in nature
2 there are a lot of sea creatures that are bioluminescent
3 most of these creatures live in the deep ocean
4 or just lighting your way as you move around
5 an electrical force in the phytoplankton's body causes a chemical reaction
6 the electricity is generated by motion in the water

> ▶ **HEDGING LANGUAGE**
>
> It seems/appears that … ,
> … tend(s) to …
> This suggests that …
> It's reasonable to assume that …
> We can probably conclude that …
> There are estimated to be …
> There are thought to be …
> Arguably …
> Probably / Possibly / Most likely / Perhaps …

6 You are going to make a news podcast about a new discovery. Work in two groups of three.

Group A: Turn to page 154. Read the information.

Group B: Turn to page 155. Read the information.

- Discuss what you are going to say and prepare the story. Remember to use hedging language.
- Practise reading the story aloud, concentrating on pace and clear pronunciation.

my life   THE IMPACT OF DIGITAL MEDIA   ▶ BRANDS   ▶ ATTITUDES TO SECURITY   ▶ MAKING A PODCAST
▶ A NEWS REPORT

writing a news report • writing skill cautious language   Unit 7 **Digital media**

7e The Invisible Man

Writing a news report

1 Read the advice given to journalists below. Then look at the photo and title of the article and, with your partner, write six questions.

> A good news report should answer the five Ws and the H – *who*, *what*, *where*, *when*, *why* and *how* – as quickly as possible for the reader before giving further details or information.

2 Read the news report and check your answers. Did you find the answers quickly?

3 Which paragraph does the following:
 a gives the writer's opinion?
 b gives essential information?
 c explains the details?

4 Writing skill cautious language

a News reports (and academic reports) use cautious language when the information given cannot be verified 100%. Find an example of each of the following types of cautious language in the report.

 1 the verbs *seem* or *appear*
 2 passive reporting verbs
 3 adverbs that make generalizations
 4 adverbs that speculate about a fact
 5 modal verbs that express possibility

b Rewrite these sentences using the words given to express more caution about each of the facts presented.

 1 His pictures carry a strong social message. (generally)
 2 He became internationally famous when a New York art dealer bought some of his works. (apparently)
 3 His work makes people think more about their surroundings. (might)
 4 He wants to draw our attention to what we cannot see in a picture. (seems)
 5 Bolin used friends at first to help him paint his pictures. (believed)

5 Write a short news report about something that happened in your town or school recently. Use the five 'W's and the 'H' to know what information you should include and follow the structure in Exercise 3. Write around 150 words.

THE INVISIBLE MAN

In his work created in the summer of 2011 at his Beijing studio, Chinese artist Liu Bolin blends into a background of a supermarket soft drinks display. When his assistants had finished painting him in, he seemed to have disappeared. Entitled 'Plasticizer', the piece expresses Bolin's shock at the discovery of plasticizer in food products. Plasticizer is normally used to make materials like cement more flexible.

Such pictures have made Bolin internationally famous, which is ironic because it is said he used them originally to make a statement about feeling ignored by society. Bolin loves the challenge of blending into any surroundings: a building site, a telephone box, a national monument. No trick photography or Photoshopping is used and careful planning is needed for each image. First, before entering the scene, he tells the photographer how he would like the picture to look. Then he asks his assistant to paint him in. This process can take up to ten hours while Bolin stands completely still, presumably in some discomfort.

The pictures may be unusual, but they appear to have appealed to people all over the world because more recently, Bolin has received commissions to do similar paintings in New York, Paris, Venice, Rome and London.

6 Exchange news reports with your partner. Use these questions to check your reports.

- Does the report answer the six basic questions?
- Does it follow the paragraph structure in Exercise 3?
- Does it use cautious language appropriately?

my life ▶ THE IMPACT OF DIGITAL MEDIA ▶ BRANDS ▶ ATTITUDES TO SECURITY ▶ MAKING A PODCAST
         ▶ A NEWS REPORT

7f Talking dictionaries

A man and his son, Tuva Republic, Russia

Before you watch

1 Work in pairs and discuss the questions.

1. Can you think of three languages which are spoken in more than one country? Which is the most widespread?
2. Is your language spoken in another country? If so, where?
3. Is another language, such as English, replacing or influencing your language or other languages in your country?

2 How can we save lesser-spoken languages from being dominated or replaced by 'world' languages? Is it important to do this? Why? / Why not?

3 Key vocabulary

a Read the sentences. The words in bold are used in the video. Guess the meaning of the words.

1. Because so many have been killed for their ivory, the elephant is now an **endangered** species.
2. He said that he would not have won the award without the **collaboration** of his university colleagues.
3. They published a **lexicon** of terms used in the digital media field.
4. Swallows are **migratory** birds which travel from northern Europe to North Africa each autumn.
5. There are very few **indigenous** people left on the islands: most are foreign settlers.

b Match the words in bold in Exercise 3a with these definitions.

- a a dictionary or word list
- b regularly travelling from one place to another
- c native
- d at risk (of dying out)
- e working together

While you watch

4 ▶ 7.1 Watch the video and compare your answers from Exercise 2 with what the speaker says.

5 ▶ 7.1 Watch the first part of the video (0.00 to 1.02) again. Answer the questions.

1. How many of the world's languages are endangered?
2. Why are these languages dying out?
3. What are the more technologically aware communities doing to preserve their languages?

6 ▶ 7.1 Watch the second part of the video (1.03 to 2.29) again. Then complete the summary of the Talking Dictionaries project using one word per space.

The aim of *Talking Dictionaries* is to give endangered languages a first-ever ¹_____ on the ²_____. An example is Siletz Dee-ni from Oregon, USA, which has only one ³_____ speaker. Words are recorded and made into a talking dictionary. The rich vocabulary helps you appreciate the cultural ⁴_____. The dictionary can then be used to ⁵_____ the language.

7 ▶ 7.1 Watch the last part of the video (2.30 to the end) again. Answer the questions.

1. What did the Papuan New Guinea villagers ask the Enduring Voices team?
2. What message did seeing the Matukar talking dictionary on the internet send to people?
3. What is special about the Tuvan talking dictionary?
4. Who do the Talking Dictionaries team want to spread the message of the importance of linguistic diversity to?

8 Which words do you remember from the two talking dictionaries that you saw? What did they tell you about those particular cultures?

1. Siletz Dee-ni (Oregon, USA)
2. Matukar Panau (Papua New Guinea)

After you watch

9 Vocabulary in context

a ▶ 7.2 Watch the clips from the video. Choose the correct meaning of the words and phrases.

b Complete the sentences in your own words. Then compare your sentences with a partner.

1. I always feel revitalized after …
2. Talking to … gave me a real insight into …
3. We mustn't devalue … because it/they play a really important role.

10 Work in groups of three or four. You are going to make your own small talking dictionary.

- Think of words or short phrases which are typical of your language and culture (e.g. social life, food, geography, weather).
- Make a list of five or six of these and write an English translation for each.

Read your phrases and their translations to your group. Then ask each other questions about why you chose these particular phrases.

11 Do you think that the internet helps promote cultural diversity or does it make cultures more similar and homogenous? Give examples to support your arguments.

UNIT 7 REVIEW AND MEMORY BOOSTER

Grammar

1 Read the article. What is the Mariana Trench and what was Cameron's aim in visiting it?

2 Complete the article by making passive reporting verbs from the words in italics. You will need to use the correct verb form and tense.

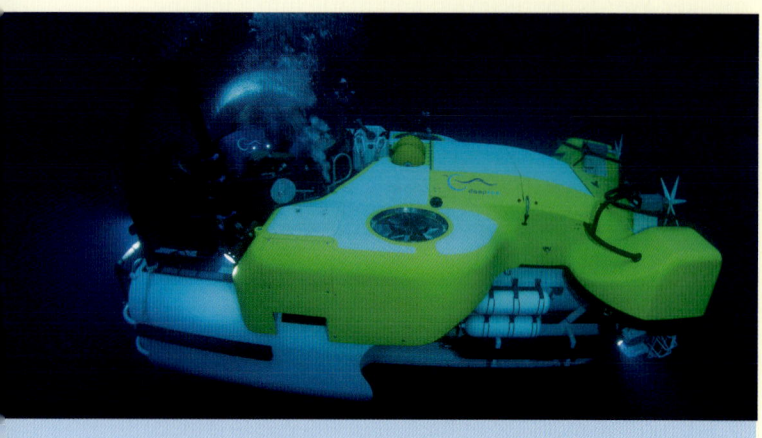

¹ *It / say / be* one of the greatest achievements in exploration since we put a man on the Moon. In March 2012, James Cameron piloted a one-person submersible to the bottom of the Mariana Trench. The trench, which ² *know / be* the deepest part of the ocean, is 120 times larger than the Grand Canyon. Although ³ *it / already / know* how the Mariana Trench was formed, Cameron hoped that he would learn more about what was living in the deep ocean. A famous Hollywood director (*Titanic* and *Avatar*), Cameron ⁴ *say / have* this ambition since he was a child. In achieving it, he became one of only three people to have dived to Earth's deepest point, and the only one to stay long enough to look around. In 1960, Swiss engineer Jacques Piccard and US navy captain Don Walsh ⁵ *report / spend* twenty minutes in the Mariana depths, but without discovering much. Their submarine disturbed a lot of mud, making it difficult to see anything clearly. Cameron's submersible was equipped with a large bank of LED lights and stereo digital cameras to take 3D shots. But it was not a comfortable expedition. The cabin of the submersible was so small that Cameron ⁶ *say / not be able* even to stretch out his arms.

3 **» MB** Rewrite these sentences from the article using nominalization. Then discuss why we sometimes use nominalization in writing.

   1 Cameron hoped that he would learn more about what was living in the deep ocean.
     Cameron's _____ was to gain greater _____ about _____ in the deep ocean.
   2 The submarine disturbed a lot of mud, making it difficult to observe the seabed.
     The large _____ of mud made _____ of the seabed difficult.

I CAN	
report what has been said (using passive reporting verbs)	
form nouns from other parts of speech	

Vocabulary

4 Complete these sentences using the correct verbs. You have been given the first letter.

   1 I've u_____ the wedding photos onto this website. Just c_____ on the link here.
   2 I think RT were the first channel to b_____ the news.
   3 I've never met him, but he's always p_____ comments on my social networking page.
   4 Don't you know her? She w_____ a really funny blog about life in Ireland.
   5 Before you buy a new laptop, you should see which ones have been favourably r_____ .
   6 Readers of online newspapers o_____ readers of print newspapers by ten to one.

5 **» MB** Match the two parts of these business buzz words. Then discuss the meanings with your partner.

   1 ballpark   a practice
   2 rocket   b check
   3 best   c science
   4 reality   d figure
   5 going   e win
   6 win   f forward

I CAN	
talk about different digital media	
understand business buzz words	

Real life

6 Rewrite the sentences using the words in brackets so that the speaker sounds less certain of the facts.

   1 Gorillas are shy creatures. (tend)
   2 There are around 340 different breeds of dog. (estimated)
   3 We can conclude that this is the main cause of the problem. (reasonable)
   4 No one knows the real reason. (appears)
   5 This demonstrates that the current regulations are ineffective. (suggests)
   6 She is the greatest actor of her generation. (arguably)

7 **» MB** Work in pairs. Use the hedging phrases in Exercise 6 to make four statements about exploration of the deep sea and James Cameron. Then compare statements with another pair.

I CAN	
use hedging language	

Unit 8 The music in us

Buskers playing in the old town in Havana, Cuba

FEATURES

94 World music
A musician talks about cultural influences

96 Healing music
The power of music

98 One love
Bob Marley

102 A biopic
A video about a film documentary of the life of Bob Marley

1 Look at the photo. What is a busker and what kind of music do they play? Is it common to see buskers in your country?

2 ▶ 57 Listen to a busker talking about her experiences. Make notes on the following points.
1 why she started busking
2 how her career developed
3 what the future holds for her

3 Complete the pairs of expressions (1–7) using these words. Discuss the differences in meaning between each pair.

| acoustic | amateur | gifted | hum | live | lyrics | solo |

1 **recorded** music and .... music
2 an **electric** guitar and a(n) .... guitar
3 to **sing a song** and to .... **a tune**
4 a **professional** musician and a(n) .... musician
5 to write the **music** and to write the ....
6 a **trained** musician and a **naturally-**............... musician
7 a **band** and a(n) .... artist

4 Work in groups. Discuss these questions.
1 How important is music to you? When do you listen to music?
2 What kind of music do you like? Who are your favourite singers/musicians?
3 Do you often sing or hum to yourself? What kind of tunes?

my life ▶ THEMES OF SONGS ▶ HOW TO RELAX ▶ A CHARITY CONCERT ▶ YOUR FAVOURITE MUSIC
▶ A DESCRIPTION

93

reading **music and cultural influences** • grammar **the adverb** *just* • pronunciation **expressions with** *just* • speaking **themes of songs**

8a World music

WORLD MUSIC

INTERVIEW OF THE WEEK

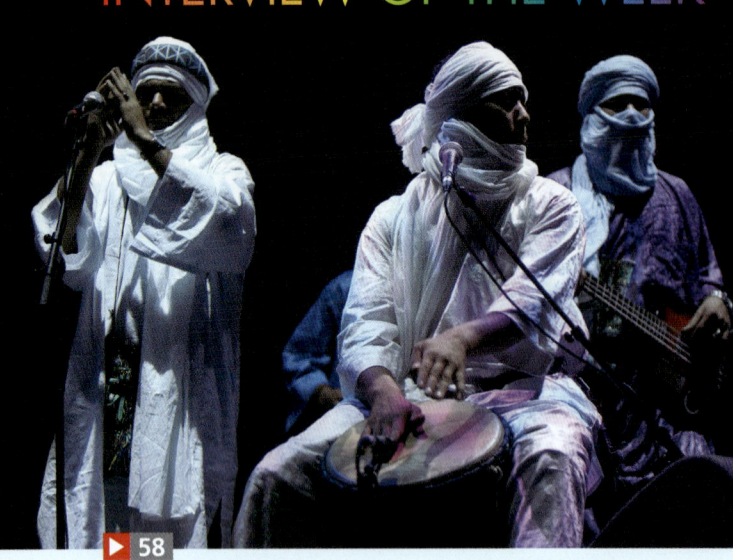

▶ 58

He has been travelling around the world for just under two years, collecting ideas for his new album, so we thought it was time to catch up with Justin Cape.

WM: Justin, you've just spent a lot of time studying and experimenting with musical styles in other countries. What's your aim? Are you trying to make music with a more universal appeal?

JC: No, that's not my goal really. International, that's to say commercial, pop music already has mass global appeal. I just get very excited when I hear new types of music and that's an excitement I'd like to share with others.

WM: But for many people, those different styles aren't very accessible, are they?

JC: No, they can be difficult to appreciate, but I don't think that's so surprising. Tastes are often just a question of habit, like the food you eat. Not many American teenagers listen to Indian sitar music, in just the same way that not many Indians eat hamburgers and fries. But I think if you get over that initial strangeness, discovering new musical styles can be incredibly rewarding.

WM: So, what music is 'exciting' you at the moment?

JC: I've been listening to a lot of music from Mali, particularly a group called Tinariwen, who play an upbeat mix of Middle Eastern and African music. Actually, I'm just working on a song that incorporates those influences. I've also been listening to a collection of Mexican-Irish songs produced by Ry Cooder. He's also a bit of a musical nomad with pretty eclectic tastes. You probably know him already from his collaborations with African and Cuban artists.

WM: Yes, I do. And do you find the things people sing about vary a lot from culture to culture?

JC: Not really. Themes are pretty universal: love, heartbreak, hopes for the future, nostalgia, challenging social rules and often just daily life. But themes are also linked to the times: western rock music in the sixties was often about independence and breaking out, whereas music in the noughties was more introspective and about personal feelings. What I do find, though, wherever I go, is that each new generation feels that 'their' music is speaking just to them, as if the same feelings hadn't been experienced before.

noughties (n) /ˈnɔːtiz/ the years from 2000 to 2009

Reading

1 Work in groups. Answer the questions.
1 How important is music in your culture? Is there one style of music that dominates?
2 How different are musical tastes between different generations (e.g. you and your parents)?
3 Do you listen to music from other countries and cultures? If so, who or what?

2 Read the interview with a musician. Which of the statements (a–c) best represents his main message?
a International pop music has damaged musical diversity.
b It's fascinating to study music from other cultures.
c You find out a lot about people from what they are singing about.

3 Match the references (1–4) with the point they illustrate (a–d).
1 American teenagers and sitar music
2 International pop music
3 Ry Cooder and Mexican-Irish songs
4 60s rock

a Other people are interested in researching different musical styles.
b Some music is a product of its time rather than its country or culture.
c There is some music which is universally popular.
d Musical tastes depend on what you are used to hearing.

4 Find adjectives in the interview with these meanings.
1 involving a large number of people
2 easy to relate to or understand
3 satisfying
4 positive or cheerful
5 varied and diverse
6 looking inwards, analysing yourself

Grammar the adverb *just*

> **THE ADVERB *JUST***
>
> **just + verb**
> You've **just** spent a lot of time studying musical styles.
>
> **just + preposition**
> He has been travelling around the world for **just** under two years.
>
> **just + noun**
> It's **just** a question of habit.
>
> For further information and practice, see page 170.

5 Look at the grammar box. Find at least one more example of each use of *just* in the text. Then answer the questions.

1. What is the position of *just* when the word it adds meaning to is:
   a. a verb?
   b. a preposition?
   c. a noun?
2. In which sentences (from the article) does *just* have the following meaning:
   a. a little   d. exactly
   b. simply   e. recently
   c. only   f. right at the moment

6 Put *just* in the most appropriate place in these sentences. There is sometimes more than one possible answer. Work in pairs. Discuss the meaning of *just* in each sentence.

1. If you took the time to listen to Ry Cooder, you'd definitely like him.
2. I've been listening to a live concert on the radio.
3. It's over five years since they performed in New York.
4. Hearing her sing gives me goosebumps.
5. The concert is in an old theatre behind the bank in the High Street.
6. If you like Stevie Wonder, I have the thing for you: a CD of his early recorded songs.
7. I don't listen to the lyrics; I like the music.
8. It's an idea, but why don't you try to get the tickets on eBay?

7 Complete these sentences with *just* in your own words. Then compare your sentences with your partner.

1. If you don't mind, I'll just …
2. Don't worry. It's just (a) …
3. My home is just …
4. I'll call you back. I'm just …
5. I've just …

8 Pronunciation expressions with *just*

a Work in pairs. Look at the phrases and discuss in what situations would people say them. What was each phrase a response to, do you think?

1. Just a minute. I'll get my coat.
2. Phew! Just in time.
3. It's OK. It's just one of those things.
4. Thanks. That's just the job.
5. No, thanks. I'm just looking.
6. Oh, I was just about to call you.
7. No, we're just good friends.
8. No particular reason. I just wondered.
9. Yes, do bring some, just in case.
10. It just goes to show no one's perfect.

b ▶ 59 Listen to the conversations and compare your answers. Then practise saying the phrases in Exercise 8a with the same pronunciation.

c Work in pairs. Choose five of the phrases and make new short conversations using the phrases.

Speaking my life

9 Work in groups. The list below contains the hundred most used words in pop song titles in the last 100 years (with common words like *the, to, I, you, my, don't*, etc. filtered out). First check you know what the words mean. Then follow this procedure.

1. Each person should think of five of their favourite pop song titles (including any you know in English).
2. Check if the song titles contain one or more of these words.
3. Discuss what the most common themes are in the songs that you thought of.

> ain't alone angel arms around away baby
> bad beautiful believe blue boy change
> christmas comes crazy cry dance days dear
> dream ever everybody everything eyes fall
> feel fire fool forever girl gone gonna
> goodbye happy heart heaven hey hold kiss
> la lady leave life light lonely love lover
> mama man mind mine miss moon moonlight
> morning mr music night nobody oh people
> play please rain red remember river rock
> roll rose sing smile somebody something
> song soul star stay stop street summer sun
> sweet sweetheart talk tears theme things
> think tonight town true walk wanna wish
> woman wonderful world young

my life ▶ THEMES OF SONGS ▶ HOW TO RELAX ▶ A CHARITY CONCERT ▶ YOUR FAVOURITE MUSIC
▶ A DESCRIPTION

listening music therapy • idioms music • grammar purpose and result • speaking how to relax

8b Healing music

Listening

1 Work in pairs. Answer the questions.

1 How do different types of music affect your mood?
2 Think of examples of when you use music to affect your mood (e.g. when driving a car).

2 ▶ 60 Which of the following therapeutic benefits do you think music has? Explain your reasons. Then listen to a talk by a neuroscientist and say which properties she mentions.

a relieving stress
b relieving pain
c helping sleep
d preventing heart disease
e increasing well-being
f improving memory
g helping with speech difficulties

> **dyslexia** (n) /dɪsˈleksɪə/ a condition that makes it difficult to read and write words correctly
> **stroke** (n) /strəʊk/ interruption of blood flow to the brain, causing loss of movement or speech

3 ▶ 60 Work in pairs. Complete the notes. Then listen to the neuroscientist again and check your answers.

1 Area of the brain activated by music: _____
2 The body releases endorphins to _____ and produce _____
3 The same parts of brain used to praocess _____ and _____
4 Music could help people with _____ and other _____
5 Gottfried Schlaug treated people who _____
6 The results of Schlaug's music therapy were _____
7 Music therapy for dementia and memory loss is important because _____

Idioms music

4 Look at the idiom in bold from the talk. What do you think it means?

'This news should be **music to our ears**.'

5 Match the music idioms (1–6) with the correct meaning (a–f).

1 You**'ve changed your tune**. You've always said you don't like foreign holidays.
2 Her talk about working unsociable hours **struck a chord with** the audience of nurses.
3 It's a mistake to plan what you are going to say at a job interview. Just **play it by ear**.
4 I don't want to **blow my own trumpet**, but actually, I think I did an excellent job.
5 Sooner or later someone will find out that he cheated and he'll have to **face the music**.
6 In the end he did help us to clear up, but he **made a big song and dance about it**.

a accept the consequences
b give a different opinion from your original one
c seemed very relevant to
d made a fuss or protested loudly
e shout about one's achievements
f take things as they come

6 Think of examples of the following. Then work in pairs and compare your ideas.

1 a person who likes to blow their own trumpet
2 a time when you (or someone you know) made a mistake and had to face the music
3 something you read that really struck a chord with you
4 a situation where it is best to play it by ear

Grammar purpose and result

> **▶ EXPRESSING PURPOSE**
>
> *to, in order (not) to, so as (not) to*
> 1 If you're not having to strain **in order to** hear what others are saying .
> 2 We clearly need to find a solution **so as not to** let it get any worse.
>
> *for*
> 3 It's used in hospitals now **for** the relief of* pain after an operation.
> * or **for** relieving
>
> *so that / in order that*
> 4 I'm not saying you should take up a musical instrument **so that** you can hear people better at parties …
>
> **▶ EXPRESSING RESULT**
>
> *so … that*
> Its power to relax us is **so** strong **that** it's commonly used in hospitals now.
>
> *such … that*
> The therapy produced **such** a dramatic improvement **that** even sceptics were impressed.
>
> *so much, so many, so little, so few …. that*
> There's **so much** noise **that** it's difficult to hear the person right next to you.
>
> For further information and practice, see page 170.

7 Look at the grammar box. Answer the questions.
  1 What grammatical form follows:
     a *to / in order to / so as to*?
     b *for*?
     c *so that*?
  2 Which sentence describes the function or use of a thing?
  3 What type of words follow a) *so* and b) *such* in a result clause?
  4 Do we use *so* or *such* when the word before the noun is *much, many, little* or *few*?

8 Use the words in brackets to rewrite the clauses expressing purpose.

> When pronouncing words in a new language, we often use sounds that are similar to those in our own language ¹ *because we don't want to sound silly* (so as). But ² *if we want to pronounce* (order) the new sounds properly, we must overcome this fear. Here are a few ideas ³ *so that you can improve* (for) your pronunciation.
> First, try to get the sounds right from the very beginning ⁴ *because otherwise you will develop* (avoid) bad habits. Secondly, exaggerate the sounds of the new language ⁵ *because then you get* (so that) as close to native pronunciation as you can. Thirdly, sing songs in the target language ⁶ *because it will help you lose* (to) your inhibitions.

9 Work in pairs. Write three tips of your own about learning English. Use expressions of purpose. Then share your ideas with the class.

10 Rewrite these sentences using a result clause with *so* or *such … that*. Write two versions of each sentence (one with *so* and one with *such*) where possible.
  1 The queue for taxis was very long. For that reason we decided to walk.
  2 I've worked there for over fifteen years. I really need to move on.
  3 I feel really nervous about this trip because I have very little experience of travelling.
  4 She's very determined. So I think she's bound to succeed.
  5 I don't think we'll ever agree because there are big differences between us.
  6 He has a lot of good ideas. That's why he never knows which ones to develop.

11 Complete these sentences in your own words using a clause with *so* or *such*. Then compare your answers with your partner.
  1 … that I can't stop listening to it.
  2 … that I can't wait to go there again.
  3 … that I felt better almost immediately.
  4 … that I've decided to find out more about it.

12 Read this example of a musical therapy game for elderly people. Explain what its purpose is and what results you could expect from it.

> In two teams, the group hears an extract of a well-known song from the past. The first team must try to name the song to win one point. If they cannot name it, the other team has the chance to answer. For an extra point, the team which has named the song can sing or say the next line in the song.

Speaking my life

13 What do *you* do to: a) relieve stress; b) feel better when you're down; c) generally relax; or d) help yourself remember things? Discuss with a partner and try to use expressions of purpose and result in your answers.

I get so stressed by my work sometimes that I can't think about anything else. I find the best thing to get it off my mind is just to chat and joke with friends.

reading **Bob Marley** • critical thinking **identifying key points** • word focus *hit* • speaking **a charity concert**

8c One love

Reading

1 Work in pairs. Think of four famous pop artists. What do you know about them? Discuss these points with your partner.

- nationality/background
- type of music / names of songs
- other things they are known for

2 Read the review. Then look at the headlines about Bob Marley. Do you think the writer of the review agrees, partly agrees or disagrees with them?

1 THE MAN WHO BROUGHT REGGAE TO THE WORLD

2 MILLIONS IN THIRD WORLD LOOK TO MARLEY AS A HERO

3 SOCIAL DISADVANTAGES INSPIRE MARLEY SONGS

4 MARLEY WAS AN ABSENT FATHER

5 NEW FILM REVEALS MUCH ABOUT REGGAE STAR'S LIFE

6 SINGER WHO SPREAD MESSAGE OF HARMONY

3 Find words in the review with the following meanings.

1 someone who rescues or saves people (para 1)
2 sections of film or a short film (para 2)
3 a poor, neglected area of a city, often with high crime (para 3)
4 a person who doesn't fit in to a group (para 3)
5 taken from your home or homeland (para 5)
6 suffering from lack of money (para 6)
7 different sides in a dispute (para 6)
8 in a state of great happiness (para 7)

Critical thinking identifying key points

4 Work in pairs. Identify in the text at least five key events or factors in Bob Marley's life that you think contributed to making him the person he was and the superstar he now is.

5 Work with another pair. Compare your ideas. Did you identify the same key points? Is there one thing that makes Bob Marley stand out as a pop artist? Does the author think so?

Word focus *hit*

6 Look at this sentence from the review. What does the word *hit* mean in this context?

"His first **hit** came when he was only eighteen years old."

7 Look at the sentences using expressions with *hit*. Match the expressions in bold with the correct definition (a–f).

1 The recruitment process is a bit **hit and miss**, I think: it doesn't guarantee that we're going to get good people.
2 They **took** a big **hit** when the stock market crashed.
3 The video game that you bought was **a real hit** with Luis; he hasn't stopped playing it.
4 I think you **hit a nerve** when you told Pedro that he needed to study harder. Did you see his expression?
5 You **hit the nail on the head** there, Kirsten. Damien really is just a kid in a grown-up's body.
6 The joke he told didn't really **hit the right note** with the audience. In fact, I think they were a bit offended.

a be appropriate
b a big success
c suffer a financial loss
d mention a sensitive point
e not consistently successful
f sum up something exactly

8 Make sentences of your own using two of the expressions from Exercise 7. Then read the sentences to your partner missing out the phrase with *hit*. Can your partner guess which phrase is missing?

Speaking my life

9 Work in groups. In 1976, Bob Marley organized a concert for peace called 'Smile Jamaica'. You are going to organize a charity concert to raise money for children in poverty. Decide on the following elements.

- the name and venue
- what age group you want to attract
- which artists you will invite to perform
- how it will raise money
- how you will link the event to the theme of children in poverty

ONE LOVE

Why is Bob Marley such an important figure in popular music? Globally, perhaps only Elvis, the Beatles and Michael Jackson are bigger names. Marley was not the first person to introduce reggae to a wider audience outside the West Indies, but he remains the only global reggae superstar. Yet, unlike the artists above, Marley and his music represent more than just great pop. Indeed, in many developing countries, he is celebrated as some kind of saviour, a symbol of hope. To understand why this is, one needs to know more about the man and his background.

This is where the documentary, *Marley*, fascinates, even if it does not provide all the answers. Containing a lot of previously unseen footage – interviews, performances, recording sessions – the film provides an insight into the mind and motivation of a musician whose life was cut tragically short: Marley died of cancer in 1981 aged 36.

Born in a poor ghetto of Kingston, Jamaica, Marley had a passion for music and began recording at a young age, his first hit coming when he was only eighteen. His difficult environment instilled in him a keen sense of social justice, which came to be expressed in his music. His mixed race origins taught him what it felt like to be an outsider: his father was a white Jamaican who worked as a British marine officer; his mother a black Jamaican who married at eighteen.

His father was rarely present, travelling as he did for his work, and died when Bob was only ten years old. Did this absence have any bearing on Marley's behaviour towards his own children, of whom there were eleven in all? In the film, his daughter, Cedella, talks about her difficulty in getting her father to notice her. But neither she, nor any others in the family, has a bad word to say about him. There is no sense that he did not have time for them; simply that he was prioritizing, because Marley's duty was first and foremost to music and its power to effect change.

Shortly after his marriage to Rita Anderson in 1966, Marley became a Rastafarian, a faith that champions the right of black Africans taken into slavery in the West Indies to return one day to Africa. So while themes of social injustice and hardship in the shanty towns of Kingston, Jamaica characterize early songs like *Trenchtown Rock* and *I Shot the Sheriff*, it is the theme of a displaced people that is dominant in later songs: *Exodus* and *Redemption Song*.

But whether the songs deal with injustice or with dislocation, they still contain the sentiments of unity and love that run through all his work. Marley himself maintained that, 'People want to listen to a message. This could be passed through me or anybody. I am not a leader, but a messenger.' This is too modest. Marley experienced genuine hardship and even put his life on the line for justice. In 1976, he took great risks to organize a free concert in his home town of Kingston called 'Smile Jamaica'. The concert was intended to unite the warring political factions in Jamaica, but while preparing for it, he was the victim of an assassination attempt that left him wounded.

A heartfelt message and an appeal to people in hardship are certainly a key to Marley's enduring status as a songwriter. But what really strikes you watching this film is the magic of his performances. The music sounds as fresh as it was when it was first recorded and Marley himself is lost in it, living each note as he spins and jumps ecstatically around the stage.

Even after two and a half hours of this documentary, you still feel there are many unanswered questions about the man who became the first Third World superstar. But isn't that the nature of great people who die young? They leave us wanting more. Kevin Macdonald's *Marley* is in selected cinemas from 3rd May.

real life your favourite music • speaking skill responding to questions • pronunciation intonation to express uncertainty

8d Desert Island Discs

Real life your favourite music

1 Work in pairs. Read the description of a popular radio show in the UK. Do you have a similar programme in your country? What is it? Discuss with your partner.

Desert Island Discs is a radio programme that has been running on BBC radio since 1942. Each week a guest is interviewed about their life. The basis of the show is that the guest is 'invited' to be a castaway on a desert island. They are allowed to take with them eight pieces of music, a book and one luxury item. During the programme they talk about their life and the reasons for their choices of music.

2 ▶ 62 Listen to a 'castaway' talking about himself and answer the questions.

1 What is this man's job?
2 In what way has he been successful?
3 What kind of music is the record he chooses and why does he choose it?

3 Speaking skill responding to questions

▶ 62 Look at the expressions for responding to questions. Then listen to the castaway again and answer the questions.

a What questions does the interviewer ask?
b Which phrases does Frank Steel use in his answers?

> ▶ **RESPONDING TO QUESTIONS**
> That's a good / an interesting question.
> I've never really thought about it.
> It's not something I've often thought about.
> I don't really look at it like that.
> I honestly don't know.
> I couldn't tell you really.
> That's difficult to say.
> Frankly, I've no idea.

4 Work in pairs. Think of three questions to ask your partner about their life (e.g. about their choice of career, their favourite things, their hobbies, their lifestyle). Try to make questions that really make your partner think. Then answer each question using one of the phrases in the box.

Do you think your parents influenced your choice of career?

5 Pronunciation intonation to express uncertainty

a ▶ 63 We often use a 'wavering' intonation – rising and falling in the same phrase or sentence – to express uncertainty. Listen to the phrases in the box and notice the rise and fall of the speaker's intonation. Then practise saying the phrases.

b ▶ 64 Say these phrases with a 'wavering' intonation. Then listen and check.

1 perhaps
2 maybe
3 I'm not sure
4 I can't say

6 Work in pairs. You are going to act out a *Desert Island Discs* interview. Follow these steps.

- Write down some details about yourself so that the 'interviewer' has some information to work with. Include your job and education, interests and personal achievements.
- Exchange notes with your partner and each prepare questions to ask each other.
- Think of two records you would like to take to a desert island and your reasons for choosing them. Also think of one luxury item.
- Act out the interviews, taking it in turns to play the parts of interviewer and castaway.

7 Did you find out anything interesting or new about your partner?

my life ▶ THEMES OF SONGS ▶ HOW TO RELAX ▶ A CHARITY CONCERT ▶ **YOUR FAVOURITE MUSIC** ▶ A DESCRIPTION

writing a description • writing skill parallel structures

Unit 8 The music in us

8e Fado

Writing a description

1 Work in pairs. Describe a traditional form of music in your country to your partner, giving a few details: its style, its themes, its history, its popular appeal now.

2 Read the description of Fado, a traditional style of music from Portugal, and answer the questions.

 1 How would you sum up what this style of music is?
 2 With whom is it popular?

3 Look at the elements of a description and find an example of each one in the text.

 1 It uses powerful adjectives.
 2 It describes feelings.
 3 It tries to convey an atmosphere.
 4 It uses similes.
 5 The author speaks to his audience as one of them.

4 Writing skill parallel structures

a Look at the sentences from the description. Notice how the words that follow the phrases in bold balance. For example, in 1, *either* and *or* are followed by a pronoun + verb. What parallel structures are used in the other sentences (2–4)?

 1 … **either** you'll love it **or** you'll hate it.
 2 **Like** the blues, Fado songs tell of … , **but unlike** the blues, the songs focus on …
 3 … of being separated from **either** a loved one **or** your home, **or** something you can never regain.
 4 Mariza has broadened Fado's appeal **by** fusing it with other musical traditions … and **by** touring the world with her music.

b Rewrite these sentences using parallel structures.

 1 Mariza is young, talented and she has lots of energy.
    Mariza is young, talented and energetic.
 2 She sings both traditional songs and she sings more modern songs.
 3 You can either book in advance or it's possible to pay on the door.
 4 You can spend hours wandering around the old town, visiting cafés and you can listen to live music.
 5 The music fuses traditional Spanish folk music and there are elements of north African music.

THE *FADO* OF LISBON by Jay Rowsell

People say about Fado that either you'll love it or you'll hate it. One thing is certain: you can't ignore it. It has been compared to the 'blues', because the songs are sad, but with Fado the intensity of the emotion is greater, piercing the listener's body like a knife. Like the blues, Fado songs tell of pain and hardship, but unlike the blues, the songs focus on the pain of separation: of being separated from either a loved one or your home, or something you can never regain. Perhaps that is not surprising when you consider that Portugal is a country with a long tradition of sailors and voyagers.

When I first saw a *fadista* perform in a dimly lit café one sultry evening in Lisbon twenty years ago, I was ignorant both of the Fado music tradition and of the Portuguese language. But that didn't matter, because the sheer drama of the music told its own story. In those days, Fado was a style of music that was known only in Portugal and a few of its former colonies: Brazil, Angola and Mozambique. Now, with the help of stars like Mariza, it has an international following. Mariza has broadened Fado's appeal by fusing it with other musical traditions – Spanish flamenco and Brazilian jazz, for example – and by touring the world with her music. But to hear traditional Fado, you should go where its roots are – the Alfama district of Lisbon. You may hate it, but I suspect you will love it.

5 Write a description of a traditional type of music or music and dance. Write 150–200 words and include the following details.

 • information about the history of this tradition
 • a description of how it is performed, what its appeal is and the feelings it arouses
 • where you can still find it being performed

6 Exchange descriptions with your partner. Use these questions to check your descriptions.

 • Does the description give a sense of the atmosphere?
 • Does it include strong descriptive language?
 • Does it speak to the reader personally?
 • Does it use parallel structures correctly?
 • Would you want to listen to this kind of music?

my life ▶ THEMES OF SONGS ▶ HOW TO RELAX ▶ A CHARITY CONCERT ▶ YOUR FAVOURITE MUSIC
▶ A DESCRIPTION

8f A biopic

Musicians walk the beach in Jamaica, West Indies.

Before you watch

1 Work in pairs or groups. Each pair/group takes a different quotation (a–f) by the singer Bob Marley and discuss what it means. Then explain your quotation to the rest of the class.

a 'Just because you are happy it does not mean that the day is perfect but that you have looked beyond its imperfections.'
b 'The truth is, everyone is going to hurt you. You just got to find the ones worth suffering for.'
c 'Some people feel the rain. Others just get wet.'
d 'Love the life you live. Live the life you love.'
e 'The day you stop racing is the day you win the race.'
f 'Better to die fighting for freedom than be a prisoner all the days of your life.'

2 Key vocabulary

a Read the sentences. The words in bold are used in the video. Guess the meaning of the words.

1 The people were so poor that they were dressed in **rags** rather than proper clothes.
2 It was a great **privilege** to meet the Prime Minister and speak with her about our concerns.
3 Although they took a big cut in salary, the employees found **solace** in the fact that they still had jobs.
4 Being famous has benefits, but there are also many **tribulations** to deal with in not being able to live a normal life.
5 They are an **oppressed** group: not allowed proper housing and ignored by the rest of society.

b Match the words in bold in Exercise 2a with these definitions.

a comfort or consolation
b treated very badly and discriminated against
c honour
d pieces of old cloth, often torn
e troubles or suffering

3 Work in pairs. If you were going to interview the director of a documentary about a famous musician's life, what questions would you ask? Write three key questions. Then compare your questions with another pair.

While you watch

4 ▶ 8.1 Watch the interview with Kevin Macdonald, the director of *Marley*, and compare your questions from Exercise 3 with the ones the interviewer asks.

5 Watch the first part of the video (0.00 to 0.55) again. Answer the questions.

1 What aspect of Marley's life did Kevin Macdonald feel had not been covered yet?
2 How does he describe the way we react to his music?
3 What does he hope the film will achieve?

6 ▶ 8.1 Watch the second part of the video (0.56 to 1.51). Underline the adjectives and expressions Kevin Macdonald uses when he describes Bob Marley's life.

touching	fascinating	extraordinary
tough	rags to riches	family troubles
racial issues	personal suffering	crime
violence	gangsters	political activity	amazing

7 ▶ 8.1 Watch the third part of the video (1.52 to the end). Complete the sentences about Bob Marley.

1 The first thing people like about him is that he is ....
2 More significantly he is very ....
3 He tries to offer people in hardship some ....
4 Because he's lived through tough times himself, you ....
5 He's the most listened to artist because his message is ....
6 The things he sings about are things we can all ....

After you watch

8 Vocabulary in context

a ▶ 8.2 Watch the clips from the video. Complete the collocations. Then discuss your answers.

b Complete the sentences in your own words. Then compare your sentences with a partner.

1 … music doesn't really appeal …
2 When I …, I took on more than I bargained for.
3 … went through a difficult time when …

9 Work in pairs. Discuss these questions.

1 What situations can you think of where music brings people together?
2 What examples can you think of in your own culture?

10 Work in groups. Think of a famous person to make a documentary about. Decide what you want to include in your documentary and what message you want to communicate. Then present your ideas to the class. Think about these areas:

- who you will interview
- where you will film the documentary
- how you will present the information – through narration or interviews

UNIT 8 REVIEW AND MEMORY BOOSTER

Grammar

1 Read the article. Then complete the article with clauses of purpose and result.

2 What three things did the 1971 Concert for Bangladesh achieve?

The Concert for Bangladesh in 1971 was the first large concert organized ¹_____ help victims of a disaster. It was staged at Madison Square Garden in New York and the organizers, George Harrison and Ravi Shankar, were ²_____ well-known that it attracted an audience of 40,000 people and raised over US$250,000. Further income was gained from the live album of the concert that was then made. The money was used ³_____ the relief of the refugee crisis following the war and the cyclone that hit the country in 1970, and was passed to the charity UNICEF ⁴_____ that they could distribute it to where it was most needed. Other famous music artists of the day, such as Bob Dylan, Billy Preston and Eric Clapton, also performed so ⁵_____ to ensure as wide an audience as possible for the music.

But the wider aim of the Concert for Bangladesh wasn't to raise money. The organizers felt people were not aware enough of Bangladesh and its problems. Ravi Shankar later said that in this sense the response to the concert had been amazing. It also proved to be the start of a new movement in benefit concerts. Under fifteen years later, Live Aid, a response to the Ethiopian famine, was staged in London and Philadelphia, attracting a global TV audience of almost two billion.

3 **>> MB** Read the last paragraph of the article again. Put the word *just* in an appropriate place in each sentence. Then compare answers with your partner. Explain what *just* means in each case.

I CAN
use purpose and result clauses accurately
use the adverb *just* with different meanings

Vocabulary

4 Complete the text about music. Use one word in each space.

I'm still an ¹_____ musician, but I hope to be professional one day. I play piano, and also the ²_____ guitar – never electric. I write my own songs, both the music and the ³_____. I'm basically a ⁴_____ artist, but when I play ⁵_____ (at local music venues) then I get a band together. I don't want to blow my own ⁶_____ but I think I am a naturally-⁷_____ musician. Whether that means I'll make a living out of it is another question.

5 **>> MB** Work in pairs. Discuss the difference between these pairs of words.

1 **sing** and **hum**
2 **gig** and **concert**
3 **song** and **tune**
4 **pop** and **folk music**
5 a **busker** and an **amateur musician**
6 **title** and **lyrics**
7 **chord** and **note**

I CAN
talk about music
use music idioms

Real life

6 Read the conversation and complete the responses to the questions.

A: How often do you actively listen to music each day?
B: I've never really ¹_____ about it. Um … probably three or four times a day, I ²_____ think.
A: Do you use music when doing certain things, like doing housework or working at your computer?
B: That's an ³_____ question. I guess I do often listen to music when I'm working.
A: And does it help you work: make you more productive?
B: I couldn't ⁴_____ you really. I suspect that it's more of a distraction, actually.
A: How do you think you would feel without music in your life?
B: That's difficult to ⁵_____. I imagine it would be less fun, but I ⁶_____ don't know.

7 **>> MB** Work in pairs. Act out a similar conversation by asking each other the questions in Exercise 6.

I CAN
talk about (my favourite) music and why I like it
give myself time to think when responding to difficult questions

Unit 9 Window on the past

The Stones of Stenness, Orkney, Scotland

FEATURES

106 Dear little daughter
What personal letters reveal about our past

108 The story of Martin Guerre
The story of an unusual crime in medieval France

110 Diamond shipwreck
A story of hidden treasure and mystery on the Namibian coast

114 Collecting the past
A video about how Chinese people are preserving their cultural heritage

1 Look at the photo. How old do you think these stones are and what was their purpose?

2 ▶ 65 Listen to an archaeologist talking about these stones. Make notes about the stones (age, location, purpose, who built them, etc.).

3 ▶ 65 What objects did archaeologists find that helped them understand more about the stones? Listen again and check.

4 Use these words related to discovery to complete the summary.

| clues   deduced   determine   find out   evidence |
| indicated   uncovered |

Archaeologists say it's not what you find that matters, but what you ¹_____. They couldn't ²_____ the purpose of these stones until they ³_____ other objects that gave them valuable ⁴_____. The rich soil ⁵_____ that this was a wealthy farming community, while pieces of flint and glass were ⁶_____ of a trading society. From this the archaeologists ⁷_____ that the stones were monuments of great cultural importance.

5 Work in pairs. What ancient historical sites or monuments are there in your country? What do these sites tell you about the people who built them?

my life ▶ AN IMPORTANT PAST EVENT ▶ A CASE OF FRAUD ▶ HISTORICAL IRONY ▶ CONFIRMATION AND CLARIFICATION
▶ DESCRIBING A PAST EVENT

reading a father's letter • wordbuilding verb + preposition • grammar linking words • speaking an important past event

9a Dear little daughter

Reading

1 Do you keep any of these things from your past? Do you ever look back at them? What do they tell you about your past?

- letters
- diaries
- old photos
- old schoolwork

2 Read the article and letter. What made Dubois write the letter and what hopes does he express in it?

3 Read the article again. Answer the questions.

1 What are the advantages and disadvantages of letters as historical documents?
2 What do we know about Dubois' own education?
3 What does the letter tell us about:
   a Dubois' view of America?
   b Dubois' view of England/Europe?
   c how life will be different for Yolande?
   d Dubois' expectations of his daughter?

Wordbuilding verb + preposition

▶ **WORDBUILDING verb + preposition**

Certain (non-phrasal) verbs have a preposition between them and their object.
to prepare for (a meeting), to focus on (the job)

For further practice, see Workbook page 75.

4 Look at the wordbuilding box. Find the prepositions used with these verbs in the article and letter.

a relate   b wait   c shrink   d believe

5 Complete the sentences with the correct prepositions.

1 He is suffering _____ exhaustion.
2 Do you approve _____ the new building?
3 Who will benefit _____ these changes?
4 I need to reflect _____ it before I answer.
5 She didn't participate _____ the game.
6 The book is aimed _____ an older audience.

Dear Little Daughter

▶ 66

Of all the types of historical document – maps, interviews, legal records, photographs, newspaper cuttings – perhaps the most engaging is the letter. Although letters don't always represent mainstream views, owing to their personal nature, they often provide a fascinating window on people's
5 values and behaviour. Moreover, the subject matter is generally something we can easily relate to – love, advice, gratitude, disappointment. This is an extract from a letter written by the American sociologist and civil rights activist, W.E.B. Dubois, in October 1914. He wrote it following his daughter's departure for boarding school in England. Dubois, who
10 was the first African-American to get a PhD from Harvard University, valued education highly and was concerned because Yolande, thirteen at the time, wasn't doing well at school. As well as having poor marks, she seemed unmotivated. So he decided to send her to a liberal private school in England, Bedales, and soon after she left, he sent her this advice.

Dear Little Daughter: 15

I have waited for you to get well settled before writing. By this time, I hope some of the strangeness has worn off and that my little girl is working hard and regularly.

Of course, everything is new and unusual. 20
You miss the newness and smartness of America. Gradually, however, you are going to sense the beauty of the old world: its calm and eternity and you will grow to love it. … 25

Don't shrink from new experiences and custom. Take the cold bath bravely. Enter into the spirit of your big bed-room. Enjoy what is and not pine for what is not. Read some good, heavy, serious books 30
just for discipline: Take yourself in hand and master yourself. Make yourself do unpleasant things, so as to gain the upper hand of your soul.

Above all remember: your father loves you 35
and believes in you and expects you to be a wonderful woman.

I shall write each week and expect a weekly letter from you.

Lovingly yours, 40

Papa

Grammar linking words

> **▶ LINKING WORDS**
>
> **linking word + clause**
> *and, after, although, as, because, but, since, when, while, when*
> **Although** letters do not always represent mainstream views, they often provide a fascinating …
> Dubois was concerned **because** Yolande was not doing well at school.
>
> **linking word + -ing form or noun**
> *after, as well as, despite, in addition to, in spite of, on account of, because of, as a result of*
> **As well as** having poor marks, she seemed unmotivated.
>
> **linking word + noun / noun phrase**
> *following, owing to*
> He wrote it **following** his daughter's departure …
>
> **linking word + new sentence**
> *afterwards, consequently, however, moreover, nevertheless, subsequently, what's more, yet*
> … window on people's values and behaviour. **Moreover**, their subject is generally something we can easily relate to.
>
> For further information and practice, see page 172.

6 Look at the grammar box. Which linking words in the box have the following functions?

   a to contrast ideas
   b to make an additional point
   c to state a reason or result
   d to show the sequence of events

7 Complete the sentences with these linking words. There are three extra words.

| after | although | and also | as well as | despite |
| following | moreover | on account of | since | |

  1 _____ having many friends at her new school, she still missed home.
  2 Being at boarding school helped her to focus on her work _____ taught her independence.
  3 She gave up playing sports at school _____ getting injured too often.
  4 She liked her fellow classmates. _____ , they liked her.
  5 _____ leaving university, she returned home to plan her next step.
  6 _____ there were no jobs she wanted to do, she decided instead to train as a lawyer.

8 Rewrite the sentences in two ways using the words given so they have the same meaning.

  1 War broke out in Europe shortly after Yolande arrived, **but** her mother decided to visit her there anyway.
     a Despite …   b … . However …
  2 The letter shows that he was a concerned father **and also** reveals that he was quite strict.
     a In addition to … b … as well as …
  3 Dubois did not see his daughter again for two years **because** he had such a busy schedule.
     a Owing to …   b Since …
  4 Dubois went off travelling himself **when** Yolande and her mother returned to America.
     a Following …   b … . Soon afterwards …

9 Read this informal letter. Link the sentences, as indicated by the words in brackets. Sometimes you will need to rewrite the sentences.

> Dear Jana
>
> Thanks for your letter and news. I was very glad to hear that you're well. [1] (*contrast*) I was really disappointed to read about Nathan's job. I do hope he's able to find another one soon.
>
> It would be great if you could visit us here. The weather's quite cold at the moment. [2] (*contrast*) It's often sunny and there's so much to see. Berlin has some fantastic museums and galleries. [3] (*addition*) It has some amazing shops. It's also just a great place to walk around. [4] (*reason*) It's not heavily populated – unlike London, which always feels too crowded and hectic. [5] (*addition*) There are loads of interesting places to eat and drink.
>
> If you don't make it here, I'll probably come back to England in the summer. [6] (*sequence*) My exams are at the end of May. I've made some good friends here. [7] (*contrast*) I really miss my old friends. Anyway, have a think about it. [8] (*sequence*) Write and let me know.
>
> Much love
>
> Harriet

Speaking   *my life*

10 Work in groups. You are going to talk about a past event using linking words. Follow these steps:

- Each choose an event to talk about from the list below; think about how you will integrate the linking words into your story.
- Give each other three different linking words to use in a story.
- Take turns to tell your stories.

  a a time in your childhood (even a short period) when you lived away from home
  b the story behind an old (family) photo
  c a letter that had a big impact on you
  d an event you recorded in a personal diary

vocabulary crime and punishment • listening an unusual crime • grammar present and perfect participles • speaking a case of fraud

9b The story of Martin Guerre

Vocabulary crime and punishment

1 Work in pairs. Look at these common crimes. Discuss what each one is and try to agree on an order of seriousness.

> assault   burglary   dangerous driving   fraud
> possession of drugs   theft   trespassing
> vandalism

2 Put these steps in the criminal justice process in the correct order. What is the next step if a person is found to be not guilty of a crime?

   a They are found (to be) guilty or not guilty.
   b They are sentenced or they are acquitted.
   c The case is heard or they go on trial.
   d Someone is accused of the crime.
   e They go (or are taken) to court.
   f They appeal against the conviction.
   g A crime is committed.   *1*
   h They are arrested and charged with the crime

Listening

3 Look at the photo and caption. What kind of crimes (from Exercise 1) do you think were common here in medieval times?

4 ▶ 67 Listen to an interview with a historian. Make notes about the following points.

   1 what this historian is particularly interested in and why
   2 who these characters are in the story
      a Martin Guerre   c Arnaud du Tilh
      b Bertrande   d Pierre
   3 why Martin Guerre left his home and family
   4 what Bertrande's attitude to Arnaud was
   5 what happened to Martin Guerre in the end

5 ▶ 67 Look at the events in the story. Put them in order. Then listen to the interview again and check your answers.

   a Martin's uncle, Pierre, took Arnaud to court to prove he was an impostor.
   b Martin was wounded in battle and lost his leg.
   c Martin got married and had a son.
   d Martin appeared in the high court and told the true story.
   e Martin escaped to Spain and joined the Spanish army.
   f Arnaud arrived in Artigat, saying he was Martin to claim the family estate.
   g Arnaud lost the case but appealed against the decision.
   h Martin was caught stealing from his father's grain store.

A medieval town, Collonges, south-west France

Grammar present and perfect participles

> **PRESENT and PERFECT PARTICIPLES**
>
> **Present participle**
> 1 We look out for that kind of unusual story, **hoping** that it will give a better idea of …
> 2 **Fearing** a severe punishment, he fled over the border to Spain.
> 3 Bertrande was left at home, **not knowing** what had happened to her husband.
>
> **Perfect participle**
> 4 **Having spent** some time doing various jobs, he eventually joined the Spanish army.
> 5 Perhaps, **having waited** so long, she was just glad to have someone to support her again.
>
> For further information and practice, see page 172.

6 Look at the grammar box. Answer the questions.
1 What is the subject of each participle?
2 Does the participle clause in each sentence describe the main event or a secondary event?
3 Do the perfect participle clauses describe an event that happened before or after the other event?

7 Rewrite the sentences (1–5) from the grammar box. Replace the participle clause with *because*, *after* or *and* + subject + verb.

8 Read the sentences. There are two ideas in each sentence. Decide which idea should be the secondary idea. Then rewrite the sentences using participle clauses.
1 Clara focuses on historical events that are unusual and examines them in great detail.
2 Martin got married very young and then had a son when he was 21.
3 He was wounded in battle while he was fighting for the Spanish army.
4 Arnaud came to the village because he hoped to inherit Martin's estate.
5 Martin's uncle suspected that Arnaud was an impostor and took him to court.
6 After Arnaud lost the first case he appealed and took the case to a higher court.

9 Work in pairs. Discuss how to complete these sentences using participles and the verb in brackets.
1 He didn't tell his parents, … (fear)
2 … , she decided that New Zealand was the place she most wanted to live. (travel)
3 I called the police, … (think)
4 I burnt my hand … (try)
5 … , he concluded that his friend must have forgotten their arrangement. (wait)
6 They sold all their possessions – their house, their car, their furniture, … (decide)

10 There are certain participles that act almost as fixed expressions. Look at this example from the story about Martin Guerre and answer the questions.

'**Given that** Martin's father had already died, the house and land now legally belonged to his eldest son.'

1 What does *given that* mean?
2 Does the clause with *given that* give the main idea or extra information?
3 Are the subjects of each clause the same or different?

11 Look at the participle expressions in bold and match the two halves of each sentence.
1 **Assuming (that)** there are no travel delays,
2 **Provided (that)** everyone else is happy,
3 **Compared to** most cities,
4 **Considering (that)** she's only eleven,
5 **Given that** he has such a strong interest in history,
6 **Seen from** the doctors' point of view,

a Vancouver offers lots of outdoor activities.
b we can have something to eat before the show.
c her performance on the piano was amazing.
d the drug has a lot of advantages.
e I don't mind being in charge of the project.
f I think a book about ancient maps would be a great gift.

12 Write new subordinate clauses for sentences a–f from Exercise 11. Use a different participle expression from clauses 1–6 in each case. Then compare sentences with your partner.

Considering it has such a wet climate, Vancouver offers a lot of outdoor activities.

Speaking my life

13 Work in pairs.

Student A: Turn to page 153.

Student B: Turn to page 155.

Read the stories and put participle clauses into them where indicated (P). Then tell the story to your partner. Ask each other questions and discuss what you think of these crimes.

14 Talk about a crime that appeared in the news recently in your country. Explain what happened and why this made an impact on you.

15 Are you (or anyone you know) good at impersonating other people's voices? If you could impersonate someone else's voice perfectly, who would you choose and why?

reading **hidden treasure** • critical thinking **unanswered questions** • word focus *board* • speaking **historical irony**

9c Diamond shipwreck

Reading

1 Look at the map showing shipping routes in the 16th century from Portugal to the East. Answer the questions.

   1 Why did ships make these voyages?
   2 What dangers did sailors face on a voyage like this?

2 Read the article about the voyage of one of these ships. Summarize the main events. What happened to the ship and crew on its voyage? Why was this ironic?

3 Read the article again. Choose the word (a–c) that does NOT fit in each sentence, according to the text.

   1 Among the objects on the *Bom Jesus* were … and … .
      a spices   b weapons   c treasure
   2 The ships themselves were … .
      a up-to-date   b well-built   c much travelled
   3 This part of the Namibian coast is very … .
      a unwelcoming b hot   c unpopulated
   4 If anyone survived the shipwreck, they would certainly have been … .
      a injured   b tired   c cold
   5 The striking thing about the diamonds in this area is how … they are.
      a big   b easy to find c numerous
   6 The voyage of the *Bom Jesus* ended in disaster because it was unable to resist the strong … .
      a tides   b currents   c winds

4 Find words in the article with the following meanings.

   1 incredible (para 1)
   2 extremely beautiful (para 1)
   3 good at their job (para 3)
   4 incomplete (para 4)
   5 piece (para 4)
   6 depressing and unwelcoming (para 5)

Critical thinking unanswered questions

5 It's important to analyse what articles say; it's also important to think about what they *haven't* said. Look at the areas below. Do you have any questions about them that the article did not answer?

   • the treasure from the ship
   • the geologist who found it
   • the wreck of the ship
   • the sailors' bodies
   • the diamonds

6 Work in pairs. Ask each other your questions from Exercise 5. Did the article give any clues at all to the answers or not? Summarize what we know and don't know about this event.

Word focus *board*

7 What does this expression with *board* from the article (line 30) mean? Discuss the meanings of the other phrases with *board*.

   " She had **on board** a fortune in gold and ivory … "

   1 The new design is great. They've clearly listened to their customers and **taken** their views **on board**.
   2 I changed the plug, but it still doesn't work. Well, **back to the drawing board**!
   3 We'll need some food, but don't **go overboard** – just a few snacks is fine.
   4 The deal was completely **above board**. The agent always takes ten per cent of the profit.
   5 The government is raising taxes not just on big houses but **across the board**.

8 Think of examples of the following. Then work in pairs and tell your partner.

   1 a time when a plan didn't work and you had to go back to the drawing board
   2 a time when someone you know went overboard in organizing a special occasion
   3 a time when you had to take different people's views on board

Speaking my life

9 Work in groups. You are each going to read two historical facts. Then ask each other to guess what the irony of each situation was.

   Student A: Read the facts on page 153.

   Student B: Read the facts on page 154.

   Student C: Read the facts on page 155.

10 Think about a subject you know a lot about. Prepare to talk about a specific point of interest in this subject. Then work in pairs. Describe the point to your partner. Your partner should ask questions to get clarification or confirmation about it.

Diamond Shipwreck

This remarkable story would have been lost forever if a company geologist had not made an astonishing discovery in 2008 in the beach sands of Namibia. While he was working in the area, he came across a copper ingot. The ingot was the type traded for spices in the East Indies in the sixteenth century. Archaeologists would later find a staggering 22 tons of these ingots beneath the sand, as well as cannons, swords, ivory, muskets, chain mail and exquisite gold coins bearing the coat of arms of King João III of Portugal. From this evidence, historians have pieced together the following story.

One bright spring day in 1533, the great ships of the Portuguese India fleet sailed grandly down the Tagus River and out into the Atlantic, flags flying. These ships were the pride of Portugal, off on a fifteen-month mission to bring back pepper and spices from distant places such as Goa, Cochin and Zanzibar, places that were familiar ports of call thanks to Portuguese navigating skills.

The ships were strong and capable; two of them were brand-new and owned by the king himself. One was the *Bom Jesus*, captained by Dom Francisco de Noronha and carrying 300 crew, soldiers and merchants. She had on board a fortune in gold and ivory to trade at a spice port on the coast of India.

But four months after its departure from Lisbon, the fleet was struck and scattered by a huge storm. Details are sketchy, because the fleet commander's report has been lost. All we know is that it mentioned that the *Bom Jesus* had disappeared in wild weather somewhere off the Cape of Good Hope. We can guess what happened next: the ship was caught in powerful winds and currents and driven helplessly northwards for hundreds of miles. Somewhere near the Namib Desert, it struck rocks 150 metres from shore. The blow broke off a big chunk of the ship's stern, spilling tons of copper ingots into the sea and sending the *Bom Jesus* down.

And the sailors? 'In a storm, getting ashore would have been just about impossible,' says the archaeologist Dieter Noli. 'On the other hand, if the weather had calmed, the ship might have drifted ashore.' And then what? This is one of the most inhospitable places on Earth, an uninhabited wasteland of sand and scrub. It was winter. Any survivors would have been wet, freezing and exhausted. No ship was likely to pass, since they were far away from the trade routes. As for getting back to Portugal – they might as well have been shipwrecked on Mars.

Yet, in spite of its bleak environment, this place held an extraordinary secret. It was a desert rich in high-quality diamonds; so rich, in fact, that in the 1900s, the explorer Ernst Reuning made a bet with a companion about how long it would take to fill a tin cup with gems found in the sand. The job took ten minutes. Over many centuries, millions of diamonds had been washed down to the shore from deposits in the mountains far inland. Only the hardest gems, some weighing hundreds of carats, survived the journey. They spilled into the Atlantic at the river's mouth and were washed up the coast, carried by the same cold current that would one day sweep the *Bom Jesus* to its end.

None of the sailors of the *Bom Jesus* ever returned home. They died somewhere near this mysterious coast, unaware that beneath their feet were more than a hundred million carats of diamonds. They had no idea of the irony of it. They had set off on a great journey in search of riches, and now here they were, on a shore of unimaginable wealth.

---

carat (n) /ˈkærət/ a unit of weight for precious stones 1 carat = 200 milligrams
fleet (n) /fliːt/ a group of ships
ingot (n) /ˈɪŋgət/ a bar of a precious metal such as gold or copper
musket (n) /ˈmʌskɪt/ an old-fashioned rifle
stern (n) /stɜːn/ the rear end of a ship

real life checking, confirming and clarifying • pronunciation silent letters

9d I'll give you an example

Real life checking, confirming and clarifying

1 Look at the photo. Describe the weather you see.

2 ▶ 69 Listen to two friends discussing a book about the weather. Answer the questions.

1. What is the subject of the history book *Fixing the Sky*?
2. How have people traditionally tried to do this?
3. How have they tried to do this more recently?
4. What probably happened as a result of the cloud-seeding experiment?
5. What point is the author of the book trying to make?

> ▶ **CHECKING, CONFIRMING and CLARIFYING**
>
> **Checking and confirming**
> So, are you saying (that) …
> So, am I right in thinking that … ?
> What do you mean by … ?
> Would you mind just going over that again?
> If I understand correctly, you're saying that …
> Let me get this straight. …*
> Perhaps I'm missing something, but …
>
> **Clarifying**
> What I'm saying is …
> The point is that …
> What I meant (by that) was …
> In other words, …
> That's to say, …
> I'll give you an example …
> * more informal

3 Work in pairs. Look at the expressions for checking, confirming and clarifying. Choose an appropriate phrase to complete each sentence.

1. _____ 'control the weather'?
2. It describes the kind of things people have traditionally done to get the weather they want – _____ , things like praying for sunshine …
3. What kind of experiments? _____ . In the 1950s …
4. But _____ when people did these experiments, they didn't see it as interfering with nature.
5. Hang on, _____ .
6. _____ the government experimented with making rain …?
7. But actually, _____ that it could be quite useful technology now?
8. We should also be aware of the history of these techniques. _____ , we shouldn't just jump into things.

4 ▶ 69 Listen to the conversation again and check your answers in Exercise 3.

5 Pronunciation silent letters

a ▶ 70 Look at the words from the conversation and underline the letters that are not pronounced. Then listen and check.

| fascinating | chemicals | straight | doubt |
| wrong | technology | know | guess |

b ▶ 71 Practise saying the words in Exercise 5a. Then practise pronouncing these other words. The silent letters have been underlined for you. Listen and check.

as<u>th</u>ma	cas<u>t</u>le	<u>c</u>haos	dis<u>g</u>uise
enviro<u>n</u>ment	<u>k</u>neel	mus<u>c</u>le	plum<u>b</u>er
<u>p</u>sychology	recei<u>p</u>t	san<u>d</u>wich	si<u>g</u>n	sub<u>t</u>le

6 Work in pairs. You are going to talk about an historical event which was affected by weather.

Student A: Turn to page 155.

Student B: Turn to page 155.

Look at the summary of the article and prepare to speak about it. Then explain the story. Your partner should check their understanding and ask for clarification if they do not understand something. Use the expressions for checking, confirming and clarifying to help you.

---

my life ▶ AN IMPORTANT PAST EVENT ▶ A CASE OF FRAUD ▶ HISTORICAL IRONY ▶ CONFIRMATION AND CLARIFICATION
▶ DESCRIBING A PAST EVENT

writing describing a past event • writing skill sequencing events   Unit 9 Window on the past

9e Krakatoa

Writing describing a past event

1 Look at the photo. What kind of island is this? Do you know any others like it?

2 Work in pairs. Read the short historical account about Krakatoa and answer the questions. Then discuss your answers with your partner.

1. What were the immediate effects of the eruption of Krakatoa?
2. What were the long-term effects and how was this unusual?

In 1883, the volcano on the island of Krakatoa erupted with such force that the explosion sent ash six kilometres into the atmosphere and could be heard 160 kilometres away. Until then, few people had heard of Krakatoa. It was just a small island passed by ships as they crossed the straits between Java and Sumatra.

The eruption took place on Monday 27th August, causing the deaths of thousands of people on neighbouring islands, and destroying two-thirds of Krakatoa itself. But the long-term climate effects were just as dramatic. In the preceding months the volcano had already been active, discharging huge quantities of ash into the sky and blocking out the sun for miles around. However, during the main eruption the ash went so high that it reached the upper atmosphere and was blown right around the world on the trade winds. The following year, scientists recorded a 1.2°C drop in global temperatures and these did not return to normal levels until some years later.

Unusual global weather patterns continued in the years following the eruption of Krakatoa. Nebraska, in the USA, suffered an extraordinary winter in 1888, when temperatures dropped 18 degrees in three minutes and 125 cm of snow fell in 36 hours – extraordinary in those days, when 60 cm was the average for a whole year.

3 Writing skill sequencing events

a Work in pairs. How does the writer sequence the different facts surrounding the eruption of Krakatoa? Put these events in the order they appear in the text.

a events following the eruption of 1883
b the events leading up to the eruption of 1883
c the eruption itself

b Read the account again and find time phrases about the past which correspond to each of the present time phrases (a–d).

Present	Past
a up to now	1 _____
b in recent months	2 _____
c next year	3 _____
d nowadays	4 _____

c Complete the sentences with the correct time phrases. Use the words given.

Viewed from the present	Viewed from a point in the past
some days ago	They had met 1 _____ . (earlier)
tomorrow	There were further eruptions 2 _____ . (following)
at the moment	No one was living on Krakatoa 3 _____ . (time)
yesterday	Loud noises were heard 4 _____ . (previous)
from now on	Krakatoa became famous 5 _____ . (then)

4 Write about an event that happened in your town or region. Use the ideas below to help you. Describe the events leading up to the main event, the main event and what happened afterwards. Write approximately 200 words.

- an extreme weather event
- the visit of an important person
- a sporting event or festival
- a special music event or festival

5 Exchange accounts with your partner. Use these questions to check your accounts.

- Is the sequence of events clear?
- Are the facts presented objectively?
- Are arguments supported by clear evidence?
- Have the correct time phrases been used?

my life ▶ AN IMPORTANT PAST EVENT ▶ A CASE OF FRAUD ▶ HISTORICAL IRONY ▶ CONFIRMATION AND CLARIFICATION
▶ DESCRIBING A PAST EVENT

9f Collecting the past

A print of China's first emperor, Qin Shi Huan

Before you watch

1 Look at the photo and answer the questions.

1. What do you think this object is and why is it important?
2. What kind of objects do you like to look at in museums? Are they from your own country or from other countries?
3. Do you or your parents own any historical or old objects? What are they?

2 Key vocabulary

a Read the sentences. The words in bold are used in the video. Guess the meaning of the words.

1. I bought these chairs at an **auction.** The starting price was $20 and I got them for $25.
2. There was a table for sale with the chairs, which I wanted too, but someone **bid** $120 and I didn't want to pay more than $100.
3. They ruled Egypt for six generations, but their **dynasty** ended when the last king died childless.
4. It is an ancient book with some beautiful illustrations and **calligraphy**.
5. The Greek government would like the statues in the British museum to be **repatriated**.

b Match the words in bold in Exercise 2a with these definitions.

a. a line of kings/queens or rulers from the same family
b. sent back to their original country
c. offered to pay a certain amount for something
d. decorative handwriting
e. a sale where people compete against each other to buy things

While you watch

3 ▶ 9.1 Watch the video. Who is collecting objects like the one in the photo and why?

4 ▶ 9.1 Watch the first part of the video (0.00 to 1.06) again. Choose the correct options to complete the table.

1	Period of objects in exhibition: *Qing dynasty / Ming dynasty*
2	Owner of objects: *Chinese state / private collector*
3	Where items were bought: *foreign auctions / foreign antique shops*
4	Location of exhibition: *a train station / a shopping mall*
5	Value of collection: *US$ 25 million / US$ 100 million*

5 ▶ 9.1 Watch the second part of the video (1.07 to the end) again. Answer the questions.

1. Who is competing for these objects?
2. What is happening to the price of this kind of item?
3. Where has the world seen this phenomenon happen?
4. What kind of items were bought as the phenomenon evolved?
5. What are the two reasons people buy?

6 Complete the summary about Chinese collectors. Use one word in each space.

There is an increasing number of private Chinese collectors who would like to [1] _____ objects that have ended up overseas. So they buy up pieces at [2] _____ all over the world and bring them back to China. Often it is one Chinese wealthy person [3] _____ against another to buy the piece and so prices have risen considerably. But dealers say there is also a market for more [4] _____ pieces which people buy either as an [5] _____ or to help preserve their country's [6] _____ .

After you watch

7 Vocabulary in context

a ▶ 9.2 Watch the clips from the video. Choose the correct meaning of the words and phrases.

b Complete these sentences in your own words. Then compare your sentences with a partner.

1. The price of … has soared in the last few years.
2. … is one of a new breed of …
3. … smashed the record for …

8 Work in pairs. Watch the video again with the sound turned off and try to supply the narration, taking turns to speak.

9 Work in groups. Think of three important objects in your country (monuments, works of art, artefacts in a museum, etc.) that best reflect your country's heritage. Describe them to your group and explain why they are significant.

---

embroidered (adj) /ɪmˈbrɔɪdəd/ decorated with patterns or images sewn onto it
finery (n) /ˈfaɪnəri/ expensive and beautiful objects
scroll (n) /skrəʊl/ a roll of paper with writing on it

UNIT 9 REVIEW AND MEMORY BOOSTER

Grammar

1 Read the article about a historical discovery. Then choose the correct options to complete the article.

2 Read the article again. Answer the questions.

1 Why did historians think children in the Middle Ages had no childhood?
2 What new evidence did the archaeologists find and how did they find it?

Historians used to think that children in the Middle Ages didn't have much of a childhood, ¹ *compared / comparing* to children today. ² *As well as / What's more*, some historians even claimed that parents 700 years ago did not form any emotional attachment to their children. ³ *Referring / Having referred* to the adult-like representation of children in paintings of the time, they said that children were treated like little adults ⁴ *and / being* sent out to work at a young age. They also assumed that ⁵ *since / because of* life expectancy was much shorter, this was a logical thing for parents to do.
⁶ *However, / Even though* a recent archaeological dig on the banks of the River Thames in London has uncovered new evidence, ⁷ *painting / having painted* a different picture of childhood in the Middle Ages. ⁸ *Using / Having used* metal detectors, the archaeologists found various miniature objects like chairs and guns and ⁹ *put / after having put* them all together, came to the conclusion that they must be children's toys. ¹⁰ *Assuming / Assumed* that they are right, we can conclude, ¹¹ *although / in spite of* earlier historians' claims, that children in this period had time for playing ¹² *in addition / as well as* working.

3 >> MB Work in pairs. Find linking words or phrases in the article that do the following:

1 contrast an idea
2 add a point
3 state a reason
4 show a sequence of events

What grammatical form follows each linking word or phrase?

I CAN	
use linking words to connect ideas	
use participles in subordinate clauses	

Vocabulary

4 Complete the conversation. Use verbs to describe the criminal justice process.

A: Did you hear that Stefania ¹ _____ the local newspaper to court last week?
B: No. What crime had they ² _____ ?
A: She ³ _____ them of using one of her photos without permission.
B: And what happened? Were they ⁴ _____ guilty?
A: Yes, they were ordered to pay compensation, but they've ⁵ _____ against the ruling.

5 Put these verbs into five groups according to the preposition that usually follows them. What is the preposition in each group?

accuse	adjust	aim	approve	belong
believe	benefit	participate	reflect	relate
rely	specialize	suffer		

6 >> MB Write sentences that are true for you or your family/friends using the verb + preposition combinations in Exercise 5.

I CAN	
talk about crime and court proceedings	
use the correct preposition after certain verbs	

Real life

7 Complete the comments for checking, confirming or clarifying information. Use one word in each space.

1 If I understand _____ , you're saying there's no difference between …
2 Perhaps I'm _____ something, but aren't the police supposed to … ?
3 Am I right _____ thinking that your country is … ?
4 Let me get this _____ . The last time you ate …
5 What do you mean _____ 'a substantial amount of …'?
6 Would you mind just going _____ what you said about … again?

8 >> MB Work in pairs. Complete the endings of the sentences in Exercise 7 with ideas of your own. Then use them to have short conversations. Use these responses to help you.

What I'm saying is …   The point is that …
What I meant (by that) was …
In other words, …   That's to say …

I CAN	
ask for confirmation and clarification	

Unit 10 Social living

People celebrating the annual Mexican festival, Cinco de Mayo, Denver, USA

FEATURES

118 A co-operative society
How ant society works

120 The power of play
Why playing is important

122 Living free?
The Hadza people of Tanzania

126 Initiation with ants
A video about an unusual initiation ceremony in Brazil

1 Work in pairs. Look at the photo and caption. What festivals or public holidays in your country celebrate particular groups or communities? What form do the celebrations take? Discuss.

2 ▶ 72 Listen to an extract from a radio programme talking about ethnic communities. Answer the questions.
   1 Which cities are mentioned and what large ethnic populations do they have?
   2 What do the communities have in common, apart from the one in London?
   3 What values define Alejandra's ethnic community?

3 ▶ 72 Listen to the radio programme again. Which adjectives are used with these words to talk about communities?

   groups   migrants   immigrant community   family   values
   community   gatherings   heritage

4 Look at the questions and discuss with your partner.
   1 Is there a strong sense of community where you live? What kind of social gatherings take place, e.g. street parties, meals with friends, dances?
   2 Do you think it's confusing to have two cultures like Alejandra, or is it a positive thing? Why?

my life ▶ BEING A GOOD MEMBER OF SOCIETY ▶ SOCIAL GAMES ▶ FEELING FREE ▶ MAKING CONVERSATION ▶ A DISCURSIVE ESSAY

reading ant society • grammar adverbs and adverbial phrases • vocabulary and speaking being a good member of society

10a A co-operative society

Reading

1 Look at the picture and humorous quotes from the animated film *Antz*. Discuss the questions.

  1 What do the quotes tell you about ants?
  2 What else do you know about ants (diet, habitat, predators, etc.)?

" When you're the middle child in a family of five million, you don't get any attention. "

" I wasn't cut out to be a worker. My whole life, I've never been able to lift more than ten times my body weight. "

2 Read the article. Which adjectives best describe ants and ant society? Why?

| co-operative | creative | cruel | efficient |

3 Answer these questions. Then read the article again and check your answers.

  1 What environment do ants *not* like to live in?
  2 Why have ants done so well?
  3 Within each ant colony, what are the most common jobs?
  4 What two examples does the writer give of ants sending 'messages'?
  5 How do ants defeat larger animals in a fight?
  6 What is the writer implying about people in line 40–41?

4 What other animals do you know that live in groups or 'societies'? How do they help each other?

A CO-OPERATIVE SOCIETY

▶ 73

Ants number approximately ten thousand trillion worldwide. Each individual ant weighs almost nothing, but together they weigh about the same as all of mankind. They are also ubiquitous, thriving everywhere except on icy mountain peaks and around the Poles. No one knows precisely how many species there are, but it is estimated to be over 20,000. For an animal of its size, ants have been incredibly successful and this success is largely due to the fact that, socially, they are such sophisticated creatures.

In colonies that vary in size from a few hundred to tens of millions, each ant plays a clearly defined role: there is a queen or queens whose job it is to reproduce, and some fertile males who die shortly after mating with the queen. The rest are sterile females who make up the main population of workers (nest builders and food gatherers) and soldiers, all beavering away in an organized manner.

How they achieve this level of organization is even more amazing. Where we use sound and sight to communicate, ants depend primarily on pheromones, chemical signals emitted by individuals and picked up by the group. Each species produces just ten to twenty such signals. For example, a foraging ant leaves a pheromone trail that leads others straight to where the food is. When an individual ant comes under attack or is dying, it sends out an alarm pheromone to alert the colony, which then mobilizes fast as a defence unit.

In fact, in the art of war, ants are probably unrivalled. They are completely fearless and will take on bigger predators readily, attacking in large groups and overwhelming their target. They are so committed to the common good of the colony that workers regularly sacrifice their own lives to help defeat the enemy.

Behaving in this unselfish and community-minded way, these little creatures have flourished on Earth for more than 140 million years. And because they think as one, they have a collective intelligence greater than the sum of its individual parts. Unfortunately, this is not something you can always say of people.

beaver away (v) /ˈbiːvə(r) əˈweɪ/ to work hard and busily at something
colony (n) /ˈkɒləni/ a group of ants that nest together
forage (v) /ˈfɒrɪdʒ/ search for food
sterile (adj) /ˈsteraɪl/ not capable of reproducing
ubiquitous (adj) /juːˈbɪkwɪtəs/ found everywhere

118

Grammar adverbs and adverbial phrases

> **▶ ADVERBS and ADVERBIAL PHRASES**
>
> 1 No one is **entirely** sure how many species there are.
> 2 Workers **regularly** sacrifice their own lives to help defeat the enemy.
> 3 They will take on bigger predators **readily**.
> 4 Ants have been **incredibly** successful.
> 5 **Socially,** they are such sophisticated creatures.
> 6 In the art of war, ants are **probably** unrivalled.
> 7 **Unfortunately,** this is not something you can always say of people.
> 8 The colony then mobilizes **fast**. manner
> 9 … all beavering away **in an organized manner**.
>
> For further information and practice, see page 174.

5 Look at the sentences in the grammar box. Answer the questions.

1 Which adverbs qualify: a) verbs or verb phrases; b) adjectives; or c) the whole sentence?
2 What type is each adverb or adverbial phrase: manner, probability, degree, frequency, viewpoint or comment?
3 Which other position in the phrase or sentence could each adverb have without changing the meaning? If none, say 'none'.
4 What is unusual about the words *fast* and *organized* in sentences 8 and 9?

6 Find at least four more adverbs in the article on page 118. Discuss their type, form and position.

7 Transform these adjectives into adverbs or adverbial phrases. Then complete the sentences.

| colourful | general | lively | slow | straight |
| technical | | | | |

1 I'll repeat the instructions _____ so that there's no confusion.
2 She tells stories _____ and the children love it.
3 _____, it's not illegal to fly a drone in the park.
4 Let me get _____ to the point.
5 I don't _____ post messages on social media.
6 The room was large and _____ painted.

8 Transform the adjectives in brackets into adverbs or adverbial phrases. Then put them in the correct place in these sentences.

1 Ants have a developed social system. (high)
2 An ant can lift objects as much as twenty times its own body weight. (easy)
3 A worker ant doesn't live – on average fifty days. (long)
4 Many brown ants don't work at all, with 72 per cent being inactive half the time. (hard)
5 Different species of ant vary. (physical / enormous)
6 Ants do not act towards each other. (necessary / friendly)
7 Some species of ants attack other ant colonies. (surprising / aggressive)

9 Write three sentences about your own social group (e.g. friends or family). Use these adverbs/adverbial phrases (or your own choice) in each sentence.

fast	financially	generally	healthily	highly
in a relaxed way		incredibly	interestingly	
late	socially			

Vocabulary being a good member of society

10 Choose the correct option to complete the collocations. Then think of an action as an example of each collocation.

1 *act / play* **a part** in society
   Using local shops and facilities, chatting to local people.
2 *do / make* **your bit** for the community
3 *bring / lend* **a helping hand** to your neighbours
4 *keep / take* **responsibility** for your environment
5 *take / show* **concern** for others who are less fortunate
6 *give / have* **a say** in decisions that affect you

Speaking my life

11 Work in pairs. Look at the statements from an international citizenship survey. Add two more statements of your own using adverbs. Then rank them in order of importance.

> **To play a full part in society, a good citizen:**
>
> 1 should always vote in elections.
> 2 should obey laws and regulations unquestioningly.
> 3 should be actively involved in clubs and community organizations.
> 4 should spend some of their free time helping people who are financially or physically less well-off.
> 5 should take responsibility for keeping their local environment clean and safe.
> 6 …
> 7 …

listening the importance of play • vocabulary having fun • grammar negative adverbials and inversion
pronunciation sentence stress • speaking social games

10b The power of play

Listening

1 Work in pairs. Match the games in list A with the categories in list B. Then think of other examples for each category. Discuss which games are:
a) the most social   b) the most international
c) the most enjoyable   d) ones you play yourself

A	B
1 Minecraft	a outdoor games
2 sudoku	b board games
3 basketball	c team sports
4 frisbee	d party games
5 chess	e puzzles
6 charades	f computer/video games

2 Look at the photo and in sixty seconds, list as many benefits of this kind of play as you can. Then compare your list with another pair.

3 ▶ 74 Listen to a podcast about the importance of play. Note down the four main benefits that the speaker mentions.

4 ▶ 74 Try to complete these expressions that the speaker uses in the podcast. Then listen again and check.

1 Play seems more like a _luxury_ **to indulge in** when we have spare time.
2 Play increases our ability to solve problems and to **think outside the** _box_.
3 Laughter improves blood circulation and increases the body's _resistance_ **to disease**.
4 With play, there's just a shared feeling of enjoyment and of **letting** _go_.
5 Play has the power to **break down** _barriers_ between people.

6 A lot of the time, **our minds** _wander_ and we find ourselves thinking about things in the past.
7 But when we're engaged in play, … **we** _lose_ **ourselves** in the present.
8 Play doesn't have to be a specific activity; it's also **a** _state_ **of mind**.

Vocabulary having fun

5 Complete the expressions with these prepositions. Discuss what you think each expression means.

| about | against | of | on | on | out of |

1 Try to **see the funny side** _of_ it. At least you didn't lose any money.
2 I love watching TV quizzes and seeing contestants **pit their wits** _against_ each other.
3 They **played a joke** _on_ him by swapping his jacket with Gino's which was identical but two sizes smaller.
4 Don't tell me the answer. It **takes the fun** _out of_ doing the crossword.
5 Shop owners love **making a play** _on_ **words**. My local bike shop is called 'Cycloanalysts'.
6 I had a great evening with Eman. We **had** such **a laugh** _about_ the old days.

6 Work in pairs. Describe a time when someone:

• played a joke on you
• didn't see the funny side of something
• made a funny play on words

120

Grammar negative adverbials and inversion

▶ **NEGATIVE ADVERBIALS and INVERSION**

seldom, rarely, hardly ever
1 In fact, we **seldom** think of play as something necessary.
barely, scarcely, hardly
2 In many ways, it **scarcely** matters what kind of play it is.
3 In casual play, there's **hardly** any formality.
Inverted negative adverbials*
4 **No sooner** have we started to relax **than** our minds **also** begin to think differently.
5 **Not only** does it relieve tension, studies have **also** shown that laughter improves blood circulation.
Other inverted negative adverbials include:
Barely/Scarcely/Hardly … when/before;
Under no circumstances …; In no way …;
Only when / Only if / Only by …; Never …; Little …

* We use inversion in slightly more formal speech or writing.

For further information and practice, see page 174.

7 Look at the grammar box. Answer the questions.
1 What is the position of the adverbs in sentences 1–3?
2 How would you express the same idea in sentences 2 and 3 using *almost* instead of the adverbs in bold?
3 What do you notice about the word order in sentences 4 and 5?
4 How would you write sentences 4 and 5 without inversion (use *as soon as* and *not only*)?
5 What effect does inverting the word order like this have on each sentence?

8 Pronunciation sentence stress

a ▶ 75 Listen to the sentences in the grammar box. Which of the words in bold are stressed?

b ▶ 76 Work in pairs. Underline the words you expect to be stressed in these sentences. Then listen and check.
1 In no way was I surprised.
2 But I hardly know her!
3 We rarely see each other now.
4 Not only is it cheap, it's also delicious.

9 Rewrite the sentences using the negative adverbials in brackets. When the adverbial is at the beginning of the sentence, you will need to use inversion.
1 As soon as we had set out on our walk, it started to rain. (No sooner)
2 Sorry, I haven't really had a minute to think about it. (barely)
3 It is only possible to access the bank's website by using a special card reader. (Only by using)
4 You mustn't mention this to her under any circumstances. (Under no circumstances)
5 We hardly ever went out in the evenings, because it was so expensive. (Only very rarely)
6 He doesn't only look like George Clooney; he sounds like him too. (Not only)
7 We don't really go out dancing at all anymore. (hardly ever)
8 You couldn't find such a spectacular view anywhere else in America. (Nowhere else in America)

10 Complete the text about being playful as an adult using these words. Then compare your answers with a partner.

do	hardly	never	not	only	seldom
should	when	will	you		

Children are naturally playful. They
¹ _seldom_ worry about the reactions of others. Only ² _____ we reach adulthood
³ _____ we become self-conscious about what others think and stop playing so much. Sadly, some adults ⁴ _____ play any games at all. But it's ⁵ _____ too late to develop your playful side. Begin by setting aside time to play. Then think of something that you'd like to do. On no account ⁶ _____ you feel under pressure – just pick a game you used to play as a child. And then just enjoy it. ⁷ _____ by letting go ⁸ _____ you experience the benefits of play. If you keep doing this, ⁹ _____ only will
¹⁰ _____ enjoy it, you will find the more you play, the more you will laugh.

Speaking — my life

11 Work in groups of eight and play this game. Follow the steps below. Discuss if you think this game is a good 'social' game.
1 One person makes up a sentence, ideally an unusual one, using an adverbial from the grammar box.
2 They whisper the sentence to the person next to them only *once*. That person whispers the sentence they think they heard to the next person and so on until it reaches the last person.
3 The last person then says aloud the sentence they think they heard. Has the original sentence changed in any way?

12 Your group is going to present a good or bad game. Follow these steps.
1 Make a list of games you've played that are good (or bad!) for social relationships (e.g. Monopoly, Twister).
2 Describe and explain any game your partners do not know.
3 List the benefits (or shortcomings) of each game.
4 Present the most (or least) social game to the rest of the class.

Unit 10 Social living

my life ▶ BEING A GOOD MEMBER OF SOCIETY ▶ SOCIAL GAMES ▶ FEELING FREE ▶ MAKING CONVERSATION
▶ A DISCURSIVE ESSAY

reading the Hadza of Tanzania • critical thinking reading between the lines • word focus *free* • speaking feeling free

10c Living free?

Reading

1 What is meant by the term *hunter-gatherer*? How is a hunter-gather's life different from a farmer's?

2 Work in pairs. Look at the map. In what kind of places do hunter-gatherers still live today?

3 Read the article and say which statement best summarizes what the author thinks about the Hadza way of life.

   a It's a good life but not practical for us nowadays.
   b It's a way of life that guarantees both health and harmony in society.
   c It's a sustainable way of life that we ought to imitate.

4 Read the article again quickly. Find out which of these things the Hadza have, and which things they do not have. Then compare answers with your partner.

   • working animals
   • enemies
   • sufficient food
   • basic tools
   • a lot of free time
   • a government
   • their own strict routines
   • a difficult environment

5 Work in pairs. Explain what these phrases from the article mean.

   1 Agriculture's rise, however, **came at a price** (para 2)
   2 social divisions between **haves and have nots** (para 2)
   3 they have scarcely **left a footprint** on the land (para 3)
   4 the Hadza are such **gentle stewards** of the land (para 5)
   5 what was once their **exclusive** territory (para 5)
   6 Their entire life is one **insanely committed** camping trip. (para 6)

Critical thinking reading between the lines

6 Sometimes in articles, an author's views are not explicitly stated and have to be inferred. Underline the sentences in the article that help you to infer the answers to these questions.

   1 Does the author admire the Hadza and their way of life?
   2 Does the author have particular views about what should happen to the land the Hadza live on?

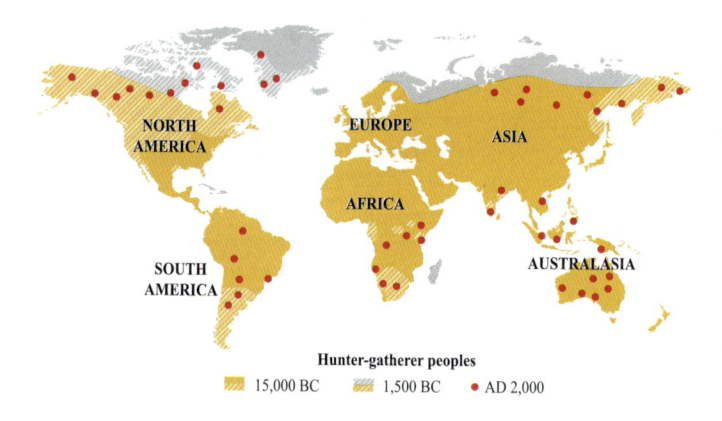

Hunter-gatherer peoples
15,000 BC   1,500 BC   • AD 2,000

7 Work in groups. Compare your answers from Exercise 6, referring to the parts of the article that support your view. Did you agree or not?

Word focus *free*

8 Look at this quote from the article. What does it tell you about the Hadza?

*There are many things to envy about the Hadza – principally, what **free spirits** they appear to be.*

9 Work in pairs. Look at these other expressions using *free* and discuss what each one means.

   1 **Feel free** to make yourself a cup of coffee.
   2 Did you really think he wouldn't want to be paid for his help? **There's no such thing as a free lunch**, you know.
   3 It was supposed to be a civilized debate but the chair lost control and it became **a free-for-all**.
   4 They were very particular about the text, but they gave us a **free hand** with the design.
   5 Although there was a lot of evidence to suggest he was guilty, he **got off scot-free**.

10 Choose two of the following and talk about them from your own experience.

   • a discussion that became a free-for-all
   • a time you were given a free hand in a task
   • a time you got off scot-free
   • someone who is a free spirit

Speaking my life

11 Work in pairs. Discuss the questions.

   1 What aspects of the Hadza lifestyle appeal to you? Which don't appeal?
   2 In which area(s) of your life do you feel 'free'? In which area(s) would you like to have more freedom?

122

Unit 10 **Social living**

▶ 77

Living free?

The Hadza hunter-gatherers of Tanzania live a life that has not changed much in 10,000 years. They have no crops, no livestock, no permanent shelters. In spite of long exposure to nearby communities who farm both crops and animals, the Hadza have maintained a nomadic, foraging lifestyle.

The spread of agriculture is linked to the growth of population. First villages formed, then cities, then nations. In a relatively brief period, the hunter-gatherer lifestyle disappeared in all but a few places. Agriculture's rise, however, came at a price: social divisions between haves and have nots, the spread of disease, famines and even war. Professor Jared Diamond of UCLA has called the adoption of agriculture 'the worst mistake in human history' – a mistake, he says, from which we have never recovered. Looking at people like the Hadza, you can see why he came to this conclusion. They do not engage in warfare. They are too few and too spread out to be threatened by infectious disease. And they have no history of famine because their diet is more varied and adaptable than that of most of the world's citizens.

The Hadza also have hardly any possessions. The things they own – a cooking pot, a water container, an axe – can be wrapped in a blanket and carried over a shoulder. They enjoy an extraordinary amount of leisure time, because their 'work' – gathering food – takes only four to six hours a day. Hadza women gather berries and baobab fruit and dig for tubers. Men collect honey and hunt. They will eat almost anything they can kill, from small birds to zebras. What is more, in the thousands of years they have followed this lifestyle, they have scarcely left a footprint on the land.

There are no official leaders in Hadza society. No Hadza adult has authority over any other and none accumulates personal wealth. Nor are there social obligations – no birthdays, no public holidays, no anniversaries. People sleep when they want, generally staying up late at night and dozing opportunistically during the heat of the day.

doze (v) /dəʊz/ to sleep lightly
intolerable (adj) /ɪnˈtɒlərəb(ə)l/ unbearable, can't be endured
tuber (n) /ˈtjuːbə(r)/ an edible part of the stem of a plant (like a potato)

The chief reason the Hadza have been able to maintain this lifestyle is that their homeland is not an inviting place. The soil is poor, fresh water is scarce and the bugs can be intolerable. For tens of thousands of years, it seems no one else wanted to live here. Recently, however, the pressure of a rising population has brought a flood of people into Hadza lands. The fact that the Hadza are such gentle stewards of the land has, in a way, hurt them, as the region is generally viewed by outsiders as an unused place badly in need of development. Up to now, the Hadza, who are by nature peaceful, have simply moved on rather than fight for the land. But now there is nowhere else to go and they are being forced to share what was once their exclusive territory.

There are many things to envy about the Hadza – principally, what free spirits they appear to be. Free from schedules, jobs, bosses, bills, traffic, taxes, laws, social duties and money. Free to grab food and run shirtless through the bush. But who of us could live like them? Their entire life is one insanely committed camping trip. It's incredibly risky. Medical help is far away. One bad fall from a tree, one bite from a snake, and you're dead. Women give birth in the bush and nearly half of all children do not make it to the age of fifteen. They have to cope with extreme heat and swarming tsetse flies. The fact is that it's too late for us to go back to a Hadza lifestyle. Of greater concern is that soon it may be impossible for them to remain in it.

my life ▶ BEING A GOOD MEMBER OF SOCIETY ▶ SOCIAL GAMES ▶ FEELING FREE ▶ MAKING CONVERSATION
▶ A DISCURSIVE ESSAY

123

10d Showing interest

Real life making conversation

1 Work in pairs. Discuss which of the following points are characteristic of a good listener.

　a　trying to predict what you will hear
　b　waiting before giving your view
　c　asking questions / check understanding
　d　relating what you hear to your experience
　e　maintaining eye contact
　f　showing appreciation
　g　keeping the conversation moving

2 Are you a good listener? Which of the points in Exercise 1 are you good or bad at doing?

3 ▶78 You are going to hear two conversations between university students. Listen and answer the questions for each conversation.

　1　What does each female speaker want?
　2　How does her friend respond to this?

4 Speaking skill showing interest

▶78 Work in pairs. Look at the expressions for showing interest. Which phrases did the speakers use to show interest and respond to each of these statements and questions? Then listen again and check your answers.

　1　Fancy a game of tennis this afternoon?
　2　Why? What are you doing?
　3　I need to get an essay in …
　4　I'm really enjoying it, actually.
　5　Great party, last night.
　6　That's not your job, is it?
　7　You couldn't lend me a hand with it later, could you?
　8　I've got to wait in this afternoon …
　9　I'm always missing things in lectures.
　10　I'll send you the link.

▶ SHOWING INTEREST

Showing interest

I got a 'B' for my essay.	→ Really?
I'm going to Spain next month.	→ Are you?
I've got to go to London tomorrow.	→ Have you? Why's that?
Lovely concert.	→ Yes, it was, wasn't it?
The weather doesn't look great.	→ No, it doesn't, does it?
He's quit his job.	→ He hasn't, has he?
I'll give you a call some time.	→ Yes, please do. / Yes, do please.

Responding naturally

Do you fancy a drink?	→ I'd love to, but …
I can't make this evening.	→ Oh, that's a shame.
What are you doing here?	→ Working.
Are you going to the conference?	→ I expect/hope/think/suppose so. / I'm afraid so.
Will the shop still be open?	→ I don't think so. / I'm afraid not. / I doubt it.
I've got a cold coming.	→ Me too.
I can't wait for the holidays.	→ Me neither.

---

5 Pronunciation intonation and elision

a ▶79 Listen to the intonation in the first six short responses in the box. Does it rise or fall? Which pattern shows interest (I), which surprise (S) and which agreement (A)?

b Work in pairs. Practise saying the responses in the same way.

c ▶80 Listen to how these phrases are pronounced. Notice which sounds are elided. Then practise saying them with your partner.

　1　I'm afraid not.
　2　I suppose so.
　3　I expect so.
　4　I hope so.
　5　I doubt it.
　6　I'd love to.

6 Work in pairs. Have similar conversations to show interest and respond. Follow this structure:

Student A: Suggest doing something with Student B.

Student B: Explain that you have another commitment.

Student A: Show interest and get more information about this.

---

my life ▶ BEING A GOOD MEMBER OF SOCIETY ▶ SOCIAL GAMES ▶ FEELING FREE ▶ **MAKING CONVERSATION**
▶ A DISCURSIVE ESSAY

writing a discursive essay • writing skill referring to evidence   Unit 10 Social living

10e A good start in life

Writing a discursive essay

1 Look at the items (a–h). Choose the four items that you think most help people to achieve professional success in life.

   a wealthy parents
   b a strong work ethic
   c good social connections
   d supportive friends or community
   e ambitious parents
   f good education
   g high social status
   h something else?

2 Work in groups. Discuss your answers from Exercise 1. Does social background (e.g. upbringing, education, parents' jobs) play a big part in determining a child's prospects in life?

3 Read the essay and answer the questions.

   1 What is the main argument?
   2 What evidence is it based on?
   3 Are you convinced by the argument? Why? / Why not?

4 Writing skill referring to evidence

a Work in pairs. Look at this sentence from the essay and discuss how the meaning would be affected if you replaced the phrase in bold with each of the phrases below.

This suggests that children's prospects are connected to their expectations.

   1 This demonstrates that
   2 This illustrates the fact that
   3 From this we can infer that
   4 This implies that
   5 This indicates that
   6 This points to (+ -ing)
   7 This proves that
   8 This shows that

b Complete these sentences in your own words.

   1 Their excellent exam results prove that …
   2 The fact that no one passed the exam points to the exam …
   3 From the age of the paper we can infer that the documents …
   4 His popularity with the students illustrates the fact that …
   5 The high quality of her writing indicates that she …

Is social background an important factor in success in life?

It is generally thought that to have a good chance of succeeding in life, you need certain social advantages: wealthy parents, a high social status and a good-quality education. There is truth in this, but it is not the whole story. I would argue that provided a child has the basic necessities of life – food, clothes, a warm bed, parental love and care – then their prospects are determined only by their own opinion of what is possible. And that opinion can be changed. A recent study in Baltimore, USA, where children were interviewed about their prospects, supports this view. Their ambitions reflected their own experience. Those from high-income families wanted to be lawyers or doctors, the typical professions of their parents' friends. Those from poorer backgrounds hoped to be professional sports people or music artists, because those were the people who had succeeded in their communities. However, they expected to become electricians or hairdressers. The children from higher-income families performed well at school, because they could see the connection between good grades and realizing their professional ambitions, while the children from poorer backgrounds performed much worse.
This suggests that children's prospects are connected to their expectations. As long as children have only modest ambitions, they will see no benefit in working hard at school and, as a result, will not succeed. In summary, we can say that some people always start life worse off than others, but where they end up is a question of what they believe is possible.

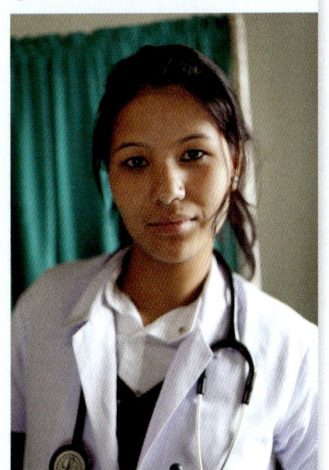

5 Work in pairs and discuss what you think is the answer to this question: *Does it help students if parents pay for their university education?* Then write an essay of 200–250 words on the topic. Use the evidence on page 190, if necessary.

6 Exchange essays with your partner. Use these questions to check each other's essays.

   • Is the main argument clear?
   • Is the essay well structured?
   • What conclusions does the essay draw from the evidence?
   • Is the main argument outlined at the beginning and end of the essay?

10f Initiation with ants

Sateré-Mawé boy during the Festival of Parintins, Tupinambarana Island, Brazil

Unit 10 Social living

Before you watch

1 Work in pairs. Look at the definition of *initiation*. Then think of an example of a ceremony for these occasions (a–f).

initiation (n) /ɪˌnɪʃiˈeɪʃ(ə)n/ a ceremony or task that gives a person formal admission or acceptance into a club, organization, community or family

a being born
b passing from childhood into adulthood
c marriage
d entering a college or school
e joining a gang
f joining a professional group or club

2 Look at the photo. What part do you think ants play in this initiation ceremony, where boys pass from childhood to adulthood?

3 Key vocabulary

a Read the sentences. The words in bold are used in the video. Guess the meaning of the words.

1 Bee keepers wear special suits to protect themselves from being **stung**.
2 The black mamba snake has a deadly **venom** in its bite.
3 Lions are **carnivores**. They don't eat plants or vegetables at all.
4 He booked an emergency appointment at the dentist because he was in **agony**.
5 It's a **gruelling** journey by road – at least seven hours over rough tracks.
6 I was really fascinated by the Japanese **ritual** of tea-making.

b Match the words in bold in Exercise 3a with these definitions.

a poison
b very difficult and tiring
c pricked or wounded by a poisonous plant or animal
d great pain or suffering
e actions (often religious) done in a specific order
f meat-eaters

While you watch

4 ▶ 10.1 Watch the video and check your answers from Exercise 2.

5 ▶ 10.1 Watch the first part of the video (0.00 to 0.51) again. Complete the table about the initiation ritual.

1	The signal for the start of the initiation:
2	Length of ritual:
3	Age of participants:
4	Animal used in ritual:
5	Purpose of ritual:
6	Number of times participant must perform ritual:

6 ▶ 10.1 Watch the second part of the video (0.52 to the end) again. Answer the questions.

1 How powerful is the sting of these ants?
2 How is it possible to place the ants in the gloves without being stung?
3 Why don't the ants escape from the gloves?
4 What is the purpose of the dance?
5 What happens after the gloves are removed?
6 How does the new initiate, Ted, react to his ordeal?

7 What does the chief say about the wider purpose of this ritual? Do you agree with him? Why? / Why not?

After you watch

8 Vocabulary in context

a ▶ 10.2 Watch the clips from the video. Choose the correct meaning of the words and phrases.

b Complete the sentences in your own words. Then work in pairs and compare your sentences.

1 I think my prospects of getting a job in …
2 My … was completely unfazed by …
3 I didn't enjoy … because I had to endure …

9 Choose one of the initiation ceremonies from Exercise 1 and think about how you would describe one or more of the rituals that take place during this ceremony. Make notes if you need to.

10 Work in groups. Take turns to describe your ceremonies. What do the rituals symbolize? What are the most difficult things to do in front of peers?

UNIT 10 REVIEW AND MEMORY BOOSTER

Grammar

1 Read the interview about a National Marine Park in Mexico. What was the key to saving the coral reef?

I = Interviewer, E = Environmentalist

I: Cabo Pulmo National Marine Park is a great example of citizens acting to effect change (¹ concerted). Was the main purpose of this project to protect the coral reef?
E: Absolutely. The reef was deteriorating (² fast). We needed to save it.
I: And did you get the help of the government?
E: Yes. It was they who set up the conservation area. Basically, by campaigning, we managed to get fishing banned (³ hard). After all the intensive fishing of the last 25 years, any fish were left (⁴ hard). And they're an important part of the fragile ecosystem that supports the coral.
I: And has that changed?
E: Yes. The project has been successful (⁵ incredible). Stocks of fish have risen by 450 per cent. It's a real victory for the environment and the community.
I: So can you relax now that you've won the battle?
E: No, we can't relax! There's a new proposal to build an enormous tourist complex with hotels and shops right next to the marine park (⁶ sadly). So we finished one campaign and we had to begin another. We're negotiating with the developers to reach a solution (⁷ currently). The negotiations are being conducted (⁸ friendly), but if they fail, we're very worried about the negative impact on the marine park.

2 Transform the adjectives (1–8) in the interview into adverbs or adverbial phrases. Then put them in the correct place in each sentence.

3 >> **MB** Rewrite these sentences using the words given. Then discuss how the new sentences differ in meaning.

1 No, we can't relax!
   In no way _____!
2 We finished one campaign and we had to begin another.
   No sooner _____.

I CAN	
use adverbs and adverbial forms correctly	☐
use inversion with negative adverbials for emphasis	☐

Vocabulary

4 Complete the descriptions. You have been given the first letter.

1 We're lucky. Our community has a r_____ cultural heritage. There are quite a few different e_____ groups; most are second or third g_____ migrants who all play their p_____ in society. People s_____ concern for one another and are always ready to l_____ a helping hand.
2 I don't have a big e_____ family, so we don't have big family g_____. But we are a close-k_____ family and we always have a good l_____ when we get together.

5 >> **MB** Give a similar description of your own community and family.

6 >> **MB** Look at the idioms in bold. Which idioms express positive ideas? Which negative? And which could be either? Give reasons.

1 The discussion became **a free-for-all**.
2 Knowing the answers **takes the fun out of** it.
3 My parents **gave me a** completely **free hand** in choice of school.
4 He's always **playing jokes on** people.
5 She **saw the funny side of** it.
6 He **got off scot-free**.

I CAN	
talk about family and community life	☐
use idioms about humour and idioms with *free*	☐

Real life

7 Match these responses with the statements and questions (1–6). There are two responses for each statement or question.

> Yes, please do.   Definitely.   Working, mostly.
> Yes, it was, wasn't it?   Thanks, I'd appreciate it.
> Really?   That's a shame.   Me neither.
> Not much.   You enjoyed it, did you?   Have you?
> What about?   I hope so.

1 I'm afraid I can't make it to the party on Friday.
2 Are you going to visit Eva when you're in Perth?
3 What are you doing these days?
4 Great show.
5 I'll let you know as soon as I hear any news.
6 I've got a meeting with the mayor on Friday.

8 >> **MB** Work in pairs. Act out the conversations in Exercise 7. Add one or two more lines to continue each conversation.

I CAN	
use short responses in conversation and show interest	☐

Unit 11 Reason and emotion

Tribal boy: beauty in simplicity, India

FEATURES

130 Emotional intelligence

Training people to recognize feelings

132 Thinking fast and slow

Rational and irrational thinking

134 Who's working for who?

Artificial intelligence in the future

138 Madeline the robot tamer

A video about bringing humans and robots closer together

1 ▶ 81 Look at the photo and describe the boy's feelings. Then listen to a photographer who specializes in photographing people and compare your answer.

2 ▶ 81 Work in pairs. What does the photographer say about the following things? Then listen again and check your answers.

1 the ingredients of a good photo
2 the types of emotion that work in photos
3 photographing children

3 Look at the adjectives for describing emotions. Put two adjectives under each heading. Which word in each pair has the stronger meaning?

| astonished | content | cross | ecstatic | livid | low |
| miserable | petrified | scared | taken aback | | |

Anger   Fear   Surprise   Happiness   Sadness

4 Choose two of the adjectives from Exercise 3 and talk about the last time or a memorable time when you felt this emotion.

I was really cross when I turned up for a concert the other week and they told me it had been cancelled. They offered me a refund, but they should have contacted people beforehand!

my life ▶ MODERN LIFE ▶ MIND GAMES ▶ TECHNOLOGY AND OCCUPATIONS ▶ RECOGNIZING FEELINGS
▶ AN EMAIL MESSAGE

reading **understanding emotions** • vocabulary **feelings** • grammar **unreal past forms** • speaking **modern life**

11a Emotional intelligence

Reading

1 What do you think *emotional intelligence* means? How might it be helpful in life?

2 Read the extract from an article about emotional intelligence. Are these sentences true (T), false (F) or is the information not given in the article (NG)?

1. The author says EI training is mainly useful for people in stressful jobs.
2. EI training helps people to know which emotions they should listen to.
3. Our level of emotional intelligence is determined by our childhood experiences.
4. It is not only negative emotions that can influence key decisions.
5. We can learn to control and prevent the micro-expressions we make.
6. The writer says that EI training will enable you to read others' micro-expressions.

Vocabulary feelings

3 The expression *on edge* (line 6) was used to describe people who feel tense in the modern world. Match the expressions in bold in the sentences (1–6) with the feelings they describe.

| confused and disorganized | exhausted |
| optimistic | sad | very happy | very surprised |

1. Don't worry about Paolo. He's just **a bit down** after failing his driving test.
2. I think I sent you the wrong document. Sorry. I'm **all over the place** today.
3. They are very **upbeat** about their prospects of winning.
4. I can't come out tonight. I've been travelling all day and I'm completely **done in**.
5. I was **speechless** when she said it wouldn't work. It was *her* idea in the first place!
6. A: Did he like his present?
   B: Yes, he was **thrilled to bits** with it.

EMOTIONAL INTELLIGENCE

▶ 82

Your IQ, or intellectual intelligence, will get you through exams, into university and also help you solve all sorts of problems in your working life. But it is your emotional intelligence (EI) that will help manage the stress in those
5　situations. So, if you are someone who often feels anxious and on edge in the modern world – and a lot of people increasingly do – and wish you were more in control of things, perhaps it's time you looked into EI training.

Put simply, EI training is about learning to understand
10　your feelings and to distinguish constructive emotions from harmful ones. In this way, you get to know when to follow your head and when to follow your gut feeling. At the same time, you develop a better understanding of how others feel, which in turn helps communication and
15　relationship-building.

Our attitude to our emotions – whether we are sensitive to them, or whether we would just as soon they remained unexplored – is often formed in the early part of our lives. The first step in EI training is to make people aware of
20　what this attitude to their emotions is. Once you are more aware of your attitude, you can begin to manage your emotions better. You can control negative feelings: gloomy predictions ('I know I'm going to mess this up') and nagging regrets ('If only I had done more preparation'). You can also learn to recognize when　25 stress, anger or excitement might be influencing an important decision.

EI training will also reveal what emotions you betray to others non-verbally through what are called micro-expressions. These are unconscious facial expressions　30 that appear for only a fraction of a second and express a concealed emotion or an emotion that has been too rapidly processed. For example, if you wish someone would stop talking to you because you are bored, you might look away momentarily. Even if you did not　35 want to send this signal of boredom, the other person will almost certainly pick up on it. Understanding these micro-expressions is very useful for managing relationships. Supposing you were in a negotiation, for example, and were trying to decide whether to trust　40 the other person; an ability to read such signals could be invaluable.

4 Work in pairs. Talk about times when you last had each of the feelings in Exercise 3.

When I didn't get the job I applied for, it was obviously disappointing, but I tried to stay upbeat about it.

Grammar unreal past forms

> ▶ **UNREAL PAST FORMS**
>
> **would rather / would just as soon**
> 1 We **would just as soon** they **remained** unexplored.
>
> **I wish / if only**
> 2 You **wish** you **were** more in control of things.
> 3 **If only** I **had done** more preparation.
> 4 You **wish** someone **would stop** talking to you.
>
> **it's (high) time**
> 5 **It's time** you **looked** into EI training.
>
> **Supposing / What if**
> 6 **Supposing** you **were** in a negotiation, for example …
>
> For further information and practice, see page 176.

5 Look at the grammar box. Match each sentence with these definitions (a–f). Then say what tense or verb form is used in each sentence.

a a wish about a past situation
b a wish for someone to do or stop doing something
c a wish about a present situation
d a description of an imaginary situation
e a statement of what needs to be done now
f a preference for what someone/something should do

6 Write these sentences in full, using unreal past forms.

1 It's high time / he / sort out / his life.
2 I wish / I / not / have to / commute to work every day.
3 If only / I / listen / to his advice, none of this would have happened.
4 I'd rather / you / show / me the letter before / you / send / it.
5 Modern life is too hectic. I wish / people / just / slow down / a bit.
6 It's time we / leave. / In fact, I wish / we / leave a while ago.

7 Complete this funny story by putting the verbs in the correct form.

A sales representative, an admin assistant and a manager are walking to lunch when they find an old oil lamp. 'Supposing we ¹_____ (rub) it?' says the sales rep. 'Do you think a Genie ² _____ (come out)?' 'I'd rather you ³ _____ (do) it,' says the manager, 'I've just washed my hands.' So the sales rep rubs the lamp and a Genie comes out and says, 'Tell me what you wish.' The sales rep says, 'I wish I ⁴ _____ (lie) on a beach in the Bahamas.' Puff! And she vanishes. 'Me next!' says the admin clerk. 'I wish the love of my life ⁵ _____ (take) me off to the Far East for a wonderful adventure.' Puff! And he too disappears. 'Now it's time that you ⁶ _____ (make) your wish,' says the Genie to the manager. And the manager says, 'I want those two back in the office straight after lunch.'

8 Complete the statements from a survey on emotional intelligence using the correct form of these verbs.

be	can / show	find	not / get
not / talk	teach		

1 I'd just as soon people _____ to me openly about their feelings. I find it awkward.
2 I wish I _____ so irritated when small things go wrong.
3 I wish I _____ more enthusiasm when people tell me their good news.
4 Supposing I _____ very excited about something. I _____ it very hard to hide my feelings.
5 I often think I understand my feelings when really I don't. I wish someone _____ me how to recognize my true feelings.

9 Read the statements in Exercise 8 again. Decide if each is true, partly true or false for you. Then work in pairs and discuss your answers.

Speaking my life

10 Work in groups. Discuss the list of things that irritate people about modern life. Think of two more things each and explain why they irritate you. Agree on the two you find most irritating.

It really annoys me when people jump queues. Supposing someone did the same to them? I bet they'd be the first to complain.

1 being stuck in traffic
2 waiting for things to download on the computer
3 receiving unwanted sales and marketing calls from companies
4 people who talk loudly on their mobile phones in public places
5 people pushing in front of you in a queue (on foot or in a car)
6 parents who embarrass you by thinking they are fashionable

listening irrational thinking • wordbuilding and pronunciation heteronyms • grammar conditionals and inversion • speaking mind games

11b Thinking fast and slow

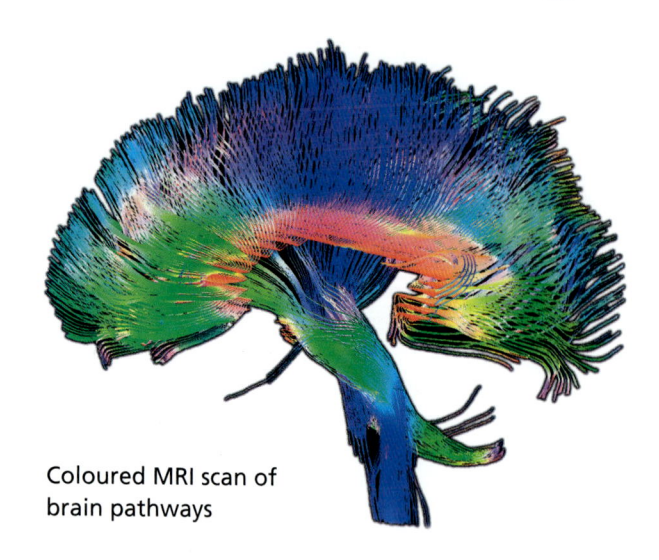

Coloured MRI scan of brain pathways

Listening

1 Work in pairs. Discuss these situations. Would you follow your first instinct? Or would you take your time before you came to a decision?

1 deciding whether to rent a nice flat you have seen (it's the first one you have looked at)
2 expressing something in English that you are not sure of
3 giving money to someone collecting for a charity in the street
4 deciding what to wear to a party
5 giving your opinion in a debate

2 ▶83 Listen to the first part of a lecture about psychologist Daniel Kahneman. Answer the questions.

1 What area has his research focused on?
2 What prize did Kahneman win in 2002?
3 What method did he use in his research?

3 Look at the three questions the lecturer puts on the screen. You have one minute to answer them. Then discuss your answers with your partner.

1 Roughly how many United Nations states are African?

2 Linda is a single 31-year-old, bright and concerned with issues of social justice. Which statement is more probable? a) Linda works in a bank, b) Linda is a feminist and works for a bank.

3a You can either have £500 for certain, or have a 50% chance of winning £1,000. Which would you choose?

3b You can either lose £500 for certain, or have a 50% chance of losing £1,000. Which would you choose?

4 ▶84 Listen to the second part of the lecture. Note the following things.

1 the answers to the questions in Exercise 3
2 what Kahneman concluded about the way our brains work

5 ▶84 Match the questions (1–3) in Exercise 3 with what it tells us about the way we think (a–c). Then listen to the second part of the lecture again and check your answers.

a that we carry a lot of preconceptions about the world with us
b that we are not logical when it comes to taking risks
c that we can be influenced in our thinking by irrelevant information

6 Have you taken any financial decisions that weren't based on a rational calculation? What were they? Did they work out for you?

Wordbuilding heteronyms

> **WORDBUILDING heteronyms**
>
> There are some words in English ending *-ate* that have the same form as an adjective and as a verb. We use pronunciation to distinguish between them.
> *deliberate*: verb /dɪˈlɪbəreɪt/; adjective /dɪˈlɪb(ə)rət/
>
> For further practice, see Workbook page 91.

7 Pronunciation heteronyms

a ▶85 Work in pairs. Look at the sentences. Which words in bold are verbs and which are adjectives? Decide where the stress falls in each word. Then listen and check.

1 a Was that a **deliberate** mistake?
  b Don't **deliberate** for too long.
2 a We need to **separate** my books from yours.
  b That's a **separate** issue.
3 a He couldn't **articulate** what he meant.
  b He's very **articulate**.
4 a I have a **duplicate** copy.
  b Let's not **duplicate** the work.
5 a That's an interesting idea. Can you **elaborate**?
  b The dress has a very **elaborate** design.

b Write two sentences using words from Exercise 7a. Then ask your partner to read them using the correct stress pattern.

Unit 11 Reason and emotion

Grammar conditionals and inversion

▶ **CONDITIONALS and INVERSION**

First conditional
1 *If you just* **look** *at the screen, you* **'ll see** *three examples.*

Second conditional
2 *If we* **were** *more aware of this influence, we* **would make** *better decisions.*

Third and mixed conditionals
3 *If someone* **had already said** *the temperature was 82°F, your answer* **would have been** *a higher number.*
4 *If you* **had read** *Kahneman's book, you* **would be** *more aware of these influences.*

Inverted conditionals
5 **Should you get*** *the answers wrong, you* **won't be** *alone.*
6 **Were** *someone* **to offer** *you the chance to win £500 for certain, you'd probably* **take it.**
7 **Were** *the same question* **to be presented** *as a logical formula, few* **would make** *this mistake.*
8 **Were it not for** *System One, we* **would make** *better decisions.*
9 **Had** *the regulators* **been** *more aware of irrational thinking, the banking crisis probably* **wouldn't have happened.**

*If you should get = if you by chance get

For further information and practice, see page 176.

8 Look at the grammar box. Answer the questions.

a Which sentences refer to i) real situations; ii) hypothetical situations?
b How has the word order been 'inverted' in the inverted conditional sentences? What word has been left out?
c What does the expression *were it not for* mean? What type of word follows it?
d Do you think inverted conditionals are more or less formal than non-inverted ones?

9 Rewrite these conditional sentences using an appropriate inverted conditional form.

1 If anyone should ask, please don't tell them it was me who told you.
2 If I had thought about it for longer, I think I would have got the answer right.
3 They wouldn't be in this situation now if they had taken my advice.
4 If you took the job, I am sure you wouldn't regret it.
5 I'd probably make fewer bad decisions if I analysed the part my emotions played.
6 I hope you will feel able to call me and ask for if you need any help.

10 Complete these texts with one word or contraction in each space. Then work in pairs. Discuss what you would do in each situation described.

A: We all like to think that we [1]_____ do the right thing if we [2]_____ faced with a moral dilemma. But no one really knows until it happens. For example, if you [3]_____ a wallet in the street, you'd [4]_____ it to the police, right? But [5]_____ you [6]_____ find a blank envelope with £150 cash in it, what then?

B: Two weeks ago I was standing in a bus queue when a cyclist lost control of his bike. If I [7]_____ not jumped out of the way, he would [8]_____ hit me. But there was also an old lady behind me who I did nothing to protect. Luckily, he missed her. [9]_____ he hit her, I hate to think what the consequences [10]_____ have [11]_____. You're probably thinking that [12]_____ such a thing to happen to you, you'd definitely not just think of yourself. But can you be sure?

11 Write about decisions you have made in your life using these sentence stems.

1 Were it not for my parents, I …
2 Had it not been so expensive, I …
3 Were I not such a … person, I think I would …
4 I would have become a … , …
5 Had I not been so young at the time, …

12 Work in pairs. Take turns to read one of your sentences from Exercise 11. Your partner should ask follow-up questions to get more information.

Speaking my life

13 Work in pairs. Look at these Kahneman puzzles, but take no more than 30 seconds to answer each one. Then check the answers on page 155. What do you think the point of each puzzle is?

1 A bat and ball cost $1.10. The bat costs one dollar more than the ball. How much does the bat cost?
2 Imagine that you bought a $30 ticket to see a play. As you enter the theatre, you discover you've lost the ticket. The theatre keeps no record of purchases. How likely are you to pay another $30 to see the play?

14 Think of one of the most difficult decisions you have had to make. Describe it to your partner. Think about:

- what you had to decide
- how you came to a decision
- how big a part your emotions played in this
- whether, on reflection, you made the right decision

my life ▶ MODERN LIFE ▶ MIND GAMES ▶ TECHNOLOGY AND OCCUPATIONS ▶ RECOGNIZING FEELINGS
▶ AN EMAIL MESSAGE

reading artificial intelligence • critical thinking analysing structure • word focus *beyond* •
speaking technology and occupations

11c Who's working for who?

Reading

1 Work in pairs. Discuss the questions.

1 How reliant are you on machines in your work or studies?
2 Think of an everyday object (e.g. a car, a newspaper). How much of the work that goes into creating it is done by machines?
3 What jobs can you imagine being done by machines (robots or computers) in the future?

2 Read the article and make brief notes on the following. Then compare notes with your partner.

- Sarah O'Connor's story
- what Sarah's story tells us
- what other jobs are done by machines and people these days

3 Read the article again. Answer the questions.

1 How did Sarah O'Connor feel her job would be affected by intelligent machines?
2 What human ability was 'Emma' incapable of?
3 When do experts in artificial intelligence believe machines will replace humans?
4 When does 'Technological unemployment' occur and where has it not yet occurred?
5 What does 'machine learning' mean?
6 Why are 'crowdworking' jobs done by people rather than machines?

4 Find words or expressions in the article that mean the following:

1 in danger (para 1)
2 was lacking (para 2)
3 delicacy or sensitivity (para 2)
4 out of date and of no use (para 3)
5 repetitive and boring (para 5)
6 strange or out of the ordinary (para 5)

Critical thinking analysing structure

5 Discursive articles, like this one, discuss problems and solutions. Answer the questions.

1 What problem did the article set out to deal with at the beginning of the article?
2 What possible solution did the article find or propose?
3 What were the problems with this solution?
4 How did the article conclude: with a different solution or a different problem?

6 Work in pairs. Compare your answers from Exercise 5. Refer to the article to show where you found the answers. Did you think this was an effective structure? Why? / Why not?

Word focus *beyond*

7 Look at this expression with *beyond* from the article. What does it mean? Then complete the other expressions with *beyond* using the words given.

'Such subtlety **was beyond it**.' (line 22)

| doubt | a joke | me | means |
| recognition | the call of duty |

1 I couldn't believe it when I went back ten years later. The city had **changed beyond** _____.
2 AI is **beyond** _doubt_ one of the most significant areas of technology in the 21st century.
3 It's completely **beyond** _____ how they manage to make create such intelligent machines.
4 I had to take a serious look at my lifestyle, because I was **living beyond my** _____ and my debts were growing.
5 I was prepared to accept a few days delay, but I've now been waiting two weeks for the delivery. It's got **beyond** _____.
6 Staying on a little to help them out is one thing, but working until 10 p.m. **is beyond** _____.

8 Work in pairs. Tell your partner about something that:

1 has changed beyond recognition
2 is beyond your means
3 seems beyond the call of duty
4 is beyond a joke

Speaking my life

9 Work in pairs. How could robots help in these areas? Which tasks in these occupations do you think they should *not* be allowed to do? Give reasons.

- police work
- healthcare
- childcare
- public transport
- legal work
- teaching

10 How could robots help in your job or studies? Discuss with your partner.

134

WHO'S WORKING FOR WHO?

▶ 86

An increasing number of people are feeling that their jobs are, if not already, then soon to be, under threat from intelligent computers or robots. *Financial Times* journalist Sarah O'Connor did not really think she was one, but decided anyway to pit her writing skills against the artificial intelligence of a piece of software called 'Emma', created by the tech company Stealth. Sarah was fairly sure that her artificial intelligence (AI) rival would be quicker than her, but at the same time felt confident that she would be able to produce a better-crafted report than Emma. The subject they had to write about was the official UK employment statistics which had been released some hours earlier. The judge, as with all stories submitted to the newspaper, was the paper's editor.

Sarah was right about Emma's speed: the program produced the story in about twelve minutes, a third of the time it took Sarah. Emma also included all the right facts, gave relevant context and even ventured an opinion: that the UK economy would see a period of growth. Where Emma fell short was in the area which actually separates accurate reporting from good reporting: the program was unable to make a distinction between significant facts and facts that readers would find interesting. Such subtlety was beyond it.

From a job security point of view, this seems reassuring. It tells us what most people who work in the field of artificial intelligence will freely admit: that AI is intelligent but not intelligent enough to make humans obsolete just yet. But it also tells us that there are more and more parts of our work that can and will be done by machines in future. Sarah doesn't actually need to do all the collecting and synthesizing of data to produce such a report. She could let Emma do it and then edit it and polish the information to make a more interesting piece of journalism.

For many employees this could be a great advantage. Machines could take over the boring parts of the work, leaving the employees more time to be creative. Or so the logic goes. Unfortunately, there are three fundamental problems with this idea. The first is what is called 'technological unemployment', which means that technology might well replace jobs faster than we can create new types of job. Technology has already largely replaced people in manufacturing. If it does the same in the services sector – banks, restaurants, shops – no one has really worked out what all the employees will do. The second is 'machine learning', the idea that machines can learn to do tasks for which they have not been specifically programmed. When this happens, machines and not people begin to determine the future of employment. This is already the case in stock market trading, where over three quarters of trades are now done by machines which have 'learned' the most effective strategies.

The third is 'crowdwork', boring tasks that machines are not good at but can be done by an army of independent human workers from their home computers. Rather than being creative high-end jobs, these are monotonous, extremely low-paid jobs which often involve checking the work done by computers, for example, checking online reviews for inappropriate content, or scanning medical photos for brown dots that could indicate a disease. The bizarre thing about this fast-growing sector is that people are doing work you would expect a machine to do. And that perhaps is the real question about AI in the future: will you be one of those lucky enough to have machines working for you, or will you be working for them?

real life recognizing feelings • pronunciation adjectives ending in -ed

11d You look concerned

Real life recognizing feelings

1 Work in pairs. Which of these statements, if any, applies to you? Which could you apply to other people you know? Give reasons.

   a I try to be sensitive to other people's feelings.
   b I'm quite guarded in my emotions.
   c I'm not very good at reading others' feelings.
   d I wear my heart on my sleeve.
   e I often get into misunderstandings.
   f I think too much about what others are thinking.

2 ▶ 87 Listen to three conversations. Answer the questions.

   1 What is the relationship between each pair of speakers (colleagues, family, friends, etc.)?
   2 What is the subject of each conversation?

3 ▶ 87 Listen again. What feelings do the speakers express? How does the other person show sensitivity to these feelings? Complete the table.

	Speaker's feeling	Comment by other speaker
1	Felipe: …	Jennie: You … fine. Is there … do?
2	Ohoud: …	Lewis: You look … . I didn't … you.
3	Megumi: …	Paola: Don't get … – I wasn't … you. I'm really … you.

4 Look at the expressions for describing feelings and misunderstandings. Which expression(s) would you use if:

   1 you wanted to offer help to someone?
   2 someone had a concerned expression?
   3 someone had offered help and you had forgotten to thank them?
   4 someone was laughing when you were speaking?

▶ RECOGNIZING FEELINGS

Recognizing feelings
You look a little puzzled/surprised/troubled.
You seem a bit distracted/worried.
Is there anything I can do?
Did I say something funny?
Did I say something to upset you?

Expressing feelings
I'm really excited/confused/annoyed about …
Sorry if I seem a bit distracted. It's just that …

Misunderstandings
Sorry, perhaps that sounded a bit abrupt.
Sorry, that came out wrong.
Don't get me wrong …
I didn't mean to be rude / sound ungrateful …
I'm OK. I'm just a bit tired/frustrated/upset …
Sorry, I hope I didn't offend you.

5 **Pronunciation** adjectives ending in -ed

a ▶ 88 Work in pairs. How are these adjectives pronounced? Listen and check.

   annoyed   confused   embarrassed   distracted
   frustrated   offended   preoccupied   puzzled
   shocked   troubled   worried

b What rules can you make about the pronunciation of adjectives ending -ed?

c ▶ 89 Look at these words which are exceptions to the rules of -ed endings. How do you think they are pronounced? Listen and check.

   busied   naked   readied   rugged   sacred

6 Work in pairs. Have short conversations using the adjectives in Exercise 5a and the expressions for describing feelings and misunderstandings. Try to keep each conversation going for at least four lines.

   A: *Are you OK? You look a bit annoyed.*
   B: *Oh, sorry, I'm just a bit frustrated by …*

7 Act out a conversation based on one of these situations with your partner. Use expressions for describing feelings and misunderstandings.

   • a friend who is worried because they have mislaid some money
   • a colleague who annoys you by being very late for a meeting; it turns out they had an emergency at home
   • a friend who is very excited about getting a job interview with a company which you think is terrible to work for

my life ▶ MODERN LIFE ▶ MIND GAMES ▶ TECHNOLOGY AND OCCUPATIONS ▶ RECOGNIZING FEELINGS ▶ AN EMAIL MESSAGE

writing an email message • writing skill avoiding misunderstandings   Unit 11 Reason and emotion

11e Don't get me wrong

Writing an email message

1 Work in pairs. Discuss the questions.

1. It's said that up to forty per cent of all emails are misinterpreted in some way. Why do you think this happens?
2. When was the last time you had a misunderstanding in an email exchange with someone? What happened?

2 Read the extract from a business communications forum and compare your ideas from Exercise 1.

> It's very easy to be misunderstood in an email. That's because people generally treat an email like a face-to-face conversation, where exchanges can be short and to the point. But of course they are *not* the same. In face-to-face conversations, we are able to communicate feelings with gestures, facial expressions and tone of voice, as well as words.
>
> In email writing, both the writer and reader must imagine the tone. So if the reader is feeling sensitive, he or she might take offence at something intended to be a joke. Or when the writer tries to express urgency about something, the reader might misinterpret this as impatience or anger when really it's nothing of the kind.

3 Read the extracts from emails (A–F) which caused misunderstandings. Match the emails with how it was interpreted by the reader (1–6). Would you have interpreted it in the same way? Why? / Why not?

1. You have ignored my wishes.
2. You are inviting me as a last option.
3. You think I can't spell.
4. You think I'm always slow to get things done.
5. You think my ideas are worthless.
6. You think I'm ignoring you.

A Thanks. I got your report. I honestly didn't expect to see it until the end of the month.

B Thanks for letting me know about Jessica's farewell party next Saturday. I hoped you were going to change the day of the party to one I could manage, but never mind.

C Thanks for your suggestions, but we're going to stick to the original plan.

D Fergus can't come with us to the races next week and everyone else seems to have made other arrangements already. Would you like to come?

E Thanks for the email asking for my 'oppnion'. Personally, I think the blue curtains look nicer.

F I know you're very busy, but could you reply to the email I sent two days ago? The deadline for a decision is today.

4 Writing skill avoiding misunderstandings

Rewrite each email extract to make it clear in tone and more polite. Use the phrases below in your emails.

> Please don't take this the wrong way, (but) …
> I don't want to pressure you.
> It took me rather/slightly by surprise.
> I do/really appreciate your help with this.
> Without wanting to be rude …
> I'm joking, of course.
> It would be great if you could.
> I am not offended though.

5 You work for a company which publishes books. A colleague has told you that your department, foreign dictionaries, is going to be closed down. Write an email to your boss to find out:

- why the decision has been taken
- if he had anything to do with it
- what is going to happen to the employees in your department

6 Exchange emails with your partner. Use these questions to check your emails.

- Is the email clear in its purpose?
- Does it contain any mistakes (grammar or spelling)?
- Is the tone clear and polite, i.e. it cannot be misinterpreted?

my life ▶ MODERN LIFE ▶ MIND GAMES ▶ TECHNOLOGY AND OCCUPATIONS ▶ RECOGNIZING FEELINGS ▶ AN EMAIL MESSAGE

11f Madeline the robot tamer

'Mimus' is a robot featured in the Design Museum 2017, as part of the Fear and Love: Reactions to a Complex World exhibition, London.

Unit 11 Reason and emotion

Before you watch

1 Work in pairs. Look at the list (a–e) of machines and programs that are 'intelligent', i.e. they make decisions for themselves. Which do you find useful and which do you find annoying?

a a parking sensor on a car
b a warning system in a car that tells you when you are not wearing a seatbelt
c an automatic spelling checker on a computer
d speech recognition systems (e.g. in a car)

2 Look at the photo. What kind of robot is this – domestic, industrial, a toy? What kind of things do you think it can do?

3 Key vocabulary

a Read the sentences. The words in bold are used in the video. Guess the meaning of the words.

1 We're going to **open-source** the computer program so anyone can modify it.
2 The reason that the iPad has been so successful is that the way we interact with it is **intuitive**.
3 Our new flat is great – a bit dark, but with a few **tweaks** to the lighting it'll be perfect.
4 I'm always amazed at how well deaf people can communicate with a few simple **gestures.**
5 We work on the **premise** that the customer is always right.

b Match the words in bold in Exercise 3a with these definitions.

a you act without thinking about it
b movements or signs made with the hands
c assumption
d make available for everyone to see and adapt
e small adjustments

While you watch

4 ▶ 11.1 Watch the video. What has Madeline programmed this robot to be able to do? Why has she done this?

5 ▶ 11.1 Watch the first part of the video (0.00 to 2.19) again. Complete the summary. You have been given the first letter.

Madeline says humans and robots ¹n_____ each other. We must find a win-win situation where robots don't ²r_____ humans, but ³e_____ the possibilities of what we can do. A global community of researchers, designers and ⁴a_____ is trying to rethink what robots do, putting ⁵p_____ at the centre. Madeline is working with an ABB robot that can move at ⁶s_____ metres per second and lift 300 hundred kilos. She used ⁷c_____ and special software to help it 'see' so then people could use ⁸g_____ to communicate with it.

6 ▶ 11.1 Watch the second part of the video (2.20 to the end) again. Then answer the questions.

1 What kind of experience between robot and human is Madeline trying to create?
2 Why would people who've seen industrial robots be surprised at Mimus?
3 Madeline describes two sides to the project: one is working at the computer ten hours a day. What is the other?
4 Why did Madeline say it was important to experiment with and 'misuse' existing technologies?
5 Who does she hope to inspire to be more interested in robots?

After you watch

7 Vocabulary in context

a ▶ 11.2 Watch the clips from the video. Complete the collocations.

b Complete the sentences in your own words. Then work in pairs and compare your sentences.

1 I don't know what's going to happen with my job. The ideal scenario would be …
2 … is a company / organization that's always trying to push the boundaries of technology.
3 An example of when everything came together for me was when …

8 Which of these adjectives best describes your reaction to Mimus and what you saw in the video? Give reasons.

| beautiful | negative | positive | predictable |
| scary | touching | weird | |

9 Work in pairs. Think about robots you have seen in films or in documentaries. Answer the questions.

1 What was the job of these robots?
2 Did the film give a positive or negative image of robots? In what way?
3 How likely is it that this kind of robot will become common in the future?

dry docks (npl) /draɪ dɒks/ an area next to the sea where ships can be repaired on dry land
gripper (n) /ˈɡrɪpə(r)/ a tool for holding something very firmly
spot weld (v) /spɒt weld/ to fuse two pieces of metal together

UNIT 11 REVIEW AND MEMORY BOOSTER

Grammar

1 Complete the article by putting the verbs in the correct form. Note that the 7th and 8th verbs are examples of inversion in conditional sentences.

2 Answer these questions about the article.
  1 What is the problem with this type of test?
  2 What information are we least likely to give away?

Look at these statements from a test of emotional intelligence and choose one of the following answers: certainly true, probably true, probably untrue or certainly untrue.
  1 I'd rather not _____ (give) my opinion if it risks offending someone.
  2 I'd rather others _____ (tell) me the truth even if it is sometimes painful.
  3 I wish I _____ (can) control some of my bad habits, but I can't.
  4 I wish people _____ (not / ask) me personal questions.
  5 If I _____ (have) to list my main strengths, I'd have no trouble thinking of them.
  6 Unless someone _____ (praise) my work, I am not happy with it.
  7 _____ (I / be asked) to do something unethical, I would refuse.

Now ask yourself: 'Did you answer them honestly?' The answer is probably 'not altogether'.
8 _____ (you / be instructed) to be as honest as possible before you started, your responses might have been more truthful, but only a little. Why is this? Like other personality tests, the problem with measuring emotional intelligence is that it relies on the respondent a) knowing their own feelings, and b) being truthful in their responses. Most of us are inclined to give untruthful responses about our weaknesses, because we would just as soon other people 9 _____ (not / know) them.

3 >> MB Work in pairs. What are the three different forms that follow the word 'wish' in English? Which are used in the article?

I CAN
talk about hypothetical or 'unreal' situations in the present/future using the past tense (unreal past)

use inversion in conditional sentences

Vocabulary

4 Choose the correct option to complete the sentences about feelings.
  1 I'm not panicking. I just feel *a bit on edge / a bit down*.
  2 I wasn't just cross. I was absolutely *all over the place / livid*.
  3 Was I surprised? Well, I was a bit *done in / taken aback*.
  4 I felt *thrilled to bits / upbeat* when I got the job. It's what I've always dreamed of.
  5 Don't be *speechless / down*. Second place is a fantastic achievement.
  6 I hate heights. I was absolutely *petrified / scared* that I would fall.

5 >> MB Make sentences with the words that you didn't underline in Exercise 4.

I CAN
talk about feelings

Real life

6 Work in pairs. Read the situations and complete the phrases that recognize other people's feelings.
  1 *The other person is looking anxious.*
     _____ concerned. Are you OK?
  2 *The other person is laughing and you don't understand why.*
     Sorry. Did I _____ ?
  3 *You are aware that what you said was quite direct.*
     Sorry, perhaps that _____ a bit _____ .
  4 *You want to decline an offer politely.*
     I don't mean to _____ , but I think I can manage.
  5 *The other person looks a little hurt by what you said.*
     Sorry, I hope I _____ .
  6 *You said something that you didn't intend to say.*
     Sorry, that came _____ .

7 >> MB Act out a short conversation where there's been a misunderstanding. Use this situation or your own ideas.

You borrowed your friend's laptop and now you've left it at someone else's flat. They speak to you about it.

I CAN
recognize other people's feelings in a conversation and respond appropriately

Unit 12 Mother nature

A hiker looks out over Lake Ringedalsvatnet, Norway.

FEATURES

142 The why of where
The importance of geo-literacy

144 Nature close up
Observing small events in nature

146 Rise of the urban animal
How wildlife are moving into our cities

150 Three years and 6,000 miles on a horse
A video about a journey of self discovery

1 Look at the photo and describe what you see. What is your favourite high point and view? What can you see from there?

2 ▶ 90 Listen to three people describing the landscape where they live. Answer the questions.
   1 Where is each person from and what kind of landscape surrounds them?
   2 What reason(s) did each person give for the landscape being special to them?
   3 Which speaker is describing the landscape in the photo?

3 ▶ 90 Listen to the speakers again. Write the adjectives that are used to describe these features of landscapes.

1	sky	vegetation	landscape
2	scenery	hillsides	mountains
3	farmland	valleys	terrain

4 Work in groups. Think of examples of the following in your country and tell the rest of the group.
   • a landscape that you associate with a particular period in your life
   • the most dramatic scenery you have seen
   • something you consider to be a blot on the landscape

my life ▶ NATURAL AND MAN-MADE FEATURES ▶ EVENTS IN NATURE ▶ THE ANIMAL AND HUMAN WORLDS ▶ A DEBATE ▶ A LETTER TO A NEWSPAPER

reading geo-literacy • wordbuilding adverb + adjective collocations •
grammar approximation and vague language • speaking natural and man-made features

12a The why of where

Reading

1 Work in pairs. Answer the geography quiz questions (1–6). Then check your answers on page 190. Did any of the answers surprise you? Why?

1 Which country's flag has a white star and crescent moon on a green background?
   a Qatar   b Nigeria   c Pakistan
2 Which country has the most billionaires per head of the population?
   a Monaco   b USA   c Kuwait
3 Which country has the greatest number of active volcanoes?
   a Nicaragua   b Japan   c Indonesia
4 Which is the most abundant gas in the Earth's atmosphere?
   a carbon dioxide b nitrogen   c oxygen
5 Which of these is the oldest city?
   a Aleppo, Syria   b Beijing, China   c Varanasi, India
6 Which of these land types covers the largest part of Africa?
   a grassland   b desert   c rainforest

2 Work in pairs. Make a list of all the reasons you can think of for why geography is important.

3 Read the extract from an interview about geo-literacy. What reasons does the interviewee give for why geo-literacy is important? Were these reasons similar to yours?

4 Read the interview again and answer the questions.

1 What does being geo-literate enable a person to do?
2 Why didn't northern Africa experience its normal rainfall in the 1970s and 80s?
3 How do you think people in the northern hemisphere felt about what was happening in Africa?
4 How could an understanding of urban planning be of practical use to us?
5 What mistake do some people who are not informed make about India?

▶ 91

The Why of Where *Geo-literacy explained*

Q What is 'geo-literacy'?

Geo-literacy is basically an understanding of how our world and the Earth's systems work. It's a newish term but not necessarily a new concept.

Q Why is it important?

For people who don't have this understanding – no mental map of the Earth's surface and the distribution of people across it – the world is kind of confusing. It's just a mixture of unrelated physical phenomena and more or less random human activity – political, cultural and economic. Geo-literacy gives you the ability to use geographic knowledge to make connections between things and to understand how changes in nature and how our own actions affect us all.

Q Can you give us an example?

I can give you dozens of examples – how long have you got? I'll give you three very different ones, just to give you an idea of the scope and importance of this. Back in the 1970s and 80s we saw the appalling consequences of drought in the Sahel region of Africa, which killed hundreds of thousands of people and left a million or so dependent on food aid. In the northern hemisphere, we threw up our hands and asked, 'What can we do?' But what we didn't realize at the time was that our own pollution in the north, all the stuff we were pumping into the air from factories and aerosols, had contributed to this drought by changing the climate. By cooling the air over Europe and the Atlantic, it had forced the tropical rains that usually fall in this part of Africa further south.

Another example would be an understanding of how cities are organized, with residential and commercial areas and so on. If, for example, workplaces are far from homes, then that has an impact on transport and on quality of life in general. That kind of awareness helps to inform our life choices.

And lastly, there's cultural understanding. Someone not geo-literate might be inclined to think of Indians as just one homogenous group. And when they met an Indian might make an inappropriate remark like 'Do you speak Indian?' or something, not knowing that India is actually an ethnically, geographically and economically diverse country with over fifteen different recognized languages.

142

Unit 12 Mother nature

5 Work in pairs. Discuss the questions.
1 Can you think of any other examples where being geo-literate could be useful?
2 What aspects of geography would you like to know more about? How do you think this might help you in your future?

Wordbuilding adverb + adjective collocations

▶ **WORDBUILDING adverb + adjective collocations**

We often use adverb + adjective collocations to describe places and communities.
ethnically diverse, politically aware

For further practice, see Workbook page 99.

6 Cross out the adverb in each group that does not collocate so well with the adjective that follows.
1 ~~ethnically~~ / physically / politically active
2 economically / industrially / ~~internationally~~ advanced
3 ~~geographically~~ / politically correct
4 internationally / ~~socially~~ famous
5 environmentally / ~~visually~~ friendly
6 ~~humanly~~ / musically / ~~socially~~ gifted
7 geographically / ~~humanly~~ / ~~physically~~ remote
8 culturally / intellectually / ~~politically~~ rich

7 Work in pairs. Think of people, communities or places that fit the collocations in Exercise 6.

The city I live in is very culturally rich.

Grammar approximation and vague language

▶ **APPROXIMATION and VAGUE LANGUAGE**

Numbers
It killed **hundreds of thousands** of people.
It left a million **or so** people dependent on food aid.
I can give you **dozens of** examples.
… with **over** fifteen different recognized languages …
Also: *around/about/roughly, as many as, up to, some, under, -odd*

With adjectives (+ noun)
It's a new**ish** term but not a new concept.
The world is **kind of** confusing.
… and **more or less** random human activity …

Vague words
… all the **stuff** we were pumping out into the air …
… with residential and commercial areas **and so on**.
… might make an inappropriate remark **or something**.

For further information and practice, see page 178.

8 Look at the grammar box. Answer these questions.
1 Which words, expressions or suffixes make another word less precise and which are less precise words themselves?
2 Which words, expressions or suffixes are more informal or conversational, do you think?

9 ▶ 92 Work in pairs. Read the text and discuss what expressions of approximation could go in each space. Then listen, compare and write what you hear.

> ¹_____ five years ago, I took a trip to Madagascar to photograph the landscape. A guy I met at a party (he was a journalist ²_____) had told me that it had the most wonderful scenery. Normally, I spend six months ³_____ researching a place before I go there, but in this case, I only spent ⁴_____ a week reading about it. Not long after, feeling ⁵_____ unprepared, I threw my ⁶_____ into a bag and left for Madagascar. During the trip, I must have taken ⁷_____ 2,000 pictures, some of them a bit amateur ⁸_____, but a lot of high-quality ones too. The landscape is incredibly varied. It's ⁹_____ like a different country in each region – desert, marshes, rainforest, sandy beaches. Incredible! And all of this is home to ¹⁰_____ 200,000 different species of plants and animals.

10 Complete these statements using your own ideas and an expression from the grammar box. Then compare answers with your partner.
1 The outside of my house/apartment is a _____ colour.
2 I can walk _____ kilometres before I begin to feel tired.
3 The landscape near us is _____.
4 From where I live it's _____ kilometres to the sea.
5 My town has grown at a _____ rate. Today _____ people live there.
6 At weekends I do _____ like _____.

Speaking my life

11 Work in groups. Each person should describe a natural geographical feature (e.g. a mountain range, a coastline) and a man-made 'system' (e.g. an underground railway, a business park, a leisure park) that they know. Use the questions below when planning what to say. Ask each other follow-up questions about the features and places.

- Where is it and what does it consist of?
- What makes this thing special or important?
- How do people interact with this place or thing?

143

listening Basho's journey • idioms adjective collocations • grammar *would* • speaking and writing events in nature

12b Nature close up

Listening

1 The Japanese poet, Basho, is famous for his haiku poems about nature. Look at the poem and say what the form of a haiku is: how many lines, how many syllables per line and how many syllables in total.

2 ▶93 Listen to an extract from a radio interview with a biographer of Basho. Answer the questions.

1 What kind of writing does the biographer normally do?
2 When did Basho live?
3 Why did Basho make his long journey across Japan?
4 What did Basho's poetry make her realize?

3 ▶93 Work in pairs. What did the biographer say about each of these things? Discuss with your partner, then listen again and check.

1 a particular flower
2 the spray from a waterfall
3 a floating leaf
4 a frog
5 an old military fort

Idioms adjective collocations

4 Look at the expression from the interview. Does 'crystal clear' mean *extremely clear* or *moderately clear*?

'… the reflection of a floating leaf in a **crystal clear** stream …'

5 Look at these other expressions which have an intense meaning. In all cases except two, the first word does the intensifying. Underline the two expressions where the second word intensifies.

bone dry	rock hard
brand new	scared stiff
fast asleep	sopping wet
freezing cold	stone cold
lightning quick	wide open
pitch black	worried sick

An old silent pond …
A frog jumps into the pond,
splash! Silence again.

Basho

6 Work in pairs. Match the collocations in Exercise 5 with the things they commonly describe.

a baby   a car   a cave   a child   dinner   eyes
ground/earth   old bread   a parent   reactions
a towel   a winter's day

bone dry: ground/earth

7 Choose three of the collocations from Exercise 5 and put them into sentences that describe situations from your own experience. Then work in pairs and compare your ideas.

Once on holiday in France, we went out for a long walk. But we got lost on the way home and had to find our way back in the dark. It was pitch black and I was worried sick that we'd never get home.

Grammar *would*

> ▶ **WOULD**
> 1 Q: Could you tell us a bit more? A: *I'd* love to.
> 2 *I'd* imagine that's the sort of thing you usually write about.
> 3 He **wouldn't** allow his celebrity to distract him from his real interests.
> 4 He decided that he **would** escape in search of a more peaceful existence.
> 5 He **would** stop and observe 'nature's modest dramas'.
> 6 It **wouldn't** really have worked if I had made that the focus of a travel guide.
> 7 **Would** you give us an example?
>
> For further information and practice, see page 178.

8 Look at the grammar box and match the sentences to the following uses of *would*.

   a to make a polite request
   b to describe a hypothetical situation in a conditional sentence
   c to respond to a request or invitation
   d to report an intention, expectation or decision
   e to describe a habitual action in the past
   f to indicate a person or thing's refusal to do something
   g to express an opinion or hope less forcefully

9 Work in pairs. Discuss why *would* is used in these sentences.

   1 My mother would sit on a bench reading while we played.
   2 The key wouldn't fit in the door.
   3 He promised me he wouldn't say a word.
   4 I'm afraid that'd be difficult for us.
   5 It's up to you, I'd say.
   6 I would have come earlier, but I had to finish some work.
   7 Would you mind giving me a hand to move this table?

10 Complete the conversations using expressions with *would* and the words in brackets.

   1 A: How about a drink this evening?
     B: Yes, _____ . (great)
   2 A: Do you think Olivia will want to come to the film?
     B: No, I _____ so. It's not her type of film. (thought)
   3 A: I had to take the bus to work because the car _____ this morning. (start)
     B: You should have called me. I _____ you a lift in my car. (given)
   4 A: I wish I'd asked you for your help.
     B: I do too, but I distinctly remember you saying _____ OK on your own. (be)
   5 A: Do you know this area well, then?
     B: Yes. I used to come here with my parents. We _____ on long walks in the hills. (go)

11 Use expressions with *would* to write sentences about each of the following topics. Use the sentence openers below to help you. Then share your ideas with the class.

   • going for long walks
   • reading poetry
   • how easy it is to enjoy nature in your area

   1 When I was younger …
   2 If I had (had) more …
   3 I promised myself …

Speaking and writing `my life`

12 Work in pairs. Choose one of the tasks below.

   • Think of two more examples of 'nature's modest dramas': small things that strike you as interesting or beautiful.
   • Take a photo of 'nature close up' and bring it to the next class. Describe this to your partner and explain why you chose it.

13 Choose one of your ideas from Exercise 11 and try to put it into the form of a haiku. Follow the rules of a haiku from Exercise 1.

12c Rise of the urban animal

Reading

1 Work in pairs. Answer the questions.

1 What animals do you see in a typical day? Where do you see them?
2 Which are wild and which are tame or domesticated?
3 What animals do you associate with cities?

2 The article on page 147 is about the rising number of animals living in cities.

a Give three possible reasons for this trend.
b Match these urban animal names with the pictures. Then try to pronounce each name.

boar   coyote   falcon   fox   pigeon

3 Read the article. Compare the reasons you gave in Exercise 2 with the ones given in the article. Is this a trend that we can stop?

4 What facts did you learn about these animals (1–6) and how their behaviour has changed? Read the article again and make notes.

1 peregrine falcons
2 wild coyotes
3 foxes
4 ants
5 mountain lions
6 bears

Critical thinking different perspectives

5 Summarize what the article says about animals living in cities as seen from these perspectives:
a a historical perspective
b an environmental perspective
c a safety perspective
d the perspective of animal welfare

6 Considering the perspectives in Exercise 5, is the trend of more animals moving to cities a) positive, b) negative or c) neither positive or negative?

7 What conclusion does the author make about the trend?

Word focus *move*

8 Look at this sentence from the article (line 24–26). What does the expression in bold mean?

"And where small animals have **moved in**, some of their predators have followed."

9 Complete the sentences with the verb *move* with these prepositions. Then check the meaning of each 'move' phrase with your partner.

around   in   off   on   on   out   over   to

1 Why have you **moved** the furniture _____? I liked it the way it was before.
2 That documentary about refugee children was very upsetting. It **moved me** _____ tears.
3 The house is empty. The last tenants **moved** _____ three weeks ago.
4 It's six months since George split up with his girlfriend, but he still thinks about her all the time. He really needs to **move** _____.
5 Sorry, would you mind **moving** _____ so I can sit down here?
6 **Get a move** _____, will you? We're going to be late.
7 I haven't found a flat yet, but Natasha said I can **move** _____ with her while I'm looking.
8 I shouted 'Wait a moment' as the car **moved** _____, but the driver didn't hear me.

10 Choose two of the expressions from Exercise 9 and make sentences about your own experience. Then work in pairs and compare your sentences.

Speaking my life

11 Work in groups. Discuss what you think could be done, if anything, about the following problems. Then share your ideas with the class.

- animals' native habitats being lost because of human (especially urban) development
- urban animals which are a danger to humans
- animals, e.g. tigers, which are in danger of extinction because of human activity
- the hunting of animals (e.g. elephants and rhinos), for valuable body parts (e.g. tusks and horns)

12 Do you have any of the problems in Exercise 11 in your country?

Unit 12 Mother nature

A mountain lion, Hollywood, USA

THE RISE OF THE
URBAN ANIMAL

▶ 94

There are now more peregrine falcons per square kilometre in New York City than anywhere else on Earth. In northern Mumbai, an estimated 35 leopards roam freely in Sanjay Gandhi National Park. Suburban Chicago is home to over 2,000 wild coyotes; some have even been seen hanging around the international airport. In Berlin, wild boars forage for food in people's gardens and raise families in local woods. In Los Angeles, mountain lions tiptoe invisibly past tourists in the Hollywood hills. And walking the streets of London in the early hours of the morning, you are as likely to see an urban fox as a domestic cat.

Rodents and insects, such as ants, have long been city-dwellers, living in sewers or under pavements and feeding on our discarded food. But there is now a trend for bigger animals, many of them carnivores, taking up residence in our towns and cities. 'I grew up in London,' says Tristan Donovan, one of many ecologists studying the phenomenon, 'and it didn't seem like there were that many foxes around when I was a kid. And that made me wonder: is this happening everywhere?' The answer is yes. But the real question is why?

It seems the main attraction for these creatures is the abundance of food in cities. Seagulls have come inland to scavenge from land-fill sites and foxes have abandoned the countryside in favour of back alleys and rubbish bins. And where small animals have moved in, some of their predators have followed. Peregrine falcons sit high up on New York's skyscrapers and watch the pigeons below, waiting to swoop on any which venture into the open.

There are other factors too. Urban sprawl and climate change have meant that animals' native habitats are shrinking or disappearing. The mountain lions of Hollywood, who in the wild typically roam an area of around 1,000 square kilometres, are limited there to a mere 65 square kilometres. At the same time, the animals feel less wary of their human neighbours than in the past and with good reason, because animal hunting is far less popular.

But if they are less scared of us, should we be any less scared of them? Certainly not, according to wildlife ecologist, Stan Gehrt, who says that when predators lose their instinctive fear of humans, they actually become more likely to attack us. He urges anyone who sees a large wild cat or coyote to shout or throw stones. To ensure our own safety, he says, we must establish our authority over these animals, because they are 'not going to go away'. Fortunately, incidents of urban animals attacking residents are relatively rare, though attacks on domestic pets are common.

Co-habitation with humans has caused other adaptations in animal behaviour. Some have even started to take on human traits, like the coyotes in Chicago, who were spotted waiting at a traffic light before crossing the road. Bears around Lake Tahoe in the United States feed so well on discarded food all year round that they no longer need to hibernate in winter.

But is this a case of animals evolving to meet the demands of a new environment or just a case of certain animals having the right personality to suit the circumstances? Gehrt thinks it might be the latter. What he has observed is that animals which are naturally cautious or neophobic (afraid of new things) tend to do much better in cities than those which are bold. So, not so much a case of fortune favouring the brave, as you would expect, but fortune favouring the timid.

City life is not for everyone and some animals will never adjust to it. But for those that have, it is time that we began to view them as one of us. As Seth Magle of Chicago's zoo puts it, 'We started from this narrative in which the city is an evil landscape that chews up the landscape and leaves nothing behind. But the reality is that we're not going to stop urbanizing the planet, so how do we turn cities into something good, something positive for wildlife?'

hibernate (v) /ˈhaɪbə(r)neɪt/ (of animals) go to sleep for the winter
sewer (n) /ˈsuːə(r)/ underground channels for carrying waste water away
swoop (v) /swuːp/ dive down towards something from above
urban sprawl /ˈɜː(r)bən sprɔːl/ the spreading of cities onto undeveloped land

my life ▶ NATURAL AND MAN-MADE FEATURES ▶ EVENTS IN NATURE ▶ THE ANIMAL AND HUMAN WORLDS ▶ A DEBATE
▶ A LETTER TO A NEWSPAPER

real life a debate • speaking skill interrupting • pronunciation intonation in interruptions

12d A blot on the landscape

Real life a debate

1 Work in pairs. Look at these facts about five of the world's most congested cities and guess which cities they are. Then check your answers on page 190.

   1 This capital is the noisiest city in South America and also one of the most congested.
   2 The longest traffic jam ever recorded was on the way to this Asian capital in 2010. It lasted for twelve days.
   3 This European capital, called the 'Paris of the East', is Europe's most congested city.
   4 In 2016, this was the world's third most congested city and the only Asian capital without a metro.
   5 This North American city is the world's most congested and also has the highest 'commuter pain' (stress, lost time and ill health).

2 Think of two ways traffic congestion could be reduced in big cities.

3 Speaking skill interrupting

a ▶ 95 Listen to an extract from a local meeting about traffic congestion in a city. Answer the questions.

   1 What two ideas to reduce traffic congestion are presented?
   2 What are the three aspects of the first idea that they discuss/debate?
       a   the _____ of the zone
       b   what the _____ will be
       c   who will be _____

b ▶ 95 Look at the expressions for interrupting. Then listen to the extract from the meeting again. Underline the phrases that the speakers used to interrupt and prevent interruptions.

> ▶ INTERRUPTING
>
> **Interrupting**
> Sorry, can I just interrupt you there?
> Can I just say something in answer to that?
> No, hang on a minute …
> No, I'm sorry. I have to stop you there …
> Yes, but …
>
> **Preventing interruptions**
> Sorry, can I just finish what I was saying?
> Just a moment, please …
> OK, you can make your point in a moment.
> You've had a chance to speak. Can I just have my say?

4 Pronunciation intonation in interruptions

a ▶ 96 It is important when interrupting or preventing interruptions not to sound aggressive. Listen to how the phrases in the box are pronounced with a firm but gentle tone.

b Work in pairs. Practise saying the phrases to each other. Tell your partner if their tone sounds too hard or unfriendly.

5 Work in groups. Use the ideas you discussed in Exercise 2 and prepare to participate in a debate. Think about the main issues and possible objections or concerns. Take the roles of Chair and the participants at the meeting. Use the expressions in the box to help with interruptions.

Unit 12 Mother nature

12e To the editor

Writing a letter to a newspaper

1 What subjects do you feel strongly enough about to write a letter to a newspaper or post a comment online? What kind of subjects do people usually write comments about?

2 Read the letter to a newspaper. Answer the questions.
1 What situation prompted the person to write this letter?
2 Why, according to the writer, is nothing being done about this problem?
3 What solution does the writer propose?

To the editor:

I was shocked to read in today's edition (13th May) that over 1,500 people in our city now die each year from problems directly related to air pollution. You would think that would be a wake-up call for the government to prioritize public health, but it won't be because there is no political will to regulate private cars and commercial vehicles.

Economic arguments always win over environmental ones and none of the solutions to the problem are economically attractive: restricting (or even banning) cars and lorries from the city; taxing people who pollute; redesigning the city to reduce the need for transport. But there must be a point where people's health wins over economics. Because unless we are all going to live in sealed apartments and walk around wearing pollution masks, a solution must be found.

The problem is public awareness. People only act when they understand the source of a problem and how bad it is. I used to drive my big SUV into the city each day – until a friend gave me an air pollution monitor. And that was that. We desperately need more air pollution displays in public places so that everyone can see the levels of pollution. So whether we are in the street, our office or our local park, we will be aware of the risk to our health. And when the risks are high, people will act.

---

3 Use this checklist. Does the letter follow these tips?
- Respond the same day or the next
- Give details of the article that you are responding to
- Be brief and to the point
- Take a strong position (state your points boldly)
- Use humour, where possible, rather than anger

4 Writing skill persuasive language

a Match the persuasive techniques (1–6) with the extracts from the letter (a–f).
1 making strong claims/statements
2 using short, clear sentences
3 appealing to shared experiences
4 telling a personal story
5 giving a view of what the future could be like
6 using emotive words

a So whether we are in the street, our office or our local park, we will be aware …
b I used to drive my big SUV into the city each day …
c Unless we are all going … to walk around wearing pollution masks, a solution must be found.
d … there is no political will to regulate private cars and commercial vehicles.
e We desperately need more air pollution displays …
f The problem is public awareness.

b Choose two (different) persuasive techniques from Exercise 4a (1–6). Use the techniques to write two sentences on one of the subjects you discussed in Exercise 1.

5 A newspaper has published an article criticizing a company for building a wind farm in an area of natural beauty. Work in pairs. Brainstorm a list of pros and cons of wind farms.

6 Write a letter to the editor expressing your views about the situation in Exercise 5. Look at the tips in Exercise 3 to help you.

7 Exchange letters with your partner. Use these questions to check your letters.
- Does the letter refer to the article it is responding to?
- Is it brief and to the point?
- Does it use persuasive techniques?
- Did you find the letter persuasive?

my life ▶ NATURAL AND MAN-MADE FEATURES ▶ EVENTS IN NATURE ▶ THE ANIMAL AND HUMAN WORLDS ▶ A DEBATE
▶ A LETTER TO A NEWSPAPER

12f Three years and 6,000 miles on a horse

Horseman on the Mongolian Steppe

Before you watch

1 Work in pairs. Discuss the questions.

a How many miles could you comfortably walk in a day (1 mile = 1.6 km)?
b How many miles could you comfortably ride on a bike or horse in a day?
c Roughly how fast (miles per day) is travelling 6,000 miles in three and a half years?

2 Key vocabulary

a Read the sentences. The words in bold are used in the video. Guess the meaning and pronunciation of the words.

1 I am very sensitive to the weather. It **dictates** my moods.
2 She sailed around the world in a **yacht** measuring thirty metres in length.
3 There's a **saying** in English: 'No man is an island'.
4 He fell ten metres from the roof to the ground, but, **miraculously**, he didn't break a single bone.
5 I guess I've had quite a **nomadic** life. I've never really lived anywhere for more than a couple of years.
6 I think we must be **cursed**. The motorway is closed, the bus has been delayed and the trains aren't running.

b Match the words in bold in Exercise 2a with these definitions.

a moving from place to place, without a fixed home
b a sailing boat
c suffering bad luck all the time
d influences or decides
e amazingly
f a proverb or common piece of wisdom

While you watch

3 📹 **12.1** Look at these topics. Watch the short video with the sound turned off. Then discuss with your partner what you saw about each topic.

- the landscape
- the weather
- the people
- the animals

4 📹 **12.1** Read the questions. Watch the video again, this time with the sound turned up. Then discuss the answers with your partner.

1 What inspired Tim Cope to make this trip?
2 What did he want to achieve by making the trip?
3 What was the obstacle to achieving this?
4 Why were his horses stolen and how did he get them back?
5 How did this event change his attitude to his trip?
6 How long had he originally planned to travel for?

5 📹 **12.1** Try to complete these phrases that Tim Cope used. Then watch the video again and check your answers

1 'My idea was to ride through …, learning to look at the world _____ a nomad's _____.'
2 '… within five days my world had come crashing _____. The horses were stolen.'
3 'Life on the Steppe without a horse is like being on the _____ without a _____.'
4 'And there's this Mongol saying that 'If you ever have to rush in life, _____.'
5 'And that was the _____ point for me on this trip.'
6 '… time's more measured by the _____ and _____ of the sun, the seasons, …'

After you watch

6 Vocabulary in context

a 📹 **12.2** Watch the clips from the video. Complete the collocations. Then discuss your answers.

b Complete the sentences in your own words. Then work in pairs and compare your sentences.

1 Did you get to … when you were on holiday?
2 Once you have … , there's no turning back.
3 You need to let go of … Otherwise, …

7 How do you think this trip changed Tim Cope's life?

8 Work in pairs. You are going to plan a life-changing journey. Discuss the following points. Then present your ideas to the class.

- What will be the 'theme' of your journey?
- What transport will you use (a single or multiple means)?
- What is the scope (e.g. different countries) and distance of your journey?
- How much time will you attempt to complete this trip in?
- How will you record your experiences?

UNIT 12 REVIEW AND MEMORY BOOSTER

Grammar

1 Look at the photo. Where do you think this is? What is the man doing? Read the article and check your answer.

2 Use these words to approximate the expressions in italics (1–6) in the article.

   1 -ish   3 dozens of   5 kind of
   2 a bit   4 or so   6 roughly

3 >> MB Underline all the places where *would* (or the abbreviated form *'d*) is used in the article. Then explain to your partner why *would* is used in each case.

Iceland has some of the most unspoilt, dramatic scenery anywhere on Earth, and you'd think, some of the most unchanging. But that's where you'd be mistaken, because it's actually very dynamic. Nowhere is this more evident than on the Westman Islands, a small archipelago of fifteen volcanic islands [1] *ten kilometres* south of the main island. In the last [2] *fifty years*, they've seen huge changes. One, Surtsey, rose out of the sea in 1963 after a volcanic eruption, while Heimaey, the only inhabited island, grew by 2.1 kilometres after its volcano erupted in 1973.

I visited the islands last year because I'd heard about their extraordinary puffin population. These [3] *small* black and white birds with unmistakable faces perch in their thousands on the cliffs and steep grassy slopes above the sea. I went to photograph them and each day I was there, locals came to practise their traditional art of 'sky fishing'. Using large nets on long poles – [4] *like* butterfly nets – the hunters would stalk the puffins, dangerously close to the cliff's edge, and just at the moment they took flight, they'd sweep them up in their nets. [5] *Puffins* were caught in this way each time. It was an incredible sight and I would have asked to try it myself, but I felt sorry for the puffins! The risk doesn't deter local hunters (at least, none of the ones I talked to would admit to feeling afraid) because puffin meat is a staple food for them. The meat itself is odd – it tastes [6] *fishy* – but locals love it.

I CAN
use approximate language
use *would* appropriately in different situations

Vocabulary

4 Complete this description of a landscape. Use these words.

   hilly   lush   monotonous   rich   sparse

We drove for hours through the desert: a flat, [1] _____ landscape with [2] _____ vegetation. Then quite suddenly it changed and became more [3] _____ . As we drove over one hilltop we came into a [4] _____ green valley with [5] _____ farmland and a wide river at the bottom.

5 >> MB Work in pairs. Complete the adjective collocations. Then think of examples of things each phrase could describe.

   1 bone dry and _____ wet
   2 completely fearless and scared _____
   3 wide awake and _____ asleep
   4 boiling hot and _____ cold
   5 dazzlingly bright and _____ black
   6 utterly unconcerned and worried _____

I CAN
describe features of a landscape
use adjective collocations

Real life

6 Put the words in brackets in the correct place in the sentences to make polite but firm phrases for interrupting and preventing interruptions.

   1 Could I interrupt you there? (just)
   2 Can I just say something to that? (in answer)
   3 I'm sorry. I need to stop you. (there)
   4 Can I finish what I was saying? (just)
   5 OK. You can make your point. (in a moment)
   6 A moment, please. (just)

7 >> MB Work in pairs. Explain to each other what you think is most important when learning English. Try to interrupt when the other person is speaking and prevent interruptions when you are speaking.

I CAN
interrupt politely and prevent interruptions

UNIT 1c Exercise 11, page 14
Group A
1 **misgiving** (n) /mɪsˈgɪvɪŋ/ doubt or apprehension about something
2 **spurn** (v) /spɜːn/ reject
3 **zany** (adj) /ˈzeɪni/ eccentric and unconventional, even a little crazy

Example:
If the word was 'immortal', a true definition could be: '*Immortal* means living forever, never dying. So we say, for example, "the immortal words of Shakespeare" or "Shakespeare has achieved immortal fame".'
A false definition could be: '*Immortal* means behaving in a way which is not right. So we say, for example, "Earning that much money when others earn very little is immortal."'

UNIT 2c Exercise 10, page 26

Quiz

How would you feel in the following situations? Read the questions and answer A, B or C for each one. Then look at the key on page 190 to find out what your comfort zone is. Discuss if you agree with the answers.

A comfortable and keen on the idea
B a little uncomfortable, but willing to try
C uncomfortable and reluctant to do it

1 At a Karaoke club, a friend forces you to go on stage to sing Frank Sinatra's 'My Way'.
2 You are asked to give a 45-minute talk about your organization to a group of 250 pre-university students next month.
3 A famous person you admire is sitting near you on a train reading a book. You would love to speak to them and get their autograph.
4 A friend, who is a cycling fanatic, has invited you to go on a cycling holiday with them in the mountains.
5 A group of your friends has organized an adventure weekend, involving canoeing in white water rapids, rock climbing and caving in underground caves.
6 You are asked if you would mind being filmed at work by a TV crew who are making a fly-on-the-wall documentary about your organization.
7 You are unexpectedly offered a promotion to a job with more pay, but also much more responsibility and less security (you will be judged by your results).
8 Your next-door neighbour's daughter practises the violin for two hours every evening and the sound is very distracting. You need to speak to them directly about it.

UNIT 4d Exercise 6, page 52
Student A
A typical coffee shop selling fresh coffee produces over two tonnes of waste coffee grounds each year. Your idea is to use these coffee grounds to grow mushrooms, which you can then sell to shops and supermarkets. Currently, cafés throw away the used coffee grounds into the general waste. By using them to grow mushrooms, you would be a) recycling the waste coffee and b) reducing the cost of the compost you need to grow your mushrooms.

UNIT 6c Exercise 9, page 74
Student A
You are a marketing manager. Your company has developed a face cream for women in their 40s. It moisturizes the skin, protects against the sun, and helps to prevent wrinkles forming.
Because women in their 40s are keen to remain looking young, you want the advertisements to feature a single young model in her 30s who is fair-skinned and very beautiful: a universally recognizable image of beauty. It will also encourage men to buy the product for their wives. Beauty sells, as far as you are concerned.

UNIT 9b Exercise 13, page 109
Student A
Rewrite the sentences marked 'P' as sentences with a participle clause. Then tell the story to your partner.

In 1925 Hungarian-born Victor Lustig read an article which said that the Eiffel Tower was in need of repairs and that the city of Paris lacked the funds to maintain it. (P) After he had created some fake government documents to show he was responsible for selling the tower, he then looked for some buyers.
Having created ... he then looked ...
(P) He claimed that it was a secret that the government was going to sell the metal from the tower and he persuaded two scrap metal dealers to pay him $100,000 each to give them the contract to dismantle the tower. (P) Lustig took the money and then returned to the United States.
(P) He continued a career as a fraudster and even cheated the famous gangster Al Capone out of money.

UNIT 9c Exercise 9, page 110
Student A
Read the facts. The underlined words give a clue, if needed.
1 Fact: Alfred Nobel was the man after whom the Nobel peace prize was named, but he also invented …
   Irony: He was also the inventor of dynamite.
2 Fact: Jim Fixx, the author of *The Complete Book of Running*, was the man who popularized jogging as a way to get healthy exercise. But at the age of 52, while out jogging …
   Irony: He had a heart attack and died.

Communication activities

UNIT 1c Exercise 11, page 14

Group B
1 **howl** (v) /haʊl/ let out a long cry like a dog or wolf
2 **jaded** (adj) /ˈdʒeɪdɪd/ bored with something, lacking enthusiasm
3 **reprieve** (n) /rɪˈpriːv/ a delay in a punishment

Example:
If the word was 'immortal', a true definition could be: 'Immortal means living forever, never dying. So we say, for example, "the immortal words of Shakespeare" or "Shakespeare has achieved immortal fame".'
A false definition could be: 'Immortal means behaving in a way which is not right. So we say, for example, "Earning that much money when others earn very little is immortal."'

UNIT 3d Exercise 8, page 40

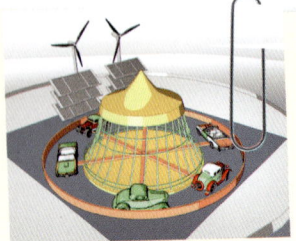

By Francesca Martelli: A children's carousel powered by wind and solar power. The carousel will have little carriages in the shape of historic cars made over the decades by the city's car manufacturer. Francesca hopes the project can be part-funded by the car manufacturer.

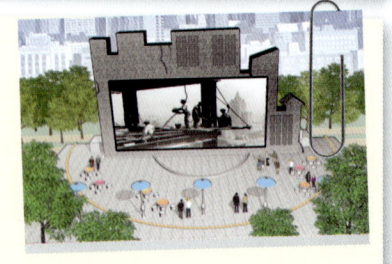

By Rana Suweilah: A giant LED screen mounted on a black granite wall (granite being the rock found in the nearby mountains). In front of the wall will be a large paved area, where people can skate or play games, with seating around it. The screen will show video footage of construction workers in the 1950s, building skyscrapers in the city centre.

UNIT 4d Exercise 6, page 52

Student B
Your idea is to make it easier for people to scrap their old cars. Currently, the owner has to pay a scrap metal dealer £100 to collect the old car from their house. You would offer to collect people's scrap cars for free. You will then a) try to recycle as many parts as possible before b) taking it to the scrap metal dealer to get money for the remaining metal or parts.

UNIT 7c Exercise 10, page 86

Security survey

1 Do you know all your neighbours and do you talk to them about questions of security?
2 Have you recorded the make and serial number of all your valuable electronic items?
3 Do you leave any lights on in your house when you are away? Do you take any other precautions?
4 Do you keep any personal information – addresses, bank details, passwords – on your phone?
5 Do you keep spare keys for your car and house with a trusted neighbour?
6 Do you always lock your car, both when you're driving and when you leave it?
7 Do you have secure locks on all your windows and doors and an alarm system fitted to your house?
8 Do you have different passwords for email, bank, online shops, etc. and do you change them at least once every three months?
9 Do you use passwords with a mixture of characters (upper case and lower case), numbers and symbols?
10 Do you ever use your computer or phone on public (unprotected) networks?
11 How many of your personal details do you think are known by a) the government and b) commercial organizations?
12 Do you keep a list of emergency numbers that you could call in the event of a breach of security?

UNIT 7d Exercise 6, page 88

Group A

Why do stars twinkle? The traditional answer is that the light from them is disturbed by movement of air in our own atmosphere. If that is true, why don't planets twinkle too? Now some scientists think the real reason must be to do with the distance (planets are much nearer) and that there is something getting in the way. What that 'something' is no one knows yet.

UNIT 9c Exercise 9, page 110

Student B

Read the facts. The underlined words give a clue, if needed.

1 Fact: Henry VIII of England (1492–1547) had six wives because he desperately wanted a son and strong male successor. But his successor …
   Irony: Edward, his only son, was a weak child and he died when he was fifteen, being King for only six years; his greatest successor was his daughter, Elizabeth I, who ruled for 45 years.
2 Fact: Einstein had one of the most brilliant minds of the twentieth century. Yet when he was seventeen, he …
   Irony: He failed his university entrance exam.

UNIT 4d Exercise 6, page 52

Student C

It is very annoying to return home in the evening and find the postman has been unable to deliver a package because no one was at home. Your idea is to provide an evening redelivery service for parcels and big letters. Currently, if no one is at home, the package is returned to a depot on the outskirts of town, which people have to visit in person to collect their post. Using your system, people would pay an annual fee for you to collect these packages and redeliver them at a more convenient time.

UNIT 6c Exercise 9, page 74

Student B

You are a sales manager. Your company has developed a face cream for women in their 40s. It moisturizes the skin, protects against the sun, and helps to prevent wrinkles forming.

You think that women don't want to see an impossibly beautiful model in the advertisements, but women that they can identify with: that are average, with some wrinkles and blemishes, and that represent diverse ethnic backgrounds. You think you could even use members of the public in the advertisements.

UNIT 7d Exercise 6, page 88

Group B

Why do people yawn? People yawn not to show they are sleepy, but to try and stay awake. Research says that people yawn to cool the brain so it can operate better. That explains why others yawn when they see us yawning. It is part of ancient behaviour that helps groups to stay awake and be alert to danger.

UNIT 9b Exercise 13, page 109

Student B

Rewrite the sentences marked 'P' as sentences with a participle clause. Then tell the story to your partner.

Frank Abagnale is one of the most famous impostors in recent history. In the 1960s he ran away from home after his parents split up.
(P) After he ran out of money, he began a career as an impostor and pretended to be a lawyer, an airline pilot and a college professor in order to make money and live an extravagant lifestyle.
Having run out of money, he began ...
(P) Since he had no qualifications for any of these jobs, he created fake certificates.
(P) What's more, he used false identities and cashed over $2.5 million dollars with fake cheques before the age of 21.
Despite his criminal activity, he was a charming and charismatic character and his story was made into a film, *Catch Me If You Can*, in 2002.
(P) He was finally arrested and sentenced to twelve years in prison, but spent very little time in jail, because instead he spent most of his sentence helping the FBI to catch similar criminals.

UNIT 9c Exercise 9, page 110

Student C

Read these facts. The underlined words give a clue.

1 Fact: In the US civil war, General John Sedgwick said to his soldiers, 'Don't worry. The enemy couldn't hit an elephant at this distance.' However, …
Irony: He was shot by an enemy bullet.
2 Fact: Alexander Bell worked hard at creating new inventions. He came up with the telephone, for example. But he refused to have one in his own study because …
Irony: He said that it got in the way of his work.

UNIT 9d Exercise 6, page 112

Student A

Studies have shown that high temperatures can have the effect of making people more aggressive. Many of the riots and violent protests that have taken place in the northern hemisphere in the past 60 years have occurred in warm or hot weather. In the UK, summer riots took place in 1981 and 2011. In France, the student riots of 1968 took place in May, and the particularly hot summer of 1967 sparked a series of protests across the USA. The worst of these was the five-day riot in Detroit which resulted in 7,300 arrests, and property damage of $60 million.

UNIT 9d Exercise 6, page 112

Student B

The Stradivarius is the world's most famous violin because it produces a quality of sound that no other violinmaker has managed to create. For years, musicians and scientists have suggested different reasons for what makes these instruments so special: the varnish that Stradivari used, the shape of the violin. But recently, two scientists, Henri Grissino-Mayer and Lloyd Burckle have said that the secret is in the quality of the wood that Stradivari used. They claim that the drop in temperatures during the period that the violins were made (17th and 18th centuries), known as the Little Ice Age, changed the nature of the wood in the trees and produced a wood for violins that was exceptional and has not been seen since.

UNIT 11b Exercise 13, page 133

1 The bat costs $1.05. If you got the puzzle wrong (most people say $1.00), don't be discouraged – so did more than 50 per cent of students at Harvard, MIT and Princeton. $1.00 is the intuitive, but incorrect answer.
2 Most answer yes, but according to probability it should be an equal number of yes and no. The point of the first puzzle is a lesson to stop and think before giving a quick answer. The point of the second puzzle is that we are influenced by more than just simple logic. We already have the disappointment of losing $30, but we don't want the added disappointment of not seeing the show.

GRAMMAR SUMMARY UNIT 1

Time phrases

There are particular time words and phrases that we often use with each different tense.

Tense	Time phrases
present simple I **often read** books about history.	often, never, every week/month/year, nowadays, generally
present continuous I'**m currently working** in South America.	now, at the moment, while, currently, this week/summer/year
past simple I **saw** Jack **three days ago**.	three days ago, a few years ago, last week, at the time, in (+ year), once, when
past continuous I once visited Berlin. I **was living** in Germany **at the time**.	while, at the time
present perfect simple I'm quite fit because I'**ve been working** out a lot **recently**.	just, recently, so far, in recent years, over the last two years, how long, for, since (2010 / I left school), already, yet, ever, never
present perfect continuous I'**ve recently started** to learn to play the piano.	how long, for, just, recently, since (2010 / I left school), for some time
past perfect simple and continuous They asked me to dinner but I'**d already eaten**.	already, before that / the 1990s, up to then, prior to the 1990s
will, going to, present continuous (for future) **In the long term**, I believe the plans **will fail**.	next week, in three days / in three days' time, soon, in the long term, from now on, on Friday

Note that some time words and phrases can be used with more than one tense.

I was four **when** Nelson Mandela was released from prison.
The Prime Minister will make an announcement **when** she arrives back in the country.
I lived in Mexico City **for** five years.
I've been living in Mexico City **for** five years.

▶ Exercises 1, 2 and 3

The continuous aspect

We use the continuous aspect to describe actions that happen over a period of time. They are often temporary or incomplete, and in some cases are repeated. We don't normally use the continuous aspect with stative verbs (e.g. *belong*, *prefer* and *seem*).

Does this jacket belong to you? (not ~~Is this jacket belonging to you?~~)

We use the present continuous to describe:

- an action in progress at the time of speaking
  I'**m** just **finishing** some work – I'll call you back later.

- an action around the time of speaking
  Laura's **looking** for a new job.

- a current trend
  More and more people **are doing** voluntary work.

- a situation which happens regularly and is irritating, especially with the adverb *always*
  My boss **is always asking** me to stay late after work.

We use the present perfect continuous to talk about:

- an action that started in the past and is still continuing
  I'**ve been waiting** here for over an hour.

- an action that was repeated in the past and continues to be repeated now
  We'**ve been going** to that theatre for over ten years.

- a continuous past action that has an effect on the present
  I'm hot because I'**ve been running**.

We use the past continuous to describe an action that was the background to another more important event in the past. The background action may continue after the more important event, or be interrupted by it.

She **was working** as a teacher when her book was published.

We don't normally use the past continuous to describe repeated past actions. Use past simple, *used to* or *would*.

When I was ten, I **used to play** football almost every day. (not ~~I was playing~~)

We use the past perfect continuous to talk about:

- something that was in progress up to a point in the past
  She'**d been hoping** to move abroad for years when the offer came.

- an action that was repeated up to a point in the past
  We'**d been complaining** about the problem for days but nobody wanted to help us.

We use the future continuous to describe:

- something we expect to be happening at a particular time in the future
  This time next week, we'**ll be lying** on the beach!

- something we expect to be repeated around a particular time in the future
  I don't work on Thursday evenings any more, so I'**ll be coming** to football practice every week.

We also use the future continuous to make a guess or prediction about an action in progress now.
Colin **will** probably **be driving** to work now.

▶ Exercises 4, 5 and 6

Exercises

1 Choose the correct time word or phrase(s) to complete the sentences. Sometimes two words or phrases are correct.

1 People *often / at the time / sometimes* like to read on trains and buses on their way to work.
2 My home town has completely changed *when / since / for* I was a little girl.
3 He's moving house *next month / soon / recently*.
4 Henry bought a flat when he was thirty-five. He'd been living with his parents *already / up to then / in the long term*.
5 The course is going to start late *last week / next week / before that*.
6 The two companies are *currently / recently / soon* trying to negotiate a deal.

2 Complete the sentences with the correct tense of the verbs in brackets. Use the time phrases to help.

1 So you're learning Japanese! How long _____ it? (you / study)
2 She _____ a new computer when the sales start in two days' time. (buy)
3 Finding a secure job _____ harder for young people in recent years. (become)
4 The film _____ already _____ when they arrived at the cinema. (start)
5 I _____ at the moment so I'll have to call you back. (drive)
6 She found somebody's wallet on the pavement while she _____ to work. (walk)

3 Complete the text with these words and phrases.

| currently | from now on | in the long term |
| nowadays | recently | up till then |

My son is ¹_____ doing a project at school about changes in the last seventy years. I couldn't answer his questions, so I suggested that he ask his grandparents. ²_____, my son had just been using the internet. Afterwards I started to think about it more. ³_____, we get most of our information from the internet, not from speaking to other people. ⁴_____, I've been doing some DIY at home and I always search the internet for instructions. We don't ask other people for advice as much as we used to. ⁵_____, I think we'll lose a lot of knowledge if we carry on like this. ⁶_____, I'm going to encourage my children to talk to their grandparents as much as possible.

4 Read the sentences. Then choose the correct explanation (a or b) for each one.

1 Joe's always calling me to talk about his girlfriend.
   a I enjoy his phone calls.
   b I find his phone calls annoying.
2 More and more young people are staying in education for longer.
   a The situation described is changing.
   b The situation described hasn't changed for a long time.
3 I didn't go to the cinema because I was studying.
   a I was studying at one particular time.
   b I was studying every day.
4 They've been living in Russia for six years.
   a They still live in Russia.
   b They don't live in Russia any more.
5 Jennifer will be working from home on Thursday afternoon.
   a She does this every Thursday.
   b I'm just talking about Thursday this week.

5 Choose the correct words to complete the sentences.

1 I can't meet you at the same time next week as I *'ll be doing / 'll do* an exam.
2 My sister *is always / had always been* borrowing my clothes without asking me!
3 More and more people *were / are* becoming vegetarians these days.
4 He *hasn't been / wasn't* attending his lessons for the last few months.
5 They *had been / have been* driving for hours when they decided to stop for a break.
6 Sorry, I *was having / have been having* a shower when you called me.
7 A: Has Tina woken up yet?
   B: No, she *is still / has still been* sleeping.
8 A: Why are you so dirty?
   B: I've *been cleaning / cleaned* out the garage.

6 Complete the conversation with the correct form of the verbs in brackets. Use a continuous form when possible.

A: What's all that noise? Is that the workmen?
B: Yes. They ¹_____ (build) a new community centre at the end of our road.
A: How long ²_____ they _____ it for? (do)
B: For six months. They said it would be finished by now, but I think they ³_____ still _____ on it this time next year! (work) But we need something like that here. I ⁴_____ (live) on this street for ten years but I only say hello to a few people I ⁵_____ (know) since I first moved here.
A: Well, more and more people ⁶_____ (move) to big cities so you're less likely to know your neighbours. The other day I ⁷_____ (walk) down my street and I saw a neighbour on his way to work. I said hello but he was in such a rush that he just walked past me!

GRAMMAR SUMMARY UNIT 2

Perfect forms

Perfect verb forms link two periods of time. We use them to look back at an event that has an impact on a later time. They can be used in the active or passive.

We use the **present perfect simple** to describe:

- a completed event or action that might be repeated or continued and has a present connection
  *Carlo **has broken** his arm and won't be able to come to work for a week.* (= Carlo can't come to work now because of his broken arm.)

- a situation or state that started in the past and is not finished
  *I**'ve** always **loved** working as a doctor.* (= I still love it now.)

We don't use the present perfect with a finished time period. We use the past simple instead.
  *We **had** a really good time last night.* (not *We've had*)

We use the **present perfect continuous** to describe:

- a continuous completed action that has a present connection
  *Sara **has been studying** all day so she's really tired.* (= She's tired now because she studied for so long.)

- an event or action that started in the past and is not finished
  *We**'ve been living** here for five years.* (= We still live here.)

We don't use the continuous aspect with stative verbs.
  *I**'ve owned** my car for ten years so I think it's time to buy a new one.* (not *I've been owning*)

We use the **past perfect simple** (*had* + past participle):

- to describe a completed action before another action in the past
  *By the time we got to the station, the train **had** already **left**.*

- in a narrative, to talk about an action that happened before the main events of a story
  *I'd always **wanted** to visit Australia, so when I saw the competition in the newspaper, I decided to enter.*

There is a **past perfect continuous** form (*had + been + -ing*):
  *They**'d been searching** for gold for six months before they found any.*

We use the **future perfect simple** (*will + have + -ing*) to describe a completed event or action at a point in the future.
  *Call me at six thirty – I**'ll have finished** work by then.*

There is a **future perfect continuous** form (*will + have been + -ing*):
  *I**'ll have been learning** to play tennis for a year in May.*

▶ Exercises 1, 2 and 3

Passive forms

We form the passive with a form of the verb *be* + the past participle of the verb.

We can form the passive in any tense, although we do not normally use it with present perfect continuous and past perfect continuous.
  *Over 10,000 calls **are made** to the police every day.*
  *Three cars **were stolen** in our neighbourhood last week.* (past simple)
  *A new hospital **is being built** near here.*
  *When I opened the parcel, I saw that contents **had been damaged**.*
  *The safety rules **were being explained** to us when the fire alarm went off.*
  *The diamond **has been kept** locked away for fifty years.*

The passive can be used with modal verbs, and there are also gerund and infinitive forms.
  *The work should **be completed** by next week.*
  *I hate **being woken up** in the middle of the night.*
  *She hopes **to be promoted** this year.*

In informal English, we also form the passive with *get* instead of *be*. We don't normally use *get* in present perfect simple or future perfect simple passives, and we only use it to describe actions, not states.
  *Sorry I'm late – I **got delayed** in the traffic.*
  *What time does lunch **get served** in the canteen?*

When we use the active form of a verb, the focus of the sentence is on the 'agent' – the person or thing that does an action. When we use the passive form, the object of the active sentence becomes the subject and the focus changes.
                              OBJECT
  A team of authors wrote <u>this book</u>. (focus on agent)
  SUBJECT
  *<u>This book</u> **was written** by a team of authors.* (focus on 'this book')

We often use the passive:

- when the agent is obvious, unknown or not important
  *Your essays **will be returned** to you next month.*
  *Because of the snow, drivers **were asked** to avoid all unnecessary journeys.*

- when we are following a series of actions that happen to the same subject
  *La Gioconda is one of the most famous paintings in the world. It **was painted** in the 16th century by Leonardo da Vinci and **has been displayed** in the Louvre museum in Paris since 1797.*

We also use the passive when we want to give extra emphasis to the agent. We do this by using the passive, and putting the agent at the end of the sentence (after the preposition *by*).
  *The child was rescued **by the fire service**.*

▶ Exercises 4, 5 and 6

158

Exercises

1 Correct the mistake in each sentence.
1. I was a hairdresser since 2005. *I have been*
2. He hasn't been on holiday last year. *He didn't go*
3. We don't need to go to the station because her train won't be arrived yet. *won't have arrived yet*
4. I've been having this car for a long time. *I've had*
5. She couldn't pay for our coffees because she'd leave her wallet at home. *left*
6. I'm wearing glasses since I was child. *I have been*
7. Last week was the first time I saw Marion since we were students. *I've seen*

2 Complete the sentences with the correct perfect form of the verb in brackets.
1. I'm really hungry! I _____ since this morning. (not eat)
2. We didn't want to watch the film because we _____ already _____ it. (see)
3. How long _____ at this company? (you work)
4. I think by the year 2050, a lot of animals _____ extinct. (become)
5. I _____ Ella for two years. (know)
6. She arrived late but luckily the lesson _____ yet. (not start)

3 Complete the text with the correct form of the verbs in brackets. Sometimes you do NOT need a perfect form.

I ¹_____ (live) on a boat for fifteen years now, and I love it. Before moving to London, I ²_____ (not live) on a boat before, so when I first ³_____ (tell) people about my plan to live on the River Thames, they thought I was crazy. When I arrived in London, I realized I ⁴_____ (cannot) afford a normal flat, so I decided to buy a boat, and I ⁵_____ (be) here ever since. The best thing about living like this is that you see a different side to London – one that's closer to nature. However, I don't have much storage space so I ⁶_____ (be able to) buy a lot of things since I moved here. In fact, I'm hoping that by the end of this year, I ⁷_____ (save) enough money to buy a bigger boat.

4 Rewrite the sentences using the passive.
1. The prime minister announced the tax increase.
   The tax increase _____ by the prime minister.
2. The local council are building a new bridge.
   A new bridge _____ by the local council.
3. You must finish this report by the end of the day.
   This report _____ by the end of the day.
4. The manager has cancelled the football match because the pitch is flooded.
   The football match _____ because the pitch is flooded.
5. The speaker will give the lecture in French.
   The lecture _____ in French.
6. The other guests had eaten all the food by the time we arrived.
   All the food _____ by the time we arrived.
7. You need to pass the written theory test first.
   The written theory test _____ first.

5 Complete the conversation with the active or passive form of the verbs in brackets. Use *get* where possible.

A: Did you see that documentary about dangerous jobs? I never ¹_____ (know) cutting down trees was so dangerous! Every year, a lot of loggers – they're the people who cut down trees – ²_____ (kill) by falling trees or by the equipment they are using.
B: I wonder if they ³_____ (tell) about the dangers before they start working.
A: Well, I expect they must know. But why does anyone choose to do it if it's so dangerous?!
B: Maybe they ⁴_____ (like) working outdoors and they ⁵_____ (pay) well. Which other jobs were mentioned?
A: Fishermen! Especially the ones that fish for crabs. Apparently, crabs can only ⁶_____ (catch) during winter in places like Alaska. So the water is really cold and people can die from hypothermia if they ⁷_____ (hit) by heavy equipment and fall into the water. They said that they ⁸_____ (earn) a lot of money, but I'm happy working in an office!

6 Rewrite the sentences using the passive to emphasize the agent.
1. A teenager from our street broke into our car.
   _____.
2. Dr Taylor can't see you today.
   _____ today.
3. Astronomers have discovered a new planet.
   _____.
4. A fast food company is going to buy the old cinema.
   _____.
5. He got lost because the app on his phone didn't give him the right directions.
   He got lost because _____.
6. Our actions are destroying the environment.
   _____.

159

GRAMMAR SUMMARY UNIT 3

Qualifiers

We use qualifiers such as *quite*, *pretty* and *rather* to make adjectives and verbs less strong.

Qualifier + adjective

We use *quite*, *pretty* and *fairly* before adjectives to make them less strong. We use them with both positive and negative adjectives, but it is most common to use them with positive adjectives.

*It's a **fairly** interesting city to visit, but I wouldn't spend more than a day there.*
*I thought the film was **quite** good, but not great.*

When we use *quite* with *a/an* + adjective + noun, we normally place it **before** the article.

*We had **quite a good trip** but the weather was disappointing.*

We also use *quite* in the phrases 'quite a lot' and 'quite a few' to talk about an amount or number when we want to be vague.

Rather has a similar meaning to *quite*, but it is slightly stronger. We can place it before the indefinite article, like *quite*, or after it.

*I waited **rather a long time** for the bus to arrive.*
*There's **a rather nice** restaurant by the river.*

We use *not very* and *not particularly* before adjectives to give them the opposite meaning.

*It was**n't very** difficult.* (= It was easy.)
*They were**n't particularly** impressed.* (= They were unimpressed.)

▶ Exercise 1

Qualifier + verb

We use *quite* before the verbs *like*, *enjoy*, *understand* and *agree*. We often use *quite* to mean 'a bit':

*I **quite** enjoyed the film.* (= But I've seen much better films.)

We can use *quite* before the verbs *understand* and *agree* to mean 'completely'.

*I **quite** agree with you.* (= I completely agree.)
*He didn't **quite** understand what to do.* (= He didn't completely understand.)

However, we also use *quite* + verb when we are disagreeing with someone or to show surprise. In this case it doesn't change the meaning or strength of the verb.

A: I thought the food here wouldn't be very good but actually it's OK.
B: Yes, I'm **quite** enjoying it. (= I'm enjoying it.)
A: I really don't like this kind of music?
B: Really? I **quite** like it. (= I like it.)

We use *rather* in this way before the verbs *like*, *enjoy* and *hope*.

*Our hotel had received very bad reviews online, but we **rather** enjoyed it.*

We use *not particularly* before *like*, *enjoy* and *hope* to give them the opposite meaning.

*We did**n't particularly like** what she cooked for us.*
(= We disliked what she cooked for us.)

We also use *slightly*, *a little*, *a bit* and *rather* after verbs to mean 'a bit'.

*I'm going off rock music **slightly** now that I'm getting older.*
*He annoys me **a little** with his constant moaning.*
*She cooks **a bit** but her husband usually prepares the meals.*

▶ Exercises 2 and 3

Intensifying adverbs

We use intensifying adverbs before adjectives to make them stronger.

*When I got my exam result, I felt **extremely** relieved.*

The choice of intensifying adverb depends on whether the adjective is gradable or ungradable. Most adjectives, e.g. *cold*, *surprising*, are gradable. This means we can make them stronger or weaker with adverbs like *very*, *a bit*, *incredibly*, *really* or *extremely*.

*I'm **a bit** / **very** / **extremely** cold.*
*The new flats they're building look **incredibly small**.*

Other adjectives, e.g. *freezing*, *amazing* are ungradable. We cannot make them stronger or weaker in this way. Adjectives like *freezing*, *essential* and *amazing* already contain the idea of 'very' in their meaning. We use *absolutely*, *really* and *utterly* with ungradable adjectives.

*It's **very cold** today. = It's **freezing** today.* (freezing = very cold)
*I like Jann's new house, but it's got an **absolutely tiny** garden.*

Ungradable adjectives can also be 'absolute' adjectives. Adjectives like this do not have a comparative or superlative form, e.g. *right*, *wrong*, *unique* and *true*. With absolute adjectives, we use the intensifying adverbs *completely*, *entirely* and *totally*.

*I'm not going to pay them until all the work is **totally finished**.*

We can use the adverb *quite* with ungradable adjectives, including absolute adjectives. When we do this, the meaning is 'very'.

*I'm **quite** interested in that period of history.* (quite = a bit)
*I think this painting is **quite** stunning.* (quite = really)

Often, the choice of adverb and adjective combination is a question of collocation. For example, we prefer to say 'absolutely freezing' rather than 'utterly freezing', even though both are grammatically correct. There are also some exceptions, for example, we sometimes say *very/really different* (even though 'different' is an absolute adjective).

▶ Exercises 4, 5 and 6

Exercises

1 Choose the correct option to complete the sentences. In one case, both options are correct.

1. The food in that restaurant *wasn't very good / was quite good*. I won't be going there again.
2. There's *quite a / a quite* big queue in that shop. Let's go somewhere else.
3. This car *is quite / isn't particularly* cheap. We should buy it.
4. It was *a fairly / fairly a* difficult test.
5. She's had *rather a / a rather* relaxing day.
6. He'd had *pretty a / a pretty* tiring day so he decided to go straight home.

2 Read the sentences. Then choose the best explanation (a–b) for each one.

1. I quite agree with what you're saying.
   a. I agree with everything.
   b. I only agree with a few things.
2. It was freezing this morning but the weather's improving a little now.
   a. The weather is much better now.
   b. The weather is slightly better now.
3. Martina: I hate this kind of music.
   Isabella: Really? I quite like it.
   a. Isabella only likes this kind of music a little.
   b. Isabella enjoys this kind of music.
4. I don't particularly enjoy this kind of food.
   a. I dislike this kind of food.
   b. I sometimes enjoy this kind of food.
5. I rather hoped that the party would be cancelled because I'm so tired.
   a. This was my wish.
   b. I only hoped this a little bit.

3 Complete the texts with the qualifiers given. Sometimes more than one answer is possible.

| fairly | not particularly | quite | rather |

I grew up in the countryside in Poland. I suppose it was ¹ _____ a nice place to grow up – there weren't many people in the village but I had a ² _____ big group of friends and we always played a lot outside. But it was ³ _____ exciting and I used to dream about living in a big city. But now I live in one, I think I'd ⁴ _____ enjoy living in the countryside again!

| not very | pretty | slightly |

My home town is a ⁵ _____ big place, but it's not huge. It's very close to London but this means the facilities are ⁶ _____ limited because most people go to London for entertainment and shopping. It's ⁷ _____ cheap to live there, because it's so close to the city.

4 Correct the mistake in each sentence. Not all the sentences contain an error.

1. It's very freezing outside today.
2. This room is incredibly small.
3. I was utterly surprised to see Matt at the party last night.
4. I found the exam really difficult.
5. It's absolutely important that you listen to the safety instructions.
6. We've just watched an extremely amazing film!
7. You're utterly right. We needed to turn left after the traffic lights.

5 Complete the sentences with these adjectives.

| cold | exhausted | freezing | small | stunning |
| stylish | tiny | tired |

1. You should put a coat on. It's absolutely _____ outside.
2. Silvia's extremely _____ and wants to stay at home and rest.
3. That's a very _____ necklace you're wearing. It looks great on you.
4. Our hotel room is absolutely _____! I'm going to ask for a bigger one.
5. It was a very _____ winter and most of the plants died.
6. The views from the tower are quite _____. You should take a camera when you go.
7. I felt utterly _____ yesterday after our long run.
8. They've just bought a very _____ flat in the city centre. They don't have much space for furniture.

6 Choose the best options to complete the conversation.

A: How was your weekend?
B: Not great. We were flat hunting! It was ¹ *very / absolutely* frustrating because the estate agent made the flats sound ² *really / very* amazing but when we looked at them, they weren't what we'd been promised.
A: Oh no! How many flats did you look at?
B: Five. The first two were in a nice area but were ³ *utterly / incredibly* small! I just couldn't live in them! Then we saw another small flat in the town centre but it was on a ⁴ *very / totally* busy road, and I didn't like that. The fourth flat was in an ⁵ *extremely / absolutely* terrible state! We'd have to do a lot of work on it.
A: So what about the fifth one?
B: It was great – new and modern, in a lovely neighbourhood. And it has a(n) ⁶ *incredibly / very* huge garden.
A: But …
B: Well, it was ⁷ *completely / extremely* expensive, so we can't really afford it.

161

GRAMMAR SUMMARY UNIT 4

Future probability

Modal verbs

We use the modal verbs *may*, *could*, *might* to say that something is possible in the future (about a 50% chance).

*In the future, we **may** / **might** / **could** find solutions to many environmental problems.*

We can add the adverb *well* after *may* / *could* / *might* to make the event sound more probable.

*Driverless cars **may** / **could** / **might well** become available sooner than people expect.*

To say that it is possible that something will not happen in the future, we use *may not* or *might not*.

*They **may** / **might not** be able to fix the problem.*

We use *should* or *shouldn't* to say that something is probable in the future (about a 70% chance).

*We **should** arrive before 7 p.m. if there is no traffic.*

We don't use *should* to talk about something bad that we think will happen.

*I think climate change **will** be a disaster for many countries.* (not *I think climate change should be*)

Adverbs

We use *perhaps* and *maybe* to say something is possible (a 50% chance). We normally put *perhaps* and *maybe* before the subject.

Perhaps / ***Maybe*** *the weather will improve tomorrow.*

We use *probably* (*not*) to say something is probable (a 70% chance). We normally put *probably* between *will* and the main verb.

*Shin will **probably** arrive late again.*

We use *almost certainly* (*not*) when we are almost certain that something will happen (a 90% chance). We put *almost certainly* between *will* and the main verb.

*There will **almost certainly** be an election this year.*

Adjective phrases

We use the adjectives *possible*, *probable*, *likely* and *unlikely* in the structure *it's* + adjective + *that* + clause.

*It's **possible that** we will create colonies on Mars this century.* (about 50% certainty)
*Unfortunately, it's **probable** / **likely** that there will be a delay with your order.* (about 70% certainty)
*In my opinion, it's **unlikely that** the new plans will cut traffic in the city centre.* (about 20% certainty)

We also use *likely* and *unlikely* with a subject and *to* + infinitive.

*The journey is **likely to take** over ten hours.*
*The work is **unlikely to be finished** today.*

Noun phrases

We use some noun phrases + *be* + (*that*) + clause to say something is probable in the future (a 70% chance).

*The **likelihood is that** he will leave the company.*
*The **chances are (that)** they'll offer me a promotion.*
*There's a **good chance (that)** our team will win.*

Note that when we use 'there's a good chance that', the future event isn't necessarily something good.

There's a good chance that it will rain later.

▶ Exercises 1, 2 and 3

Past modals

To talk about **past obligation** we use *had to*. We cannot use *must* to refer to past obligation.

*Yesterday, I **had to** be at work at 7 a.m.*

For negative past obligation we use *couldn't*, *wasn't* / *weren't allowed to*.

*We **couldn't** leave the room during the exam.*
*Women in the USA **were not allowed to** vote until 1920.*

To talk about a lack of necessity in the past, we use *needn't have* + past participle or *didn't need to* + infinitive. This means the action happened but wasn't necessary.

*I **needn't have gone** to the meeting.*
*You **didn't need to cook** dinner.*

We can use *didn't need to* or *didn't have to*, but not *needn't have*, when the unnecessary action in the past didn't occur.

*We went by train so we **didn't need to find** somewhere to park.*

▶ Exercise 4

To speculate on past events (to make deductions or guesses about them), we use *must have*, *might* / *may* / *could have* and *can't* / *couldn't have* + past participle.

*Luke **must have had** to stay late at work – he's normally home by now.* (= I think it's probable that he had to stay late at work.)
*I **may** / **might** / **could have got** a few questions wrong in the exam.* (= I think it's possible that I got a few questions wrong.)
*They **can't have got** lost – they've been here lots of times!* (= I think it isn't probable that they got lost.)
*A: Did Joan just drive by? B: No, it **couldn't have been** her. She drives a much bigger car.*

We also use *could have* when we know that something didn't happen but we want to say it was possible.

*Why were you so careless? You **could have been** killed!*

We use *should(n't) have* + past participle when:

- we think something was advisable but didn't happen, or was inadvisable but did happen
  *You **should have called** me as soon as you knew you were going to be late.*
  *I **shouldn't have gone** to the job interview in a T-shirt.*

- we expect that something happened in the past, but we're not sure if it did
  *Luca's train **should have arrived** by now.*

We use *ought to have* + past participle when we think something was advisable but didn't happen. It is more formal than *should have*.

*We **ought to have** booked seats.*

▶ Exercises 5 and 6

162

Exercises

1 Choose the correct option to complete the sentences.

1 Matt said he *might / will / is likely to* come to the football game with us tonight but he's not sure.
2 We *probably won't / won't probably / maybe won't* know the results of the election till tomorrow.
3 In ten years, we *couldn't / may not / shouldn't* be using smartphones any more.
4 It's *likely / possible / probably* that the heating system will have to be replaced soon. It's broken down three times already this month.
5 Philip and Ruth *might / should / could* be here at 8.00 p.m. They set off at 7.30 p.m. and the journey takes half an hour.
6 There's *almost certainly / maybe / a good chance* that your flight will be delayed.

2 Rewrite the sentences so they have the same meaning. Use the words in brackets.

1 It's very probable that our train will be late today. (chance)
   _____ today.
2 He might well not come to our party this evening. (probably)
   _____ this evening.
3 In the future we might all be driving electric cars. (perhaps)
   _____ in the future.
4 Space travel will probably be a lot cheaper in the future. (likely)
   _____ in the future.
5 The government might raise interest rates this year. (possible)
   _____ this year.

3 Complete the text with these words and phrases.

| almost certainly | certainly | chances | could |
| possible | should | unlikely | |

Air pollution causes millions of premature deaths throughout the world every year, and this number will ¹_____ increase in the future. As a result, we ²_____ start to see more interesting solutions for this problem. One idea to deal with pollution is Daan Roosegaarde's 'Smog Free Tower' – a tower that sucks in polluted air and blows out clean air. Roosegaarde believes that in the future, towers like this ³_____ be used to improve the air quality in polluted cities. Roosegaarde says it's ⁴_____ to build 'Smog Free Towers' the size of buildings, for an even bigger impact. Although the towers are ⁵_____ to solve the problem of air pollution completely, the ⁶_____ are that we will need to develop many innovative ideas to keep pollution under control.

4 Choose the correct option to complete the sentences. Sometimes both options are possible.

1 I was late to work this morning because I *had to / must* stop for petrol.
2 They *didn't have to / weren't allowed to* pay to enter the museum because it was free.
3 Thank you for the flowers! You *didn't have to buy / needn't have bought* me anything!
4 I *needn't have worn / didn't need to wear* this jumper. It's so hot today!
5 We *didn't have to / weren't allowed to* speak during the exam.
6 She *didn't need to go / needn't have gone* to work so she spent the day relaxing in her garden.

5 Complete the conversation with these modal forms.

| could have | couldn't have | might not have |
| must have | should have | shouldn't have |

A: I'm so tired! Some friends came for dinner last night. I spent all day cooking, and then they didn't leave until 2 a.m.! It's my fault – I ¹_____ invited them to come during the week. It's better to invite friends round at the weekend.
B: Oh dear! You ²_____ just got a takeaway!
A: Oh, I ³_____ done that! But you know, I'm sure I ⁴_____ spent an hour just cutting up vegetables!
B: You should buy a food processor. I've got one that cuts up vegetables really quickly. I ⁵_____ lent it to you!
A: It's a good thing you didn't. You ⁶_____ ever got it back from me!

6 Complete the conversations with *must*, *can('t)*, *could(n't)*, *might(n't)*, *should(n't)* and *ought (not)* and the correct form of these verbs. You don't need to use all the modal forms.

| buy | drive | eat | leave | open | see |

1 Maia _____ to work. Her car is still outside her house.
2 I have a stomach ache. I _____ so much food earlier!
3 Oh no! We've missed our train. I told you we _____ the house earlier!
4 I thought I just saw Steve, but I _____ somebody who looks like him because Steve's on holiday in Peru.
5 I can't remember where I got this dress. I _____ it from that new shop on the High Street.
6 The bank _____ by now. It's 9.15 and it opens at 8.30.

163

GRAMMAR SUMMARY UNIT 5

Emphatic structures

We use various sentence structures to make a sentence more emphatic or to give emphasis to a certain part of a sentence.

Cleft sentences

A cleft sentence emphasizes a particular part of a sentence by splitting it into two parts. There are two patterns.

We use *it + be + emphasized phrase + that* to emphasize the subject, object or an adverbial phrase. The information we want to emphasize comes at the beginning of the sentence, after *be*.

> In Thailand, the beaches are the most popular places to visit. → In Thailand, **it's the beaches that** are the most popular places to visit. (emphasizing subject)
>
> I most want to see Mexico City. → **It's Mexico City that** I most want to see. (emphasizing object)
>
> Most people go to Greece in summer. → **It's in summer that** most people go to Greece. (emphasizing adverbial phrase)

Note that we can use a relative pronoun instead of 'that'.

> It's Jenny that/who I want to see.

We use *what* or *the thing (that) + subject + verb + be* to emphasize a subject, object, a clause with *that* or a clause with a *wh-* word. The information we want to emphasize comes at the end of the sentence, after *be*.

> I hate airports most. → **The thing that I hate most is** airports. (emphasizing the object)
>
> We need to decide which dates we can travel on. → **What we need to decide is** which dates we can travel on. (emphasizing a *wh-* clause)
>
> I hope that our train isn't delayed. → **What I hope is** that our train isn't delayed. (emphasizing a clause with *that*)

We can also emphasize a whole clause with *what + subject + verb + to do + be + (to) + infinitive*.

> My country needs to invest in tourism. → **What my country needs to do is (to)** invest in tourism.

▶ Exercises 1 and 2

do, does, did in affirmative sentences

We can add a form of *do* to affirmative sentences to add emphasis. We always stress the form of *do*.

> We hope you enjoy your stay with us. → We **do** hope you enjoy your stay with us.

We don't add *do* when a sentence already contains an auxiliary (*be* or *have*) or a modal verb. In this case, we just stress the auxiliary to add emphasis.

> We <u>have</u> enjoyed our trip.
> The train service <u>can</u> be rather unreliable.
> He <u>is</u> rude sometimes. (We use the full form, not the contraction.)

▶ Exercise 3

Avoiding repetition

We can use synonyms, e.g. *loss – defeat*, or words such as *one, that, it, so* and ellipsis (leaving out words) to avoid repetition.

one, that, it, so

We use *one* in place of a singular countable noun and *ones* in place of a plural countable noun.

> Which top do you prefer? The blue **one** or the red one?
> Here are your shoes. Are these the **ones** you wanted?

When we use an adjective before *one*, we always use the indefinite article or another determiner.

> A: This hotel's great! B: I know! And just think that you wanted to book **that** cheap **one**!

We always add an adjective when we use *ones* after numbers or determiners.

> A: Did you bring any biscuits? B: Yes, I brought **some chocolate ones** and **some plain ones**.

We use *that* to replace a phrase, clause or sentence.

> A: Ask Juan to come at 8 o'clock. B: I've already asked him **that**. (*that* = 'to come at 8 o'clock')
> A: Why don't we get a takeaway tonight? B: **That**'s a great idea. (*that* = 'get a takeaway')

We use *it* to replace a noun phrase.

> Has anyone seen <u>my bag</u>? **It**'s not where I left **it**.

We use *so* after verbs like *say, think, hope* and *expect* to replace a clause, especially a short answer.

> A: Is it going to rain today?
> B: I think **so**. (*so* = 'it's going to rain today')

▶ Exercise 4

Ellipsis

Sometimes we omit words to avoid repetition, when the context is clear which words we have omitted. We can omit words:

- when we have two verbs together, and the second verb is a *to + infinitive* form. In this case, we can omit everything after *to*.
  A: Why don't we just book a beach holiday? B: **I don't want to** [book a beach holiday]. I hate the beach!

- after verbs and phrases like *hope, suppose* and *be afraid*, when what comes after is negative. In this case, we omit everything apart from *not*.
  A: Do you think we're going to miss the flight? B: I **hope not**. (= I hope that we don't miss the flight.)

We can also omit a whole clause after a subject and auxiliary or modal verb.

> I've never been to Asia, and most of my friends haven't either. (= Most of my friends haven't been to Asia.)
> Most of my friends can speak Spanish, but I can't.

When the clause that we are replacing contains a verb in the present or past simple, we use a form of *do*.

> Magda wanted to spend the day hiking but we **didn't**. (= We didn't want to spend the day hiking.)

▶ Exercise 5

Exercises

1 Rewrite the sentences to emphasize the underlined word or phrase.

1. <u>Francis</u> called Ben last night.
   It _____ .
2. I'd like <u>more free time not money</u>.
   It _____ .
3. She doesn't like <u>the way her manager speaks to her</u>.
   It _____ .
4. The hotel we stayed in was expensive but <u>the flights cost us the most</u>.
   The hotel we stayed in was expensive, but it _____ .
5. The report is going to focus on <u>the reasons why the project failed</u>.
   It _____ .
6. The students find out their results <u>in January</u>.
   It _____ .

2 Rewrite the sentences to emphasize the underlined phrases.

1. In winter I hate <u>the cold weather</u>.
   The thing that _____ .
2. We forgot <u>to lock our front door</u>.
   What _____ .
3. I loved <u>being able to relax on a beach</u>.
   The thing that _____ .
4. She liked <u>the film's ending</u> the most.
   What _____ .
5. The airline won't <u>refund our tickets</u>.
   The thing that _____ .
6. You're now going to see <u>a summary of the research</u>.
   What _____ .

3 Rewrite the underlined parts of the sentences to make them more emphatic, using a form of *do*. When it is not possible to add a form of *do*, circle the word that needs to be stressed.

1. <u>I thought</u> the tourist office would be a bit more helpful. _____
2. <u>These snakes will bite</u> you if they get the chance. _____
3. <u>She seemed to be ignoring</u> everything the tour guide was saying. _____
4. <u>They have already paid</u> for their meal.
   _____
5. <u>They offered</u> to exchange the faulty item, but she wanted a refund. _____
6. <u>She works</u> in a bank, doesn't she?

4 Choose the correct (a–c) option to replace the underlined parts of the sentences.

1. Shall we go to the restaurant by the sea or <u>the restaurant</u> near the castle?
   a that   b the one   c it
2. A: Is the film festival starting this weekend?
   B: Yeah, I think <u>the film festival is starting this weekend</u>.
   a it   b that   c so
3. A: I had to wake up at 4 a.m. to get to the airport on time.
   B: <u>Waking up at 4 a.m.</u> must have been hard!
   a so   b that   c one
4. A: The suitcases you bought are too small!
   B: They were the biggest <u>suitcases</u> they had in the shop!
   a ones   b one   c it
5. A: What time does the tourist office open?
   B: I think <u>the tourist office</u> opens at 9 a.m.
   a one   b that   c it
6. A: Will there be a lot of people at the meeting?
   B: I expect <u>there will be a lot of people at the meeting</u>.
   a it   b so   c ones

5 Find six phrases in the email that can be deleted to avoid repetition.

> Hi Alex
>
> How's it going? Samira and I arrived on Koh Chang island a week ago and it's amazing! We'd thought about going to one of the busier islands but we decided not to go to one of the busier islands. And I'm glad because it's perfect here! On the day we arrived we'd arranged to go on a jungle hike but in the end we couldn't go on a jungle hike because it was raining! It's been sunny and hot since then – I've just felt like relaxing on a beach and Sally has felt like relaxing on a beach too! But now I'm getting bored. Tomorrow I'd like to go elephant trekking but Samira doesn't want to go elephant trekking. I think she's a bit scared! So instead we're going to visit a waterfall, and go snorkelling with a group of friends we've made. They've all been snorkelling before but I haven't been snorkelling before. (Have you?) I'm really looking forward to it! Sally thinks we should stay longer on the island. I'd like to stay longer on the island too, but there are so many other places to see!
>
> Hope to see you when we get back.
>
> Renata

165

GRAMMAR SUMMARY UNIT 6

Phrasal verbs

There are some verbs that are often followed by prepositions, and the preposition doesn't change the meaning of the verb.

*It is believed that chess originally **comes from** India.*

Other verb + preposition combinations have an idiomatic meaning. You cannot predict the meaning from the individual meanings of the verb and the particle.

*Can you **look after** my bag for a minute? (look after = take care of)*

Verb + adverb combinations almost always have an idiomatic meaning.

*I had to **give up** tennis after I injured my elbow. (give up = stop doing)*

Verb + adverb

Verb + adverb combinations can be transitive or intransitive. Intransitive phrasal verbs do not have an object.

*She **grew up** in Los Angeles.*

Transitive phrasal verbs are **separable phrasal verbs**. We can put the object after the adverb or before it, with no difference in meaning.

*Can you **turn the radio down**? = Can you **turn down the radio**?*

However, when the object is a pronoun, we always put it before the adverb.

*Can you **call me back** later? (not: Can you call back me later?)*

Verb + preposition

Verb + preposition combinations always have an object. They are **inseparable phrasal verbs**. We always put the object, including pronouns, after the preposition.

*It took two months for me to **get over the injury**. = It took me two months to **get over it**.*

Verb + adverb + preposition

Three-part phrasal verbs are made up of a verb + adverb + preposition. We always put an object after the preposition.

*He doesn't **get on with** some of his colleagues at work.*

A small number of three-part phrasal verbs take two objects. We put the first object after the verb, and the second object after the preposition.

*I've decided to **take you up on** the job offer.*

▶ Exercises 1, 2 and 3

Verb patterns

When we use two verbs together in a sentence, the form of the second verb depends on the first verb.

- **verb + *to* + infinitive:** (can/can't) afford, agree, allow, arrange, ask, begin, choose, continue, decide, expect, fail, help*, hope, intend, learn, manage, need, offer, plan, pretend, promise, refuse, seem, start, tend, threaten, want, would like, would love, would prefer
*I **need to finish** my work before I go to the gym.*

- **verb + object + *to* + infinitive:** ask, get, help, need, require, tell, urge, warn
*I **asked Luke to lend** me his bike.*

- **verb (+ object) + infinitive:** help, let and make (Sometimes we do not include the object.)
*They **made me do** a medical test before I could enter the race.*

- **verb + *-ing*:** adore, avoid, begin, can't help, can't stand, consider, continue, describe, enjoy, fancy, finish, imagine, involve, keep, mention, mind, miss, practise, recommend, risk, spend (time/money), start, suggest
*I **avoid running** on hard surfaces as it hurts my knees.*

- **verb + preposition + *-ing*:** e.g. carry on, worry about, succeed in
*Do you **worry about injuring** your body?*

- **verb + object + preposition + *-ing*:** e.g. discourage from, prevent from
*Injuries **prevented her from competing**.*

Verb + *-ing* or *to* + infinitive

After *start* and *continue*, we can use the *-ing* form or *to* + infinitive, with no difference in meaning. Some verbs change their meaning depending on whether we use the *-ing* form or *to* + infinitive.

*I'm starting a new job soon, which will **mean earning** a lot more money. (mean + -ing = involve)*
*I **meant to go** to the supermarket but I forgot. (mean + to + infinitive = intend)*

*Mia **regrets not doing** more sports when she was younger. (regret + -ing = feel sorry about something)*
*I **regret to inform** you I have decided to cancel my membership. (regret + to + infinitive = feel sorry that you have to tell someone about a situation)*

*Do you **remember playing** football here? (remember + -ing = have memories of an earlier event)*
*Did you **remember to call** the doctor? (remember + to + infinitive = not forget to do something)*

*She **stopped running** when her foot started to hurt. (stop + -ing = finish doing an action)*
*She **stopped to drink** some water. (stop + to + infinitive = finish an action to do another action)*

*I **tried training** late in the evening but I didn't like it. (try + -ing = do something to see what happens)*
*I **tried to call you** but your phone was switched off. (try + to + infinitive = make an effort)*

*I've never **forgotten swimming** in the lake at midnight. (forget + -ing = not having a memory of doing something in the past)*
*Sorry, I **forgot to bring** your present. (forget + to + infinitive = not remember to do something)*

▶ Exercises 4, 5 and 6

Exercises

1 Correct the mistake in each sentence.

1. Please pay back me the money you owe as soon as you can.
2. At 8.34 a.m., took the plane off.
3. He's been looking his phone for all morning but he hasn't found it yet.
4. If you're not watching the TV, can you turn off it please?
5. His teacher won't put up his bad behaviour with any longer.
6. They let in Adam on the plans for the surprise birthday party.

2 Choose the correct option to complete the sentences. Sometimes both options are correct.

1. His cousin is an expert in cars so he *turned to him / turned him to* for advice.
2. They arranged the meeting for tomorrow but now they've decided to *put it off / put off it*.
3. She *takes after her father / takes her father after*.
4. They've *fallen out their neighbours with / fallen out with their neighbours* because of the party.
5. I told them to *come over / come over our house* at around 9 p.m.
6. You should *throw away these old clothes / throw these old clothes away* if you never wear them.
7. I hadn't seen Michele for years but I *ran into her / ran her into* yesterday at the shops.
8. Can you *fill this form in / fill in this form* now?

3 Match the phrasal verbs in Exercise 2 with these meanings (a–h).

a. be similar to an older relative
b. complete
c. delay (postpone)
d. have a serious argument with
e. meet somebody by chance
f. put into the rubbish bin (dispose of)
g. visit somebody in their home
h. ask for support or help

4 Choose the correct verb form to complete the sentences.

1. Would you consider *doing / to do* a yoga course?
2. I told him *to wait / wait* for me outside the gym.
3. He tried *ringing / to ring* the door bell but no one answered.
4. The world champion has failed *finishing / to finish* the race.
5. We need to hurry up! I'm worried about *miss / missing* our train.
6. She regretted not *wearing / to wear* a warmer jacket. It was quite cold outside.
7. Rita made me *wake / to wake* up early to go for a run.
8. I remember *to watch / watching* this cartoon when I was a child. I used to love it!

5 Complete the second sentences so they mean the same as the first sentences. Use the correct form of the verbs in brackets.

1. Stefan doesn't play squash any more because of his injury. (stop)
   Stefan _____ because of his injury.
2. He said, 'I won't be late for the meeting.' (promise)
   He _____ late for the meeting.
3. I don't want to put you off doing the race, but it's very demanding. (discourage)
   I _____, but it's very demanding.
4. They said they really wanted us to decide by the end of the week. (urge)
   They _____ by the end of the week.
5. Julia allowed me to borrow her racing bike while she was away. (let)
   Julia _____ while she was away.
6. Are you sad now that you don't live by the sea? (miss)
   Do _____ by the sea?

6 Complete the conversation with these words and the correct form of the verbs in brackets. Add an object if necessary.

ask   decide   help   make   start   stop
think about

A: Guess what? I've ¹_____ (do) a marathon!
B: Wow! Where are you going to do it?
A: In Berlin. It's in September but I've ²_____ (train) already. I even have a personal trainer. She ³_____ (exercise) really hard for an hour every day!
B: I'm not exercising at all these days.
A: I thought you went to the gym every morning.
B: No, I've ⁴_____ (go). It just wasn't ⁵_____ (get) fit.
A: You should come and train with me! I often go running outdoors with my trainer. I could ⁶_____ (work) with you, too.
B: Thanks, that'd be great.
A: Have you ever ⁷_____ (do) a marathon?
B: I think I should start exercising again regularly before thinking about races!

GRAMMAR SUMMARY UNIT 7

Passive reporting verbs

We sometimes use verbs such as *believe, confirm, expect, know, report, say, think* and *understand* in the passive to report feelings, beliefs, opinions and rumours, especially in journalism or other formal contexts. We do this when we are not completely sure of the information we are giving or if we want to distance ourselves personally from it. The passive form shows that the information has been said by someone else or is something that people generally believe.

There are two patterns:

- it + passive reporting verb + that
  It is believed that around twenty smartphones are sold every second.

- subject + passive reporting verb + to + infinitive
  Over twenty smartphones **are believed to be sold** every second.

With the second pattern, we can also use perfect or continuous infinitive forms.
  *The singer is reported **to have cancelled** tonight's concert because of illness.*
  *XCom is reported **to be working** on a new laptop.*

We can also use the second pattern with *there is/are/was/were*.
  There are thought to be more than 7,000 languages around the world.

We can use the reporting verb in different tenses. The tense of the verb does not always match the time of the event which is reported.
  *It **is** thought that the first ever mobile phone call **was** made in 1973.* (= People have this belief now about an event that happened in the past.)
  *It **was** once believed that the earth **is** flat.* (= People had this belief in the past.)

We can sometimes include the agent when using passive reporting verbs. We usually do this when the agent is new or important information, for example if we are comparing it to something or someone else.
  *The painting is reported **by some news channels** to have been destroyed in the robbery.* (= by some, but not by others)

▶ Exercises 1 and 2

Nominalization

We sometimes change part of a sentence into a noun. This is called nominalization.

Verb or adjective nominalization

We can change an action into a noun by replacing the action verb with its equivalent noun, e.g. *complete → completion, announce → announcement*.
  *The camera **costs** $480. → **The cost of** the camera is $480.*

We can also make a noun phrase with the *-ing* form of a verb. In formal contexts, we often use a possessive form before the *-ing* form.
  *We had to reorganize the meeting because **they arrived** late.*
  *We had to reorganize the meeting due to **their arriving** late.*

We can also change an adjective into a noun.
  *I've been **interested** in photography for around ten years. → My **interest** in photography started around ten years ago.*

We often need to add *of* after the noun phrase we create from a noun or adjective.
  *The building work will cost over $500,000. → The cost **of** the building work will be over $500,000.*

Other types of nominalization

We can nominalize phrases beginning with *wh-* words (e.g. *why, where, when*, etc.).
  *We don't know **why the flight was delayed**. → We don't know **the reason for the delay**.*

Sometimes we use a noun that is not directly related to the verb or adjective in the phrase we are nominalizing. This may be because there is no exact equivalent noun, or because we want to vary the vocabulary we use to avoid repetition.
  *They **found** the painting in a disused cellar. → The **discovery** of the painting was made in a disused cellar.* (no direct noun equivalent of 'find')

  *The temperature of the planet **is increasing** every year because of pollution.*
  *The **rise** in the temperature of the planet is caused by pollution.* ('rise' instead of 'increase' to make writing more varied)

Uses of nominalization

We often use nominalization to be more concise, especially in writing. A nominalized form is often shorter than using a verb or adjective.
  The place where we put each painting is very important.
  → The position of each painting is very important.

We can also use nominalization to develop an argument or description. A verb, adjective or even a whole phrase can become a subject or object in the next sentence.
  *I studied Finance and Economics at the University of Berlin. **My studies** provided me with some crucial knowledge and allowed me to develop a number of skills.*

▶ Exercises 3 and 4

Exercises

1 Read the pairs of sentences. Then choose the correct option to complete second sentence.

1. Lots of people are saying that the Prime Minister has decided to resign.
   It *is / was* said that the Prime Minister has taken the decision to resign.
2. Most weather reports yesterday said it would be very hot today, but it was actually quite cool.
   The weather *is / was* expected to be hot today, but it was actually quite cool.
3. Some newspapers are suggesting that the new smartphone will only cost $240.
   It *is / is being* suggested that the new smartphone will only cost $240.
4. They told us to evacuate the building.
   We *were / are* told to evacuate the building.
5. Many people believed that the company's employees would receive compensation.
   It *is / was* believed that the company's employees would receive compensation.
6. People know that there are only a few thousand giant pandas left in the world.
   There *are / were* known to be only a few thousand giant pandas left in the world.

2 Rewrite the sentences with passive reporting verbs using both possible patterns. Use the underlined verb as the passive reporting verb.

1. People <u>say</u> that the director is working on a new film.
   The director _____ on a new film.
   It _____ on a new film.
2. We <u>know</u> that regular exercise is important.
   It _____ important.
   Regular exercise _____ important.
3. The police <u>claimed</u> that the suspect was carrying a gun.
   The suspect _____ a gun.
   It _____ a gun.
4. We <u>expect</u> the guests will have arrived by 12 p.m.
   The guests _____ by 12 p.m.
   It _____ by 12 p.m.
5. People <u>argue</u> that the mobile phone has had a big impact on our social lives.
   It _____ on our social lives.
   The mobile phone _____ on our social lives.
6. For a long time, people <u>thought</u> that bad smells caused diseases.
   For a long time, bad smells _____ diseases.
   It _____ diseases.

3 Complete the sentences with the correct nominalization of the underlined word or phrase.

1. I was <u>disappointed</u> with the bad service.
   My _____ was due to the bad service.
2. The company has <u>decided</u> to expand the business. This was good news.
   The company's _____ to expand the business was good news.
3. The earthquake <u>destroyed</u> many buildings.
   The earthquake led to the _____ of many buildings.
4. It was obvious that he was <u>suitable</u> for the job.
   His _____ for the job was obvious.
5. We need to make more people <u>aware</u> of the impact of car fumes on air quality.
   We need to raise _____ of the impact of car fumes on air quality.
6. People have been shocked by how the airline has <u>treated</u> its passengers.
   People have been shocked by the airline's _____ of its passengers.
7. People should be warned about how <u>dangerous</u> using a phone is while driving.
   People should be warned about the _____ of using a phone while driving.

4 Match the sentences (1–6 and a–f) to make sentence pairs. Then complete the sentences (a–f) with these words. There are three extra words.

ability	definition	disinterest	fear	hobbies
location	person	truthfulness	validity	

1. I'm trying to find out <u>what this word means</u>.
2. The audience <u>didn't seem very interested</u> in the presentation.
3. Tom was <u>scared</u> of flying.
4. Cathy liked <u>playing tennis and football</u>.
5. Police still don't know <u>who robbed the bank</u>.
6. The instructions described <u>where we needed to go</u>.

a. Their _____ was also obvious to the speaker.
b. But she only had time for these _____ at the weekend.
c. The _____ of the conference was in the city centre.
d. They believe the _____ they are looking for lives locally.
e. His _____ stopped him going abroad.
f. Unfortunately, the online dictionary doesn't give a clear _____ .

GRAMMAR SUMMARY UNIT 8

The adverb *just*

The adverb *just* has a variety of meanings and can appear in different positions in a sentence.

just + verb

We use *just* with a verb to mean:

- 'recently'
  *The band has **just** announced its world tour dates.*

- 'simply'
  *You **just** need to fill in this form if you want to become a member.*

- 'right at the moment'
  *They're **just** queuing up to buy their tickets. They won't be long.*

We use *just* before a main verb, and after an auxiliary verb, including modal verbs.
*Why don't we **just** go out for dinner so we don't have to cook?*
*It's **just** stopped raining.*
*You **must just** hold the jug still while I pour in the water.*

just + preposition/noun

We also use *just* to mean:

- 'a little'
  *They got to the concert hall **just** before the band came on.*

- 'only'
  *There were **just** twenty people at the show we went to last night.*

- 'exactly'
  *You look **just** like your brother in this photo.*

We put *just* before a noun or noun phrase, and before a preposition that it changes the meaning of.
*We've got **just two free tickets** we can offer you.*
*She left the restaurant **just in** time to catch the last train home.*

▶ **Exercises 1 and 2**

Expressing purpose and result

Expressing purpose

To give the reason for doing something (purpose), we use *to*, *in order (not) to* and *so as (not) to* + infinitive.
*I use these scissors **to** cut my hair.*
*They asked us to be quiet **in order not to** wake the children.*

We use *for* to describe the function or use of a thing. We can use *for* + noun or *for* + -ing.
*This staircase is **for access** to the roof terrace.*
*I've got a great app on my phone **for learning** new vocabulary.*

We can also use *so that* and *in order that* + clause (subject + verb) to give the reason for doing something. We often use *can*, *could*, *will*, *would* or *should* in the *that* clause.
*They got up early **so that** they could go for a run.*
*I've sent some directions to Mike in the New York office **in order that** he can find his way here easily when he comes.*

Note that if the subject of the main clause and the clause showing the purpose is different, we cannot use *to*, *in order to* or *so as to*. Use *so that* or *in order that* instead.

▶ **Exercise 3**

Expressing result

We use *so ... that* and *such ... that* to express the result of an action. We use:

- *so* before an adjective
  *Their music was **so good that** I decided to buy their CD.*

- *such* before a noun phrase
  *She hadn't seen me for **such** a long time **that** she didn't recognize me.*

Note that we use *such* before a noun phrase even if the noun phrase starts with an adjective.
*There has been **such terrible weather** that most flights have been cancelled.*

However, when the noun phrase begins with the determiners *much*, *many*, *little* or *few* before a noun, we use *so* rather than *such*.
*They have **so much money** that they could afford to buy whatever they wanted.*

When a noun phrase starts with the indefinite article (*a/an*), we can use an alternative pattern with *so*.
*It was **so nice a day** that we decided to eat outside.*
(= It was such a nice day that we decided to eat outside.)

▶ **Exercises 4 and 5**

170

Exercises

1 Choose the correct meaning of *just* in each sentence.

1 I'm just finishing making dinner.
   a right at the moment   b recently
2 This sounds just like an old *Rolling Stones* song.
   a a little   b exactly
3 This test was just too difficult for the students.
   a simply   b exactly
4 They've just bought a new car.
   a right at the moment   b recently
5 She's eaten just a sandwich today so she's really hungry.
   a only   b recently
6 He arrived just after 6 p.m.
   a exactly   b a little

2 Complete the sentences so they have the same meaning as the first sentences. Use *just*.

1 My new laptop cost $400 – that's not a lot.
   My new laptop _____ $400.
2 I've heard a great song. I heard it a few minutes ago.
   I _____ a great song.
3 He has a bag that looks exactly the same as mine.
   He has a bag _____ mine.
4 My manager is dealing with another client at the moment. She'll call you back.
   My manager _____. She'll call you back.
5 You need to arrive on time at the station – that's all you need to do.
   You _____ at the station.
6 It takes 1 hour 57 minutes to arrive at the nearest beach.
   It _____ hours to arrive at the nearest beach.

3 Complete the sentences using the word or words in brackets so they have the same meaning as the first sentences.

1 I called the doctor's surgery because I wanted to book an appointment. (order)
   I called the doctor's surgery _____ an appointment.
2 We left home early because we didn't want to be late for the show. (so)
   We left home early _____ late for the show.
3 He paid for express postage because he wanted it to arrive on time. (order that)
   He paid for express postage _____ arrive on time.
4 This site is very useful when you need to find information about historical events. (for)
   This site is very useful _____ information about historical events.
5 She wants to move house so that she doesn't live so far from her workplace. (order to)
   She wants to move house _____ so far from her workplace.

4 Complete the sentences with *so* or *such*.

1 It was _____ cold outside that we decided to stay in.
2 The band has become _____ famous that they can't go anywhere without security.
3 There was _____ good music at the festival that we've decided to again next year.
4 I've got _____ much work to do that I think I'll have to work at the weekend too.
5 The service was _____ poor that Esme complained to the restaurant owner.
6 _____ few people have bought tickets for the concert that it will most likely be cancelled.
7 The band had _____ a positive response to their song that they decided to record an album.

5 Complete the conversation with these phrases and an appropriate word or phrase for showing purpose or result.

> I fall asleep
> it's been hard to find time to study
> I don't fail it
> improve our IT skills
> I find it difficult to concentrate
> persuade him to do that

A: You seem a bit stressed today. Are you OK?
B: Yes. It's just that I have a final test for my IT course in a few days' time! I really need to revise [1] _____.
A: Oh, why are you doing an IT course?
B: Our manager wants all of us to do a course [2] _____. I've learned a lot but I have [3] _____ little free time _____.
A: Maybe you should ask your manager to give you some time off work to do the course.
B: Actually, we arranged a meeting [4] _____ but he said it wasn't possible.
A: Pity. What about the evenings after work?
B: Yeah, I do have time then. But I'm [5] _____ tired _____ on what I'm doing.
A: I read recently that you should listen to classical music while studying.
B: Interesting! I'll try it tonight. I'll just have to be careful not to relax [6] _____ much _____ !

GRAMMAR SUMMARY UNIT 9

Linking words

We use linking words to show the relationship between ideas in a sentence or between sentences. Linking words can be conjunctions, adverbs or prepositions.

We use **conjunctions** to link two clauses together into one sentence.
> We went to the cinema **but** all the tickets for the film had been sold.

Some conjunctions can go either at the beginning or in the middle of a sentence.
> **Although** it was a freezing cold day, we had great fun exploring the city.
> We had great fun exploring the city, **although** it was a freezing cold day.

We use **adverbs** and **adverbial phrases** to link ideas. We use an adverb in a separate sentence, or in a clause that has been linked to the previous one with a conjunction.
> Lucy never replied to my letter. **Afterwards**, I found out that she hadn't received it.
> Lucy never replied to my letter, **but afterwards**, I found out that she hadn't received it.

We use **prepositions** and **prepositional phrases** before an -ing form or a noun phrase.
> **After** finishing work, I went outside for some fresh air.
> I arrived late **because of** the traffic.

We often use a clause after a preposition or prepositional phrase by adding 'the fact that' to the beginning of it.
> I went out, **despite the fact that** I was so tired.

We use linking words for different functions.

	conjunctions	adverbs / adverbial phrases	prepositions / prepositional phrases
Contrasting ideas	although, but, even though, yet	however, nevertheless	despite, in spite of
Making an additional point	and	moreover, what's more, in addition (without to)	as well as, in addition to
Stating a reason or result	as, because, since, so	consequently, as a result (without of)*	because of, as a result of, on account of, owing to**
Showing the order or sequence of events	after, when, while	afterwards, subsequently	after, following***

* used to refer to the result, rather than the reason
** used with a noun phrase, not with an -ing form
*** used with a noun phrase, not with an -ing form

More formal linking words
as a result of, consequently, following, however, in addition to, moreover, nevertheless, on account of, owing to, subsequently, what's more, yet

▶ **Exercises 1, 2 and 3**

Present and perfect participles

We use participle clauses to give extra information about something in a main clause. It is sometimes possible to add an object, adjective or adverb in a participle clause, but we do not normally include a subject. Participle clauses usually describe a secondary event to the event in the main clause. The subject of a participle clause is the same as the subject in the main clause.

Present participle

We form present participle clauses using the -ing form of a verb. We use participle clauses to describe:

- an event that happens at the same time as the event in the main clause
  Opening the front door of my house, I realized how cold it was outside.

- the reason for an event in the main clause
  Not knowing the city well, I got lost several times.

- the result of an action in the main clause
  Everyone looked at me when I walked into the room, **making** me feel anxious.

We need to add the preposition by to describe how someone did something in a participle clause.
> The thieves got in **by breaking** a window.

▶ **Exercise 4**

Perfect participle and past participle

We use a perfect participle clause (having + past participle) to describe an event that happened before an event in the main clause.
> **Having won the cup final**, the players ran over to the crowd to celebrate.

We can also make participle clauses using the past participle of a verb. These often have a conditional meaning.
> **Cooked** in the right way, aubergines can be delicious in all kinds of dishes. (= If they are cooked …)

We don't use a participle clause if it doesn't refer to the subject of the main clause.
> ~~Reading a book, the cat jumped on the sofa and sat next to me.~~ (This makes it sound as though the cat was reading a book.)

Fixed phrase participle clauses

Some participles clauses are like fixed phrases. Some common examples are:

- *assuming that* (= If we assume that …)
- *provided that* (= If and only if …)
- *compared to/with*
- *considering that* (= If we remember that …)
- *given that* (= If we remember that …)
- *seen from the point of view of*

▶ **Exercises 5 and 6**

Exercises

1 Choose the correct linking word to complete the sentences. Sometimes there are two possible answers.

1. The food in the restaurant was excellent. *In addition to / What's more / Yet*, the waiters were very friendly.
2. *Yet / Despite / Although* your website claims products are delivered within five days, I still have not received my order after two weeks.
3. She was born in Greece, but *subsequently / following / afterwards* she moved to Australia.
4. The speaker is ill. We *as well as / nevertheless / consequently* have to cancel the talk.
5. We're meeting him later today *as well as / moreover / in addition to* tomorrow.
6. *Since / Because of / As* you failed the exam, you will have to repeat the course next year.

2 Complete the text with these words.

| despite | however | nevertheless | since | while |

The story of how I met my husband is quite funny. One day ¹ _____ I was at work, I received an email with a music file attached. I didn't know why I had received it. ² _____, I listened to the music and I thought it was amazing, so I replied to the sender. We started to email each other and one day he suggested meeting, ³ _____ living hundreds of kilometres apart. I wasn't sure at first, and some of my friends told me not to meet him ⁴ _____ I didn't really know him. ⁵ _____, I agreed. When we met, it was love at first sight.

3 Join the two phrases with these linking words.

| as well as | even though | however | in spite of |
| moreover | on account of |

1. most people expected Martinez to become president / Sanchez won easily
2. visiting our friends in New York / we also spent some time in Boston
3. our offices are closed on Monday / the holiday
4. many motorists went out on the roads / the police's warning to stay at home
5. the hotel is very conveniently located / it is very good value for money
6. I don't normally like classical music / I really enjoyed the concert

4 Rewrite the sentence pairs as a single sentence. Use participle clauses with the -*ing* form in the first phrase. Make deletions or any other changes necessary.

1. She wasn't very interested in the film. As a result, she left early.
2. I read the contract. While I was doing this, I realized I had made a big mistake.
3. I forgot my friend's birthday. This made her very angry.
4. They didn't want to spend too much money. Because of this, they went on holiday nearby.
5. I looked around the room. When I did this, I noticed an old school friend in the corner.
6. He walked into the house with his shoes on. Consequently, he left dirt all over the floor.

5 Complete the sentences with these phrases.

| compared | comparing | having compared |
| given | giving | having given |

1. There is less traffic in the city _____ to five years ago.
2. _____ that we don't have much time, we should only visit one museum.
3. _____ the students' results, we can see that some had studied more than others.
4. _____ all the prices earlier, we knew which shop had the best deals.
5. There was a baby crying on the train the whole journey, _____ me a headache.
6. _____ in his final university assignment, Juan could finally relax.

6 Complete the text with participle clauses using these verbs.

| assume | consider | hack | look | steal | use |

¹ _____ that the number of traditional bank robberies has fallen in recent years, you may think banks are improving security. But in reality, ² _____ at the facts, it seems that thieves are using different methods. For example, in 2013, criminals carried out the biggest ever cybercrime, ³ _____ into ATMs to steal millions of dollars. ⁴ _____ the computers of a credit card company, the thieves created fake bank cards and used these cards to take cash out of hundreds of ATMs, ⁵ _____ over $45 million. ⁶ _____ that cybercrime will continue to increase, banking security won't get any easier.

GRAMMAR SUMMARY UNIT 10

Adverbs and adverbial phrases

Adverbs (e.g. *quickly, unfortunately*) and adverbial phrases (e.g. *later that day, in a polite way*) qualify or change the meaning of another word or phrase in a sentence. They can qualify a verb / verb phrase, an adjective, an adverb or a sentence.

*The ants **quickly built** a nest in the ground.*
*It was an **extremely large** colony.*
*The snow fell **very heavily** last night.*
***Suddenly**, the sky went dark and it started to rain.*

Types of adverb and adverbial phrase

- adverbs and adverbial phrases of **manner** describe how somebody does something or how something happens, e.g. *quickly, with great skill*

- adverbs and adverbial phrases of **probability** say how likely we think it is that something happened or will happen, e.g. *probably, possibly*

- adverbs and adverbial phrases of **degree** talk about the strength or intensity of something, e.g. *almost, extremely, rather*

- **frequency** adverbs and adverbial phrases talk about how often something happens, e.g. *rarely, from time to time, sometimes, often, always*

- **viewpoint** adverbs and adverbial phrases limit the information or ideas in a sentence to a particular perspective, e.g. *on a personal level, in some cases*

- **comment** adverbs and adverbial phrases express our point of view on information in a sentence, e.g. *surprisingly, interestingly*

Adverb position

We can put adverbs and adverbial phrases in three places in a phrase or sentence:

- front position, before the subject
***Unfortunately**, they did not offer me the job.*

- mid position, after auxiliary verbs (including modal verbs) and before the main verb
*He **always** arrives late to work.*
*It'll **probably** be a nicer day tomorrow.*

- end position (can be the end of the sentence, or the end of the main clause)
*He explained the problem **carefully**.*
*I read French newspapers **three times a week** to improve my fluency.*

We normally put comment and viewpoint adverbs in front position. We can put frequency adverbs in front position, if we want to emphasize them. (Note that we never put *always* in front position.)
***Interestingly**, it's colder here than 100 years ago.*
***Occasionally**, I have lunch at a restaurant.*

We normally put frequency adverbs, adverbs of degree and adverbs of probability in mid position.
*He **always** arrives late for work.*
*I **almost** fell down the stairs this morning.*
*They'll **probably** move house soon.*

We normally put adverbs of manner in end position.
*She can speak Japanese **really well**.*

The words *friendly, likely, lonely* and *lovely* and *unlikely* are adjectives, not adverbs. We can sometimes use them in the phrase *in a … way* to make an adverbial phrase.
*The film finished **in a very unlikely way**.*

Some adverbs are irregular, and have the same form as the adjective, e.g. *fast, hard, high, long, low, near, early* and *late*. Some other adjectives, e.g. many *-ed* adjectives, also do not have adverb forms.

▶ **Exercises 1, 2, 3 and 4**

Negative adverbials and inversion

When we place an adverb or adverbial phrase that has a negative or restrictive meaning at the beginning of a sentence for emphasis, we invert the subject and the auxiliary.
*I've **rarely** received such poor service.*
***Rarely have I received** such poor service.*

If there is no auxiliary, we add a form of *do*.
We only realized how sick she was later.
***Only later** did we realize how sick she was.*

After most negative adverbial phrases, we don't need to use *not* in the main clause.
Under no circumstances can I be late for the interview.
(not ~~Under no circumstances can't I be late~~)

Types of negative adverbials

We use inversion after:

- the frequency adverbs *never* and other frequency adverbs and adverbial phrases meaning 'not often', e.g. *seldom, rarely, hardly ever*

- adverbs meaning 'almost not', or 'not much', e.g. *barely, scarcely, hardly, little*

- some adverbial phrases with *only*, e.g. *only later, only if …, only when …, only after … (I read your letter), only by (doing this), not only (but/also …)*

- negative and restrictive adverbial phrases with *no* and *not*, e.g. *no sooner (than …), under no circumstances, in no way, at no time, nowhere else, not since, not until, not once*

- after *little*

Note that we don't invert a subject and auxiliary if it appears within the adverbial phrase.
~~Only when did I read your letter …~~
Only when I read your letter …

We normally use inversion in slightly more formal speech or writing. However, there are some negative adverbials that are common in informal speech.
***No way will you beat** me at tennis this time!*

▶ **Exercises 5, 6 and 7**

Exercises

1 Put the words in the correct order to make sentences.

1. buys / birthday / my / a present/ he / rarely / for
2. podcasts / loves / she / listening to / absolutely
3. was / the job / offered / luckily / I
4. should / in my opinion / the meeting / postpone / we
5. what I said / was / by / slightly / he / annoyed
6. my email / won't / she / respond to / probably
7. go / didn't / well / my / very / driving test

2 Find examples of the following types of adverbs in the sentences in Exercise 1.

1. an adverb of manner
2. an adverb of probability
3. two degree adverbs
4. a frequency adverb
5. a viewpoint adverb
6. a comment adverb

3 Correct the mistake in each sentence.

1. Always he drinks a coffee in the morning.
2. They greeted me friendly.
3. We arrived lately at the party.
4. I will help you if I certainly can.
5. He told me that his job isn't very well going.
6. She fast drove to get to work on time.

4 Complete the conversation with these adverbs.

| always | fortunately | late | probably |
| quickly | really | | |

A: I'm ¹ _____ glad I have a cat as a pet. My alarm clock didn't go off this morning. But ² _____ my cat woke me up instead!
B: She was ³ _____ hungry!
A: Yes! We ⁴ _____ have breakfast at the same time.
B: Did you get to work ⁵ _____?
A: I had to get ready very ⁶ _____, but I arrived at the office on time – thanks to my cat!

5 Choose the correct options to complete the sentences.

1. Occasionally *does he play / he plays* video games with his friends.
2. Rarely *arrive the buses / do the buses arrive* on time here.
3. Only if *does it stop / it stops* raining *can we / we can* go out.
4. At no time *were the passengers / the passengers were* offered compensation.
5. Only after *we had complained / had we complained* several times *did our neighbours switch off / our neighbours switched off* their loud music.
6. Not only *have I won / I have won* the national tennis championship, *have I / I have* also competed internationally.
7. Not once *have they / they have* called me.

6 Complete the text with these phrases.

| no doubt | not only | only after | only by |
| rarely | under no circumstances | | |

New research is showing that ¹ _____ does watching too much TV affect children's brain development, but it also reduces how much time they spend playing, interacting with others and reading. ² _____ doing these types of activities are children able to develop essential skills which a TV can't provide, argue many experts. ³ _____ do parents think about the long-term effects of their children sitting in front of a screen. They give the following advice to parents: ⁴ _____ your child has finished their homework and had time to play should you let them watch TV. Research has also shown that electronic screens can affect sleep. Sleep is essential for a child's development so ⁵ _____ should children spend time looking at screens in the hour before bedtime. ⁶ _____ many busy parents will not be happy to hear this.

7 Complete the sentences using these prompts.

| little / she / know / did |
| no sooner / she / had |
| no way / we / can / afford |
| not until / we / will |
| rarely / we / have |

1. _____ to buy a house at the moment. They're too expensive!
2. _____ the government improves public transport, _____ use our cars less.
3. _____ what would happen to her that evening.
4. _____ arrived at the hotel than she had to set off again.
5. _____ seen so much snow.

GRAMMAR SUMMARY UNIT 11

Unreal past forms

We often use past tenses to talk about unreal situations. The situations can be in the past, but also in the present or the future.

would rather / would just as soon

We use *would rather* and *would just as soon* to express a preference for what someone or something should do.

We use *would rather* / *would just as soon* + infinitive when the subject doesn't change.
   I'**d rather** not talk about this now.

We use *would rather* / *would just as soon* + subject + past form when the subject changes.
   We'**d rather you** didn't park your car here.
   They'**d just as soon the government** spent the money on something else.

I wish / If only

We use *wish* and *if only* to talk about imaginary situations that we would like to be true or to come true. The meaning of *wish* and *if only* is the same, but *if only* is stronger.

We use *wish* / *if only* + past tense to talk about a present situation that we would like to be different.
   I wish my flat **was** a bit bigger.

We use *wish* / *if only* + past perfect to talk about a past situation that we would like to be different.
   The flat we liked was sold yesterday. **If only we'd called** the owner straight away.

We use *wish* / *if only* + someone + *would* + infinitive when we would like someone to do or stop doing something. We often use this structure to complain.
   I wish you wouldn't make so much noise.

it's (high) time

We use *it's time* + subject + past tense to talk about what needs to be done now. We often use it when we are annoyed that something hasn't happened yet. We add the adjective 'high' to make the statement stronger.
   It's time you got a haircut.
   It's high time you found a job.

We can also use *to* + infinitive after *it's (high) time* to refer to the speaker and listener together.
   It's time to go. (= You and I should go now.)

supposing / what if

We use *supposing* or *what if* + past tense to talk about an imaginary situation in the present or future. We often use them in questions.
   Supposing you won the lottery, what would you do?
   A: I can't come to dinner tonight. B: **What if I gave** you a lift?

We use *supposing* and *what if* + past perfect to talk about an imaginary situation in the past.
   Supposing you'd been born in a different country, would you still have the same personality?
   Why didn't you take your phone? What if **I'd needed** to call you urgently? (= I didn't need to call you.)

We can use *imagine* + past tense with the same meaning as *supposing*.

We also use *supposing to* and *what if* + present tense to talk about what might happen in the future.
   Supposing it rains, will they cancel the concert?

In more formal contexts, we can use *were* instead of *was* when talking about hypothetical situations.
   Supposing your boss **were** more supportive – would you still want to change job?

▶ Exercises 1, 2 and 3

Conditionals and inversion

We use the **first conditional** to talk about real situations in the present and future. We can use any logical form in the main clause (e.g. *will*, *might*, *going to* or an imperative).
   If you **arrive** at the restaurant first, **get** a table.

We use the **second conditional** to talk about hypothetical situations in the present and future. We form it with *if* + past tense + *would/could*.
   If my sister **wasn't visiting** me this week, I **would be able** to come and meet you.

We use the **third conditional** to talk about hypothetical situations in the past. We form it with *if* + past perfect + *would/could/might have*
   If we **had arrived** at the cinema early, we **would have got** good seats. (= We didn't arrive early. We didn't get good seats.)

Mixed conditionals combine second and third conditional forms.
   If you **were** more organized, you **wouldn't have missed** your flight. (= You aren't organized (present). You missed your flight (past).)

In **second and third conditionals**, we sometimes use the structure *if it wasn't/weren't/hadn't been for* + noun to mean 'if this thing or situation didn't exist or hadn't existed'.
   If it hadn't been for Tom, I would never have met Ella.
   If it weren't for tourism, I wouldn't have a job.

▶ Exercises 4 and 5

Inverted conditionals

In second and third conditional sentences, we can invert the subject and auxiliary in the *if*-clause and omit the word *if*. We do this in more formal contexts, when the auxiliary in the second conditional is *were*, or in the third conditional, *had*.
   Were he from a richer family, he would have more opportunities.
   Had we been warned about the delay, it would not have caused so many problems.

We can also use *should* + subject in first conditional sentences in place of the *if*-clause.
   Should you require any further information, please contact us.

▶ Exercise 6

Exercises

1 Choose the correct forms to complete the sentences.

1. She'd rather I *didn't / don't* come to the meeting.
2. I wish I *have / had* time to take up a new hobby.
3. I'd rather *not went / not go* to the cinema tonight.
4. He wishes he *had been / was* more careful the day he crashed his car.
5. If only the government *would stop / stopped* increasing taxes.
6. I think it's time you *move / moved* out of your parents' house.
7. What if you *could / can* visit any country in the world? Where would you go?
8. A: I don't feel like going to the cinema.
   B: That's fine – I'd just as soon *watched / watch* a film at home.

2 Complete the second sentences so they mean the same as the first. Use the words in brackets.

1. I think you should go home. You've been here a long time. (time)
   It _____. You've been here a long time.
2. He'd like to earn more money. (wish)
   He _____ more money.
3. Anna wants me to help her but I'd prefer her to ask someone else. (soon)
   Anna wants me to help her but I _____ someone else.
4. I should have stayed in touch with my school friends. (only)
   If _____ with my school friends.
5. He wants to cook the meal instead of me. (rather)
   He _____ instead of me.
6. I'd like my colleagues to knock before entering my office. (wish)
   I _____ before entering my office.

3 Complete the email with *what if, wish, it's time, would rather* or *if only* and the correct forms of the words in brackets.

Hi Helena
How are you? We have exams at the moment and I'm really anxious. Sometimes I ¹_____ (I / not decide) to come to university! And my flatmates are so loud and untidy. I really ²_____ (they / not make) so much noise at night. I think next year I ³_____ (live) alone. My stress has been affecting my studies so I think ⁴_____ (I / speak) to a student counsellor. But ⁵_____ (it/not help) me – what would I do? I ⁶_____ (we / live) closer to each other. ⁷_____ (we / decide) to go to the same university, I'm sure I'd be happier.

4 Correct the mistake in each sentence.

1. I would call you more often if I have time.
2. If they'll continue being so rude, we're going to ask them to leave.
3. If she bought fewer things, she'll be able to save more money.
4. He won't have got so wet yesterday if he'd taken an umbrella.
5. I'd eat organic food if it would be cheaper.
6. If you remembered your passport, we wouldn't have had so many problems at the airport.

5 Complete the conversation with the correct form of the verbs in brackets.

A: I bought these great cups in the sales yesterday! If you ¹_____ (put) hot water in them, they ²_____ (change) colour!
B: Do we need more cups?
A: Er … no, not really. I ³_____ (not buy) them if they ⁴_____ (not be) on sale.
B: Hmm. And what else did you get?
A: These black trousers. They're quite tight. But I'm sure if I ⁵_____ (lose) some weight, they ⁶_____ (fit) me perfectly!
B: But you already have four pairs of black trousers! You shouldn't buy things if you ⁷_____ (not need) them.
A: You're right. I'm normally so careful with money.
B: Are you sure? If you ⁸_____ (be) that careful with your money, then you ⁹_____ (not buy) all that stuff yesterday. How about going out for some lunch now?
A: Sorry, I can't really afford it.
B: You see? If you ¹⁰_____ (not spend) so much money yesterday, you ¹¹_____ (be able to) come for lunch!

6 Complete the sentences with an appropriate inverted form of these verbs.

be (x2) know not arrive sell treat

1. _____ anything _____ missing from your order, please contact us immediately.
2. _____ we _____ it would take you so long to complete the work, we would not have hired you.
3. _____ the company _____ their employees better, they wouldn't have gone on strike.
4. _____ the minister more supportive of the government's policies, he'd have more chance of being elected.
5. _____ Martin _____ so late, the meeting would have finished much earlier.
6. _____ you _____ the product successfully, you will be paid commission.

177

GRAMMAR SUMMARY UNIT 12

Approximation and vague language

We often use approximate and vague language when we do not need to give exact information or if we do not know it.

Numbers

There are different ways to give an approximate number. We use:

- *tens / dozens / hundreds / thousands / tens of thousands*, etc. + *of* + noun
  There were **thousands of people** at the protest.

- *around*, *about* and *roughly* + number, or number + *or so*
  We have **around / about / roughly** $50 to spend on a present.
  Twenty **or so** people went on the hike. (= twenty or slightly more)

- *over* (= more than), *under* (= less than), *up to* (= not more than) + number
  Up to 30 million people are expected to vote in elections tomorrow.

- *as many as* (= not more than) and *some* (= approximately) + number when the number is high, unexpected or important
  Every year, **some** two million people visit this part of the world.

- number + *odd* (= approximately) in informal, spoken contexts with numbers that can be divided by ten (e.g. 50, 100, 1,200, etc.)
  I've been working here for 30-**odd** years now.

▶ Exercise 1

Adjectives

We use *kind of*, *sort of* and *more or less* before an adjective to make it more approximate. *Kind of* and *sort of* are more informal.
  All the hotels on this road are **more or less** excellent.

We add *-ish* to the end of an adjective to make it approximate. This is most common in spoken English.
  The leaves of this plant change to a purple-**ish** colour in autumn.

We can also use *-ish* with hours of the day.
  I'll call you at **8-ish**.

Vague words

We use *stuff* instead of an uncountable or plural noun when we don't know or don't need to say exactly what something is.
  It will be cold, so bring hats, gloves and **stuff**. (*stuff* = things like that)
  What's this **stuff** all over my car? (*stuff* = substance)

We use *and so on* and *and that sort of thing* to avoid giving a list of other similar things, especially after plural or uncountable nouns.
  These valleys are full of bears, deer, wolves **and so on**.
  I really enjoy swimming, surfing, walking **and that sort of thing**.

We use *or something* to mean 'or something similar'. We use it when what we've said is just an example or we are not sure about it.
  What's wrong? Are you tired **or something**?
  I think she works for a theatre **or something**.

▶ Exercises 2 and 3

would

We use *would* (usually, especially in speech, contracted to *'d*) in a number of different ways. We use it:

- in conditionals, to describe a hypothetical situation
  I **would** ask for a pay rise if I were you.
  If you'd asked me, I **would** have helped you.

- to talk about the future in the past, e.g. to report an intention, expectation or decision
  The government promised they **would** protect the area.

- to describe a habitual action (but not a state) in the past
  When we were kids, we **would** always go camping in summer.

- to indicate a person or thing's refusal to do something in the past
  Sorry I'm late – my car **wouldn't** start so I had to find a taxi.

We also use *would*:

- in polite requests
  Would you call back later? I'm rather busy.

- in polite responses to a request or invitation
  A: Can I get you a coffee? B: That **would** be great – thanks.

- to express an opinion or hope less forcefully or in a more indirect way
  I **would** think that the later train would be better. (= I think …)
  I **would** have hoped that you'd finish by today. (= I expected …)

▶ Exercises 4, 5 and 6

Exercises

1 Cross out the option which can't be used to talk about each number.

1. 3,150 people: *thousands of people / up to 3,000 people / 3,000-odd people*
2. ten hours forty minutes: *over ten hours / under ten hours / about ten hours*
3. five years and ten days: *as many as five years / roughly five years / over five years*
4. $105: *100-odd dollars / around 100 dollars / hundreds of dollars*
5. 52 cars: *about fifty cars / fifty cars or so / under fifty cars*

2 Complete the sentences with these words and phrases.

and so on	-ish	or something	sort of	stuff
up to				

1. A: Is that the building? B: No – Lucy's house is a blue_____ colour.
2. _____ 50,000 are expected to watch today's match – that's the maximum capacity of the stadium.
3. We need to go now. Put all that _____ back in your bag.
4. Are you hungry? Do you want to stop for a sandwich _____?
5. Have you watched that new crime series? It's not very original but it's _____ interesting.
6. There's a nice shop in the centre of the village that sells traditional clothes, shoes _____.

3 Complete the second sentences so they mean the same as the first. Use the words in brackets.

1. This lift can be used by no more than ten people at a time. (up)
   This lift can be used by _____ at a time.
2. I sometimes find going to the gym a bit boring. (sort)
   I sometimes find going to the gym _____.
3. Why don't we go for a walk or do another similar activity? (something)
   Why don't we go for a walk _____?
4. He likes going to museums and galleries, the theatre and other similar places. (thing)
   He likes going to museums and galleries, the theatre _____.
5. We'll need approximately two hours to resolve the problem. (so)
   We'll need _____ to resolve the problem.
6. He only started the company last year but now he has forty employees. (odd)
   He only started the company last year but now _____ employees.

4 Which of the sentences have an incorrect use of *would*? Correct the incorrect sentences.

1. If you would study harder, you'd do better in your courses.
2. I couldn't bring a copy of the document because my printer wouldn't work.
3. It would always be very cold in winter in the old house where I grew up.
4. I think it would be a great concert tonight – I'm looking forward to it!
5. Would you help me to take these boxes to my car?
6. I would expect that most of the work on the house will be finished this month.

5 Match the phrases (a–f) with the underlined words in the sentences (1–6).

a intended to
b is extremely kind
c it might be true
d please could
e refused to
f used to

1. I would think that we could find a better price elsewhere. _____
2. He said he would be here tonight. _____
3. A: Can I help you with your suitcases?
   B: That would be great. _____
4. Would you please turn down your music a little? _____
5. When I was a bit younger, I would go running five times a week. _____
6. Sorry I'm late – my boss wouldn't let me leave until I'd finished a report! _____

6 Rewrite the conversation so it's more polite and indirect by inserting *would* in six places. Make any other necessary changes.

A: Do you want any help?
B: Yes, please. Give me some information about the park.
A: What type of information do you want?
B: Oh, about the wildlife and the plants and trees. It's such a beautiful park.
A: Well, we have these brochures.
B: I want something more detailed.
A: OK, how about one of these books?
B: This one looks interesting. How much does it cost?
A: It's 30 euros.
B: Oh, I expected it to be a little cheaper…
A: Well, I could give you a discount.
B: That's great, thanks.
A: OK, that's 28 euros.
B: Oh, er … I'll take the brochures, thanks.

Audioscripts

Unit 1

▶ 1

Speaker 1
I think the most valuable lesson I've learned was when I was starting a business at the age of 25. I used to get very frustrated with my business partner, a guy called Giles. We'd set up our own web design business and Giles would always take ages making a first design to show the customer. He was trying to get it perfect when actually, it didn't need to be. When I told my dad about it – that it was driving me crazy – he said, 'Look, you can't change other people; you can only change the way that you behave towards them.' So, from then on I just tried to accept that Giles was a perfectionist and to see it as a positive thing. And since then we've got on much better. And that's become a sort of guiding principle for me in life – not to try to change other people.

Speaker 2
I think a good rule of thumb is: 'Never get too attached to things.' But it's a lot easier said than done and sometimes it takes a big event to make you realize how true this is. Our house was flooded a few years ago and because my bedroom was on the ground floor, I lost a lot of my most valued possessions: my laptop with all my photos on it; my favourite books; all my shoes were ruined and some of my best clothes too. But in fact, what mattered at the time was knowing that everyone was safe – my parents and my little brother. We've actually moved to a new house now, and it's not nearly as nice as the old one, but it doesn't matter. You need to move on. Now, I always make a point of not getting too attached to places or things. It's just stuff.

▶ 3

How many times have you been asked the question, 'So, what do you do?' when you first meet someone? It's the classic way in which people start a conversation in order to form an idea of a person's identity, by trying to fit them into an easy-to-understand category. But while some people might like to define themselves by their job – because it's what they live for – actually for many people, their work is not their identity, and the question can make you feel as if people are always judging you by your position in society, or worse, by how much you earn.

There are of course other ways we identify people. By their background: 'Sally was brought up on a farm in Wales, not in London like the rest of her friends.' By their values: 'John's a family man, really.' Or by their hobbies or interests: 'Frank's a keen photographer.' Or sometimes by their character: 'Jack's a free spirit,' or 'Kate's always the life and soul of the party.' We also define people by their beliefs: 'Anne's a campaigner for healthy eating.' And yes, sometimes too by their work: 'Sarah's a medical researcher – she's spent most of her life looking for cures for tropical diseases.'

What do these identifying characteristics have in common? Well, identity really seems to be about the experiences that shape us. Take John, our 'family man'. When his children were born, he was working as a carpet salesman. It was a secure job – not very well paid – but it kept him and his family comfortable. At one point he'd been intending to leave the company and start up his own business, but when he thought about it he realized that it would be a risk and also would take up too much of his time – time that he'd rather spend with his two boys.

What about Jack? People call him a free spirit because he's 44 and hasn't settled down yet. He fell in love when he was 25, but the relationship ended and he hasn't had another one since. He travels a lot and lives in different places, picking up bits and pieces of work as and when he can. He keeps saying that in a few years, he won't be moving about anymore – that he's had enough of that life – but actually he's been saying that since he was 35.

Anne works for a big legal firm. She's quite a driven person. A few years ago, her flatmate introduced her to a new vegetarian diet and it made her feel great and gave her more energy. It also made her think about all the bad food she had eaten in her life, particularly at school, and so she joined a campaign to provide healthier food for school kids. It has attracted a lot of interest and is now becoming a national movement. So while there are many ingredients that go into making us what we are, it seems that what defines people first and foremost is experience.

▶ 4

1. I need peace and quiet to concentrate.
2. They all came back from their canoeing trip safe and sound. No one was injured, but most of them had a few aches and pains.
3. Try not to give a long talk. By and large, it's better to keep it short and sweet.
4. People come from far and wide to see Stonehenge. There are busloads of tourists coming to and fro all day.
5. You think my job is all fun and games, but actually now and then we do some serious work too!

▶ 6

1
A: Hi. Is it your first day at college too?
B: Yes, it is.
A: How's it going? Is it as you expected?
B: It's great, actually. I was a bit nervous before, but the teachers have been really welcoming.

2
A: So, what do you do?
B: I work for an IT company, sorting out people's computer systems.
A: Oh, really? How did you get into that?
B: By accident. I got a temporary job with a company selling laptops – one of those 'no experience necessary' ads – and then they trained me in computer networks.

3
A: Hi, I don't think we've met. I'm David.
B: Oh, hi David. Good to meet you. I'm Tara. I'm an old school friend of Kate's.
A: Oh, yeah – what school was that then?
B: Langley Secondary. It wasn't a great school, actually, but a few of us have kept in touch over the years.

4
A: Hey, I like your jacket.
B: Oh, thank you. I bought it in the sales yesterday. It was only £18.
A: £18? You wouldn't know it – it looks great. Do you like bargain-hunting, then?
B: Oh no. I like clothes, but I hate shopping for them. I find it really stressful.
A: Me too. I always end up buying things that aren't right and have to take them back.

5
A: I'm supposed to have given up sweet things, but I can't stop eating this cake.
B: I know. It's delicious, isn't it?
A: Actually, it was my New Year's Resolution to stop eating things like this. But I haven't kept it. In fact, I don't think I've ever kept a New Year's Resolution. Have you?
B: No, I gave up making them years ago.

6
A: Whereabouts are you from?
B: I live in Lublin ... in the east of Poland.
A: Really? I don't know Lublin.
B: No, I don't think many people have heard of it.
A: So, what's it like? Is it a good place to live?
B: Well, it depends. The suburbs aren't very interesting, but the old town is nice and because it's a university town, it gets quite lively at night.

▶ 8

1. Do you normally eat here?
2. What's it like living in New York?
3. What sort of apartment have you got?
4. How do you like the new building?
5. Do you fancy a coffee or something?

▶ 9

Hello, everyone. First of all, can I extend a warm welcome from me and all the staff. My name's Sarah Curtain, and I'm the Principal here at King's College. I'm very happy to see, once again, such a large and diverse range of nationalities at the college. This year we have over 60 different nationalities, speaking 33 different languages. It's that diversity and international perspective that makes King's College a unique place to study.

I'm afraid I have to mention a few administrative matters first, but then I'll give you some more general advice about how to make the most of your time here.

So, immediately after this session, there will be coffee in the Students' Union where you can meet and chat to staff and other students. That's from 11 to 12.30 p.m.

Course registration takes place on Monday morning. That is compulsory for everyone to attend and it'll be in the main university hall – this room – between 10 a.m. and 2 p.m. You must attend to officially register for the courses you are going to do this year.

Audioscripts

Also during the next week, I'd ask those of you who haven't done so already, to bring copies of all your documents to the Admissions office – Room 301 – so that we can keep them on file. So that's all official documents – secondary education certificates, student visas, bank account details – to Room 301 by the end of next week. This applies to all overseas students, that is everyone except those from the UK and the European Union. Even if you don't think you have all of these, please come and see us anyway – that's very important.

Now, as for your orientation here at King's College, …

▶ 10

OK, everyone, I'd just like to say a few words about reading – something you're going to be doing a lot of here. At the end of this session, I'll give you your reading list for this particular course. Your other tutors will do the same. There'll be thirty or so books on each list, but please don't think that means you have to read every page of every book. There are three or four key books highlighted at the top of each list, which we do recommend that you read in full, but the others will mainly be for reference – that's to say, there'll be one or two chapters in them that are relevant to a particular essay or piece of work.

So, most importantly, when I give you the list, please don't go out to the nearest bookshop and buy them all. If you do that, you'll leave yourself no money for food or anything else. All these books are, in principle, available in the library – some may be out on loan of course when you want them. You'll probably want to buy some of the more important ones. My advice to you is first to look at one of the internet booksellers and see if you can pick up any second-hand or at least cheaper copies there. There's also a second-hand section in the main university bookshop, where you might find what you're looking for.

What about strategies for reading? As I said at the beginning, you'll have a big volume of reading to do, so it's important that you get faster at it. Is there a secret to that? Well, I'm afraid the answer is not really. What I would say though is that the more you read, the faster you will get. So don't worry too much if it seems like it's taking ages at first – everyone feels that …

Unit 2

▶ 11

The animal herders of western Mongolia have been called the last nomads. Their livelihood is the horses, goats and cattle that travel with them, from which they get their food, clothing and money to buy other goods.

Among these nomadic peoples are Kazakhs. Increasingly, many Kazakhs are trying to make a better living by seeking new jobs or trades in the city, but there are some who have maintained the traditional way of life, living in tents in the summer and in small houses during the cold winters. Among their customs, the most unusual, perhaps, is eagle hunting – an art practised since the days of Genghis Khan.

Wrapped in warm clothes and fur hats to keep off the cold, eagle hunters can still be seen riding their small ponies across the plains of western Mongolia, tracking foxes and other small animals. An eagle hunter spends ten years with each bird, training it – a task which requires great skill and patience – and forming an intimate working relationship with it. They even share with the eagle the meat of the animals it kills.

For many hunters these days, eagle hunting is less an occupation and more a sport, but nevertheless, it's still a tradition that they want to keep alive.

▶ 13

My grandfather was a forestry commissioner, which meant he was responsible for managing forests. I think he'd intended originally to be a biologist, but then he got a job looking after forests in Wales. He's retired now, but he's still fascinated by trees and plants. I guess his job was a way of life for him because it occupied all his time and he spent so much of his life living in or around forests. Over the years, I've often thought about working outdoors too, but I don't think I'll follow in his footsteps.

▶ 14

P = Presenter, K = Kerry, R = Reporter

P: We'd all like to jump into a fire, right? Er, I don't think so, but that was how smokejumper Kerry Franklin explained her career choice when she was interviewed by this programme. For those of you that don't know, smokejumpers are firefighters with parachutes who are dropped into inaccessible areas to tackle forest fires. Here's what Kerry said when she spoke to one of our reporters earlier.

K: Women firefighters are well suited to this kind of work. We weigh on average around 70–80 kilos, so we're the right weight for it. If you're much heavier than that, you descend too fast and you can get injured when you hit the ground. If you're a lot lighter and there's a strong wind, you might be carried a long way from your intended landing point.

R: You mean like towards the centre of the fire itself?

K: Yeah, that's been known to happen. But personal safety's not the first thing on your mind – in this kind of job you can't wrap people in cotton wool.

R: No, I guess not. So, having landed near the fire, what do you do then? 'Cos I imagine there's no fire engine or fire hydrant nearby, so you can't start putting out the fire in a conventional way.

K: No, that's right. We're like the first line of attack before other crews get there. We get dropped in with tools – chainsaws, axes, chemicals for fighting fires; we're given water pumps too, portable ones. But first the fire needs to be assessed to see how bad it is and how it's going to develop – this information has to be relayed back to base as quickly as possible. Of course, if it's a bad fire, we've got to look for a way to try and contain it. Usually that means finding a natural firebreak.

R: What's that?

K: Something like a road, or an area of rock, or perhaps some area of thinner vegetation that the fire has to cross before it continues on its path. When we've located one, then we do our best to make sure it's going to be effective by getting anything that could catch fire out of the way. Sometimes that means using controlled burning. So, we actually start another fire to make the firebreak wider.

R: I see. And can I ask: what's it like being a woman in what's traditionally a male profession?

K: That's not an issue. The job involves being trained to a certain standard and you either make the grade or you don't. Those who come through it successfully have a natural respect for each other. I met a few guys during my training who had a different attitude, but since then? No. A smokejumper's a smokejumper, regardless of gender.

▶ 17

C = Careers Advisor, K = Katy

C: OK, Katy, so can you tell me a bit about yourself?

K: Yes, of course. So, I'm 23 years old and I live in south London. I was brought up in France 'til I was twelve – my mum's French – so I speak fluent French. I studied history at Liverpool University – that was a really good experience – and I graduated from there last June. Since then I've been looking for a job in journalism. To be honest, the media is not an easy sector to break into unless you have the right contacts – and I don't particularly. So, I decided that the best thing to do was to get more work experience in the meantime and currently that's what I'm doing – bits and pieces of office work so that I can improve my general computer and admin skills while I look for something more permanent.

C: Yes, I think that's very sensible. Companies are always worried that university graduates lack those basic skills. What kind of organization would you like to work for, ideally?

K: Well, a news company, really – either online, TV or radio, or print. That's what I'm working towards. But I'd be perfectly happy to start at the bottom and then work my way up. You know, I really wouldn't mind doing a basic job to start with – just so I could get my foot in the door.

C: Well, I think that the fact that you did a history degree rather than one in media or journalism could be a positive thing. Employers are always looking for people with a slightly different background. Have you done any blogging or written anything that's been published?

K: Yeah, I wrote a regular blog about university life when I was in Liverpool. That was quite popular.

C: Mmm. Good. And what do you see as your strengths, Katy?

Audioscripts

K: Well, obviously, I think I write well – also I'm good at spotting a story. I wrote something on my blog last year about the problem of students getting into debt, which got picked up by a local newspaper. I guess I'm very focused and conscientious – once I start something, I follow it through. For example, in my current job I've spent the last two weeks helping to reorganize the office. I went in at the weekend because I wanted to finish the job before they took in a group of new interns.

C: OK. And what would you say are your weaknesses?

K: Um, well, I'm only 23, so I realize I've got an awful lot to learn still. For example, when it comes to gathering information, I don't have all the skills or resources of an older journalist. I have some experience of interviewing people – I know that the trick is to get them to tell *their* story, not the story that *you* want to hear – just not enough yet. In the past I had a tendency to get carried away with my own ideas sometimes.

Unit 3

▶ 18

Wherever I go, I always make a point of looking up and taking in my surroundings, particularly the architecture. I'd recommend anyone to do that; it's very informative. By looking a little more closely, you learn a lot about people and how they organize their lives. In Hong Kong you can't help looking up because almost all the buildings are at least twenty or thirty storeys high.

This photo was taken from the middle of an apartment complex and two things strike you immediately. The first is the density of population here – it's incredible! People live in tiny apartments, one on top of another, because the cost of renting is so high. Those air-conditioning units sticking out from the windows also tell a story, 'cos for most of the year, Hong Kong is a really hot and humid place. Then, the other thing that strikes you about the buildings is that they're such a mixture: old and new, smart and shabby. I think you get that in any city, but here it somehow seems more marked.

Actually, when you see people out in the streets you get a different impression – like everyone seems to be doing pretty well – and that's because appearances are incredibly important for most Hong Kongers: looking your best, wearing designer fashions, carrying the latest phone. You see, a lot of people come here to make money: bankers and real estate developers and so on. It's busy, it's crowded, it's competitive and frankly, it makes a lot of other big cities seem pretty sleepy. It's not for everyone, but I found it completely addictive.

▶ 21

P = Presenter, J = Jonas Wilfstrand

P: Hello and welcome to *Your Property*. Today we're going to look at something completely different: small homes – extremely small homes, in fact. The average house size these days is half the size that it was in the 1920s and there are good reasons for that, as we'll hear. So, I'm very pleased to welcome architect Jonas Wilfstrand, who specializes in the design of compact living spaces and who's going to talk us through this a bit. Jonas, I've been looking at compact homes on your website, and I must say some of them are really stunning. The timber and glass vacation house with a built-in sauna struck me particularly. But it did make me wonder: is this just a passing fashion or is there something more behind the trend for smaller homes?

J: Oh, no, there is definitely a trend for smaller homes – in Britain, but also in other Western countries. One reason is that in large cities we're incredibly short of space – it's a really big problem nowadays. The other thing is affordability. A house or flat half the size should in principle cost half the money – although it doesn't always work out that way. I know it seems completely wrong, but that's the way it is now. Unfortunately, for some people that can mean the difference between having somewhere to live or not.

P: And where did you get the inspiration for your compact homes? Were they based on something you'd seen?

J: Yes – probably a lot of things I'd seen, in fact. But one particular source of inspiration was a people called the Dolgan who live in northern Russia. It's absolutely freezing there – it can go as low as minus 40 degrees – so a small living space is very practical. The Dolgan houses are shaped a bit like a sugar cube and they're extremely basic – a single room with two or three beds, a table and a stove. They're constructed from wooden frames and reindeer skins, which is a great insulator, and they sit on sled runners, so that they can be pulled along by the reindeer. So, when the Dolgan need to move their reindeer to find new places for them to feed, they can literally move house at the same time. It's so simple. They've made the best of available resources and just kept it very functional. I must say, I liked that.

P: I guess small often means living more simply.

J: Yes, I've seen some cabins in California of ten square metres – that's about 25 times smaller than an average American home – where people had to reduce their possessions to only what was absolutely essential. But small doesn't always equal simple. The architect Gary Chang, who is another person I've been strongly influenced by, lives in an apartment block in Hong Kong that's only 32 square metres. He's rethought the concept of living space in a totally unique way using a clever series of sliding walls and moveable built-in units so that he can transform his small apartment into any room he wants – a living room, a kitchen, a library, a bedroom. It's quite amazing really – there are 24 different rooms he can make from just the one space.

▶ 24

A: Have you seen these pictures of the artwork that's being proposed for the main square in the city centre?

B: No. Er, what is it?

A: It's a sculpture in the shape of an open book, and quotes and jokes by various famous local people appear on the page electronically.

B: Oh, I see.

A: Yeah, the quotes change every few minutes. I think it's rather clever. What do you think?

B: Well, yeah, it looks quite fun, but I have to say, I didn't get the idea straightaway – not until you explained it. Personally, I'd rather have something a bit more artistic, if you know what I mean. I'm also not convinced that it'll stand the test of time. I imagine people will get bored of it pretty quickly.

A: Oh, no. I disagree. I reckon people – both locals and visitors, that is – will really like the fact that it tells you something about the city – in the sense that it features people that have been part of our history. I don't think you should underestimate the value of the educational aspect.

B: Yeah, I see that and I'm all in favour of something that's relevant, or rather that reflects our heritage, but I'm afraid it just seems a bit ugly to me.

A: Well, for me, it's very important that it's something interactive – not just a static artwork – because that's more likely to attract people to the square. It's fairly clear that's what the artist is hoping, anyway.

Unit 4

▶ 26

A woman who has been virtually blind for the last six years has spoken about her happiness at being able to see again after surgeons at Oxford's John Radcliffe Hospital inserted a tiny electronic chip into the back of her right eye. Within seconds of switching the device on, Rhian Lewis was able to see light and colour in a way that had been impossible before. It'll probably take months for Lewis to train her brain to see properly again but the early signs are extremely positive; she can already distinguish nearby objects like knives and forks on a table.

Bionic body parts are a fast-developing technology which don't have to be only for people with disabilities. New ear buds developed by a company in San Francisco promise to help anyone hear better by allowing the wearer to choose what sounds to ignore and what to focus on. For example, they can filter out the background noise in a busy restaurant or amplify surrounding sounds when you're riding a bicycle. All this raises the question of whether it is likely that one day in the not so distant future, bionic body parts will actually be more efficient than our own biological body parts.

Audioscripts

28

P = Presenter, M = Martha Kay

P: Life must have been very different before the invention of certain things, but it's not always so easy to imagine what it was like. For example, if you're in your teens or twenties, you might never have considered how people searched for information before the internet existed. The electric light is another thing that we all take for granted. But how do such inventions come about? Is it necessity that drives innovation? Or commercial profit? Or something else? Here to discuss these questions is business historian, Martha Kay. Martha, we have so many things around us that we needn't have acquired – I mean, we could clearly live without them – so the necessity argument is not the whole answer, is it?

M: Hello, Evan. No, of course it isn't. History's full of inventions that people thought they didn't need at the time. In 1878, a British Parliamentary committee, which had to comment on the usefulness of Alexander Graham Bell's telephone, said '… it is good enough for our transatlantic friends, but unworthy of the attention of practical men.'

P: Yes, well, they probably should have been more open-minded. But in 1878 people didn't need to have phones, did they? You could conduct your daily business perfectly well without one. But now it's become a necessity – a need has been created, if you like.

M: Well, I think people in the nineteenth century felt they had to find a way to communicate at a distance more effectively; they just hadn't envisaged the telephone. Of course, there are some inventions which fill an urgent need – vaccines against particular diseases, for instance. But most innovations aren't like that. Entrepreneurs often come up with ideas to make our lives a little more convenient or comfortable and then, over time, we come to rely on them. Television is a case in point. Remote shopping – like mail-order, or these days internet shopping – is another. *Time* magazine in the 1960s said it wouldn't catch on because, and I quote, 'women like to get out of the house and to be able to change their minds'.

P: I'm sure they did – like to get out of the house, that is, and away from the housework. It can't have been easy. That certainly was a different era.

M: Another form of innovation is to take something that's at first expensive to produce and therefore exclusive to rich people, and make it available to many. There are quite a few things that we now see as everyday necessities that have come to us in this way – where an entrepreneur has found a way to produce something more cheaply, like the mobile phone or the computer. Another example, in the 1890s, the motor car was thought to be a luxury for the wealthy. *Literary Digest* predicted that it would never come into common use.

P: I see, so in that sense, it's about wants rather than needs. But what about all those things that we really don't need. I'm thinking of things like …

31

First of all, say in a few words what your product or service does, without using jargon, so that anyone could understand it. Make clear what problem it solves and say why your solution is different from the competition. Lastly, you need to convince the other person that you are a good person to implement this idea, so explain your relevant background.

32

Our idea is a phone app that makes volunteering in the community easier. It's called *Volunteer Planner*. How does it work? Basically, it's an interactive diary that links people who want to volunteer to charities who are looking for help. Why is that necessary? Well, essentially the problem is that voluntary organizations always want people to commit to a regular time – like once a week – so they miss out on all the people who have time here and there and want to help, but can't commit to anything regular. So they never come forward. Of course, there are other apps that do meeting planning like Doodle and Timepal, but ours is unique to this sector because it lists each volunteer's qualifications and skills in a separate database that organizations can easily access.

We're a team of IT experts with experience of working with charities, so we understand this sector well. So, what are we asking for? Well, we've made a prototype and now we need some funding to bring it to market. Honestly, we think it will revolutionize the field of volunteering.

Unit 5

34

Three people visit the same place and each one leaves with a different story. One remembers a romantic evening in a cosy restaurant and a long walk through a beautifully lit city by night; another remembers an argument with an officious museum curator about the closing time of an art gallery; another remembers sitting and watching the world go by on a lazy, hot afternoon in an elegant park.

Our travel experiences are influenced by so many different factors: the circumstances and state of mind in which we arrive; the people we happen to meet – an affable fellow traveller or a wary local; the preconceptions that we bring to each place we visit. The gift of a good travel writer is to capture the essence of a place in a way that we can all identify with, so that it's instantly recognizable not just superficially – in its grand architecture or lively cafés – but in the way that a particular place feels and thinks. Because the best travel writers aren't really writing about travel, they're writing about how people have shaped places and how places have shaped people.

36

1 I do regret not stopping there.
2 She does travel a lot.
3 We do miss home sometimes.
4 I did spend a lot of time at the beach.

37

I = Interviewer, M = Maggie Richards

I: The idea of a mystery tour was made famous by the Beatles' 'Magical Mystery Tour' film in which the band head off westwards out of London in an old bus in search of adventure. Since then, the idea of taking a journey to an unknown destination has been taken up by coach tour operators who offer 'exciting' locations and 'top' hotels, usually to parties of more elderly holiday-makers. But a London-based company called *Secret Adventures* is targeting a younger age group by adding a twist to the concept of the mystery tour. They have developed a number of travel experiences designed, in their words, 'to generate a sense of exploration and wonder'. *Travel Book*'s own Maggie Richards went on one of the trips and talked to me afterwards about it. So, Maggie, a magical experience or not?

M: Absolutely. Definitely one I'd recommend.

I: How much did you know about the adventure before you left? How secret was it?

M: Basically, all we were told was that we'd meet in London and that we'd need a bicycle, a swimming costume and a dry bag – oh, and also that the trip would be over two days.

I: And did you know how far you'd have to swim?

M: Yeah, I did ask that – fifty metres. I thought about asking where we'd be swimming but then I decided not to.

I: No, I guess that would've spoiled the surprise. So can you explain what the trip consisted of?

M: OK, so we all met up in Hackney in north London – eight of us and our guide, Madoc. And then we set off down the track next to the River Lea. It was a beautiful afternoon and the path was flat so it was easy cycling. And that gave us the chance to chat and get to know each other. Occasionally, Madoc would give us a clue about the trip, like 'Only fifteen miles to go' or 'Is that our island? No, I don't think so.' It all added to the anticipation. Then, as the sun was setting, he told us to stop and put our bikes in the long grass and get ready to swim. We packed our stuff into dry bags and then got into the water. It wasn't warm and a few people were screaming and gasping – I know I was – but actually it felt really exhilarating to be heading off for the night with just your swimming things and a dry bag. Madoc had gone ahead and by the time we reached the island, a fire was burning. He cooked an amazing stew for supper and we shared stories around the fire.

183

Audioscripts

I: Did you have tents?
M: No, we didn't. We slept in the open, but it was fine – it wasn't cold. In the morning, we swam back and cycled to a café for breakfast. Then we caught a train back into London. It was very strange arriving back in the busy city. It made the whole thing seem as if it had been a magical dream – actually it had .
I: Are the trips expensive?
M: Not at all. Well, it depends which one . Some of the shorter ones are less than £40. You could travel a long way and spend a lot more to create that kind of magic, but what Secret Adventures taught me was that you really don't need to .

(Based on a real Secret Adventures trip. Madoc is a real character, but Maggie is a fictional character.)

▶ 38

1 A: You have to be careful not to get overcharged in the local markets.
  B: Yes, I know that.
2 A: Would you like to drive?
  B: No, I'd rather you did.
3 A: Did he take warm clothes with him?
  B: I hope so.
4 A: Do you mind travelling alone?
  B: No, I actually prefer it.
5 A: Are there many good guidebooks about this region?
  B: Yes, there are some excellent ones.
6 A: Did she enjoy visiting Russia?
  B: Yes, she loved it.

▶ 40

I think it's a well-known fact that a lot of exposure to strong sun is a dangerous thing, particularly if you're a person with fair skin. So these days people are generally more careful – they take precautions not to get sunburned. But I'm afraid it wasn't always like that.

I have my clinic in Patong. It's on the island of Phuket in Thailand – which you've heard about, I'm sure: it's famous for having beautiful beaches and consequently, we get a lot of tourists and sunseekers here.

A few years ago, I was in my clinic and a young man with red hair and very fair skin came in. His legs were the colour of his hair – like a lobster – and he was in great pain. I applied some cream to his legs and then I wrapped them both in bandages from the ankle to the thigh. I told him to stay out of the sun and to take it easy for a few days until the redness had disappeared. The following morning, I was walking to work along the street by the beach. By chance, I happened to glance down at the people on the beach who were arranging their sunbeds and parasols for a day of relaxing by the sea and there, to my amazement, was the same man! He was lying stretched out on his back, not in the shade, but in full sun with just his swimming costume and his bandages on! It was so crazy it was almost funny.

Unit 6

▶ 42

W = Woman, R = Rashmi
W: How do you advise people to stay fit and healthy, Rashmi?
R: You know, there's so much contradictory information out there about how to keep in shape: whether you should watch your weight by controlling what you eat or by exercising; what kind of exercise regime is best, and so on. I was reading a scientific journal just this morning saying that intensive exercise, like working out at the gym is actually less effective than gentle exercise, like going for a walk regularly in the park.
W: Really? Why did it say that?
R: I think the idea is that if you do really intensive exercise, then your body demands calorie compensation afterwards – in other words, you're more likely to reward yourself with a bigger snack at the end of the session. Whereas if you just stretch your legs often or take regular gentle exercise, it doesn't have the same effect.
W: So what do you do? You're in pretty good shape.
R: Well, mainly I try not to obsess too much about my weight. I don't go on diets and I don't weigh myself every day. I just do active things that I enjoy. I've never been a fan of the gym, I have to say, and I never go for a run – I find it boring. The kids keep me pretty active anyway. But recently I've got into road cycling. Every couple of weeks a few of us go out for a ride in the countryside – forty or fifty kilometres. We often go up in the woods and hills around the South Downs. The scenery's beautiful and it's a great way to enjoy nature and stay fit at the same time.

▶ 44

P = Presenter, B = Ben Newborn
P: … thanks for those comments, Lydia. I'd like to turn now to someone who should know more about sports injuries than most and that's ultrarunner Ben Newborn. Ben, before we get into the question of injuries, can you just explain for our listeners what ultrarunning is?
B: Sure, basically ultrarunning is running distances beyond a usual marathon distance. So, it could mean running 100 kilometres in a single day, or it could involve running several marathons on consecutive days.
P: And how did you get into it?
B: I was a runner anyway and I just wanted to take it to another level – to really test myself physically and mentally. So in 2008, I registered for the Ultra-Trail race in the Alps which requires runners to run 161 kilometres around Mont Blanc.
P: Didn't you worry about doing yourself real damage?
B: Actually, I wasn't so concerned about injuries. I was more worried about failure. And I knew that if I wanted to succeed in overcoming exhaustion and the things that can make you feel sick, I had to get my diet and nutrition right. That's ultimately what would let me run in relative comfort.
P: Comfort's not a word I'd normally associate with a 161-kilometre run, but anyway … What about injuries? This must put intense strain on your body.
B: I think the most important thing in any sport is to recognize when your body's in pain. A lot of sports people try to go through the pain. I'm not talking about when they're in a really bad way, but when they have a small muscle strain or pain in a joint – an ankle, for example – they tend to take some painkillers or put on some kind of support and just carry on exercising . Because they feel they can't afford to rest . But of course that's completely wrong. Pain is your body warning you to be careful – to stop, very often – because minor problems will inevitably develop into more severe injuries. So that's the first thing: to listen to your body.
P: Yes, but we all get aches and pains. Surely that shouldn't discourage us from doing exercise?
B: Well, no, but if you do the right kind of preparation, which I'd really urge people to do , you can avoid getting injuries in the first place. I follow a method developed by a sports physiologist, which is a series of stretches and gentle exercises that strengthen the key muscles and ligaments. It's definitely prevented me from getting ankle sprains and helped with some of the other things I used to suffer from: lower back pain, runner's knee and so on …

▶ 45

1 A: I heard Sarah came off her bicycle. Is she in a bad way?
  B: Luckily she didn't break anything; she was pretty shaken up though.
2 A: Is it true that Jack nearly cut his finger off?
  B: Yes, he practically passed out when he saw what he'd done. It was quite a deep cut, but he's on the mend now, I think.
3 A: You look a bit off colour. Are you feeling under the weather?
  B: No, I'm not ill. I'm just run down from working too much.

▶ 48

C = Chair, S = Sophia, T = Tariq
C: Hello, everyone. Welcome to this brainstorming session on promoting health and fitness among employees. David Grant, our CEO, is very keen that we, as a company, take some positive action on this – not only because there's also an obvious benefit in terms of productivity and days lost through sickness, but because he genuinely believes it'll make for a happier workplace. So, with that in mind, I'd like to hear any ideas you have. Who'd like to start? Yes, Sophia …
S: Thank you. Yeah, well, as I see it, there are probably two routes we could

go down. One possibility is just to encourage people to do simple things like walking to work or not spending such long periods at their computers, that kind of thing. Or the other alternative is to spend some serious money on the problem – so, something like installing a gym or a fitness centre on site that people can use in their breaks, or after work. Having said that, I realize there may not be a budget for that kind of thing.

C: OK, thanks for that and … Yes, Tariq …
T: Yeah, for me the key is getting people to enjoy exercise. If you offer activities that people think are fun, then I think you'll get much better participation.
C: Such as …?
T: Such as team sports – football, basketball, that kind of thing – you could even have competitions. Another idea could be dance classes. Admittedly, a lot of people may do these things anyway in their free time, but I bet there are a lot more who want to and never find the time.
C: Thanks, Tariq. I think those are interesting ideas. And what about the idea of group exercises in the mornings? The kind of collective warm-up routine you used to see in companies fifty years ago. It's not a particularly original idea, I'll grant you, but it might be fun – and it would definitely build team spirit.
S: Yeah, I think you have to be careful there. People might think that you're trying to force them into some sort of exercise regime. You know, I know that isn't the intention, but it might look that way. I think it'd be better to give people incentives to do things on their own, like a 'bike to work' scheme, where you offer to pay part of the cost of a new bicycle – I haven't thought the details through exactly, but I think that kind of individual incentive probably works much better.
C: Yeah, I like that. The only problem I see is that it wouldn't be so easy to monitor how much they used the bike, but I guess that's a risk you'd have to take.

Unit 7

▶ 51

Have digital media changed the way people experience the world? Probably. They've certainly changed the way we record and share those experiences with others. Never before has so much written information been published and never before have so many photos been taken and distributed. Digital media – in the form of instant messaging, blogs, social networking sites, internet forums, online photo albums, online music and video – all of this has increased accessibility to other people's experiences enormously.

But do digital media change the experience itself? That's a more difficult question to answer. In a way, they do. If you go to a concert or a festival or even a conference these days, everyone's busy recording and sharing the experience as it happens: taking photos, sending texts or tweeting. In fact, people seem to spend almost as much time recording the experience as they do actually watching or listening to what's going on.

Does that detract from the experience itself? Some would argue that it does. I'm inclined to think that it's a question of moderation – as with any tool. It's a good thing as long as you don't let it take over your life.

▶ 53

P = Presenter, S = Sarah Palmer
P: We hear about companies being customer-focused all the time these days, but a focus on your customer is pointless if they're not focused on you. Sarah Palmer from the e-marketing consultancy firm 'Excite' is here to tell us how organizations can generate that kind of interest. Sarah …
S: Thanks, Greg. Good marketing is an ability to turn your customers into fans; in other words, making people so passionate about what you do that they want to share it with others. These days, a company has no hope of doing that unless they use social media: not just to sell their products and services, but to really involve people in what they're doing. Basically, customers these days want to know a company's story, and they want to learn something. And if you can provide those things, and use social media to get them to buy into your story, then you can create a loyal following. You can catch passing customers sometimes with pop-up ads on the internet, but the creation of a loyal following is a much more effective long-term strategy.
P: So, can you give us some examples of organizations that use social media effectively, in the way that you're describing?
S: Yes, our research into social media marketing has given us some great examples of best practice; a good one is *National Geographic*. They actively encourage fan interaction: inviting users to share travel stories, or to do surveys on how environmentally friendly their lifestyle is, and then compare their scores with their friends. You can enter competitions, there are links to different causes you can support – like helping to protect elephants.
P: Mmm, that all sounds great, but where does the actual selling come in?
S: Well, alongside that there are offers of discounts for magazine subscribers, coupons you can use for *National Geographic* products, that kind of thing.
P: OK. I see how this kind of fan-building approach works for *National Geographic*, because it has such a clear and worthy mission – that's the main reason for their success. But what about a company that's just trying to sell a regular product, like bathroom cleaner? There's no real story or mission, is there?
S: No, it's really no different – the same principles apply. Priority must be given to educating or involving customers in a way that's fun. It doesn't matter what you're selling: customer engagement will boost sales. I was recently looking at a company that sells tea and their website gave you an interactive tour of the teas of China. It was great fun and very educational: you wouldn't believe the number of varieties and how much some of them cost. It's a whole other world.

▶ 55

P = Presenter, M = Martin Roddick
P: Hello and welcome to the *Nature Today* podcast. Today we're going to look at some new evidence about glowing blue waves, which are arguably one of the most spectacular sights in nature. The tiny blue lights dotted across the water make it appear as if the sea is reflecting the light of the stars, but actually, the source of this light is small sea creatures, called phytoplankton. And how they produce the strange blue light has been a mystery. Until now, that is. Here's Martin Roddick of the Oceanographic Institute.
M: Hello. Actually, there are thought to be a lot of sea creatures that are bioluminescent, in other words, that can light up in the dark, but most of these creatures tend to live in the deep ocean. That's because it's dark in the deep ocean and so the ability to light yourself up is useful for finding food or scaring away predators, or perhaps just lighting your way as you move around. But the bioluminescent creatures that cause this effect – the phytoplankton – live near the surface. And so that's how we get this wonderful sight on beaches and in waves in places like the Caribbean.
P: And how do they do it?
M: It seems that an electrical force in the phytoplankton's body causes a chemical reaction to take place, and that in turn produces a blue light. The light is usually emitted in waves, so we can probably conclude that the electricity is generated by the motion of the water.
P: Thank you, Martin. And if you'd like to know more about this research, you can read details of the study on the OI website at …

Unit 8

▶ 57

Well, like a lot of buskers, I started busking because I wanted to get more confidence as a performer. It wasn't about the money. I'm a singer-songwriter – I don't have my own band, and it's not easy to get gigs as a solo artist. Also, I just really like live performance. I love it when you're walking down the street or in the underground and then completely unexpectedly, you hear something amazing.

So, I went out busking when I was seventeen – just me and my acoustic guitar. Not in my home town, because I really didn't want people to recognize me, but in a nearby town. It was pretty nerve-racking at first, to be honest; and I think that came across in my performance because I didn't get much attention or much money, for that matter. I think the first time I got about fifteen pounds

185

…and a cheese sandwich that someone threw into my guitar case. But I got better and it definitely helped my confidence. And then last Christmas-time when I was busking this guy approached me – a keyboard player who was already semi-professional and actually a very naturally-gifted musician – and he asked if I'd like to work with him and write songs together. And I thought, 'Why not?'

And that's how my career really got started. We play R&B mainly – he generally writes the music and I write the lyrics – and we perform the songs at gigs around the country. We've actually just made our first demo recording together and we're touring next year in some quite decent venues. So, fingers crossed.

▶ 59

1 A: Are you ready?
   B: Sure. Just a minute. I'll get my coat.
2 A: Thank goodness we're nearly there. It's starting to rain.
   B: Phew! Just in time.
3 A: I hope you're not too disappointed about the museum being closed.
   B: It's OK. It's just one of those things.
4 A: Here. I've got a little screwdriver on my penknife.
   B: Thanks. That's just the job.
5 A: Can I help you?
   B: No, thanks. I'm just looking.
6 A: Hi, Bea. Sorry I'm late.
   B: Oh, I was just about to call you.
7 A: Is she your girlfriend?
   B: No, we're just good friends.
8 A: Why do you ask if I know him?
   B: No particular reason. I just wondered.
9 A: Shall I bring some food for the train?
   B: Yes, do bring some, just in case.
10 A: I couldn't believe that he lost that match.
   B: It just goes to show no one's perfect.

▶ 60

The study of how music affects the brain is still a work in progress, but exciting things are coming to light all the time. We know that music activates many different parts of the brain – that there's no one centre that processes music. And we also know that music has the power to release endorphins, which are the chemicals that our bodies use to help us deal with stress or pain. Endorphins are actually vital to our well-being in general, because they produce feelings of happiness or even elation. So when we listen to music, we're rewarded with this boost of feel-good chemicals.

Its power to relax us is so strong that it's commonly used in hospitals now to calm people before they undergo surgery or for the relief of pain after an operation.

So that's one area in which music can help people. Another is with people who have language difficulties. Imagine you're at a party and there's so much noise that it's difficult to hear the person right next to you. Well, if you're not having to strain in order to hear what others are saying, the chances are that you are someone with musical training; and that's because we use the same parts of the brain to process music and language. In other words, people with musical training have improved their brain's ability to distinguish not only musical but also spoken sounds.

What are the implications of this? Well, I'm not saying you should take up a musical instrument so that you can hear people better at parties … or so as to be a better linguist – though that is an idea. What it means is that we could use music to help people with dyslexia or other language disorders. A neuroscientist at Harvard University, called Gottfried Schlaug, has had amazing success using music therapy on people who were unable to speak properly after suffering a stroke. Before the therapy, patients responded to questions with incoherent sounds and phrases, but after being taught to sing phrases or to speak in time to the music, they were able to recite their addresses, say their names and even sing extracts of songs. The therapy produced such a dramatic improvement that even sceptics were impressed.

Similar improvements have been recorded with patients with dementia and memory loss. This news should be music to our ears, if you'll forgive the pun, because illnesses like these are becoming a bigger and bigger problem as we all live longer, and we clearly need to find a solution so as not to let it get any worse.

▶ 62

P = Presenter, F = Frank Steel
P: Today's castaway is a disc jockey who's been hosting his own radio show for over thirty years. Where most disc jockeys come and go with the changing of fashions in music, he has managed to maintain a loyal following of listeners over the last 35 years, and to attract new ones from each new generation. He is Frank Steel. Frank, what's the secret of your continuing success?
F: That's a good question, but it isn't something I've often thought about. I don't think it's a secret really. I take an interest in what's happening now in the music world, and I look out for new trends. People do that in other fields, like science or art. It's just that with pop music, you're not supposed to stay trendy after you're thirty. But I don't agree with that.
P: So you still get excited by new music. What, for you, makes a good record?
F: I honestly don't know. What makes a particular piece of music move you is something that can't really be described or identified. I'd rather not think too much about why I like a particular song or record.
P: And what's your first record?
F: This is a song by John Etheridge, a blues and jazz guitarist. I think it was the first blues record I ever heard and it opened up a whole new world to me. I also associate it with the summer of 1976, which was a really hot summer. I was supposed to be revising for exams, but I spent most of my time lazing around in the park. It was too hot to work.
P: *Crossroad Blues* by John Etheridge. Your taste in music is very wide – eclectic some would say. How did that come about?
F: That's difficult to say. It wasn't planned, if that's what you mean. I just keep my ears open for anything interesting, and I don't confine myself to any particular source for that. It's a question of staying curious, I suppose.

Unit 9
▶ 65

Archaeologists like to say about the objects that they uncover: 'It's not what you find, it's what you find out.' The 5,000-year old Stones of Stenness on the island of Orkney in the far north of Scotland stand on a grassy hill overlooking the sea and dominating the landscape around them. They were clearly built to impress and they do. Although their exact purpose can't be determined from just looking at them, other objects found near the site have given valuable clues.

The bones of domestic animals, the pieces of pottery, the ruins of smaller buildings made of stone rather than wood, which was more common at the time, and the fertile soil itself – all these things indicate that this was a rich farming community. Archaeologists have also come across volcanic glass and high-quality flint tools that were transported from other islands. These items are evidence that Orkney was on a trading route.

Consequently, they've concluded that this was a wealthy civilization that had the time and the money to build monuments – rather like in ancient Egypt. Perhaps the Stones had a religious significance, perhaps not. Either way, we can deduce that these were monuments of great cultural importance that people travelled from far and wide to see.

▶ 67

I = Interviewer, C = Clara
I: Why are you particularly interested in the story of Martin Guerre?
C: Well, I belong to a group of historians who are interested in what's called micro-history. We focus on small single events in history, because we believe you can learn more about a society from intensive study of these events. The story of Martin Guerre is a very strange one and we micro-historians look out for that kind of unusual story, hoping it'll give us a better idea of what normal behaviour was during a particular period in history.
I: I see, that's interesting. So, can you just summarize the story?
C: Yes, of course. Martin Guerre was a French peasant who lived in a village called Artigat in the south-west of France – this was in the early sixteenth century. He was the eldest son in a family of six and he got married very young – in his teens in fact. At the age of 21, he and his wife, Bertrande, had a baby son. But a few years later, he was caught stealing grain from his father's grain store. Fearing a severe punishment (theft was considered the worst type of crime in those days), he fled over the border to Spain and having

spent some time doing various jobs, he eventually joined the Spanish army. In 1557 he was wounded in battle and his leg had to be amputated.
I: And his family?
C: Yes, so in the meantime, Bertrande was left at home not knowing what had happened to her husband and unable to remarry because no one knew if Martin was dead or alive. Then one day – and this is where the story becomes interesting – one day, a man professing to be Martin Guerre appeared in the village to claim the family estate. Given that Martin's father had already died, the house and land now legally belonged to his eldest son.
I: So this wasn't the real Martin Guerre?
C: No, the man was an impostor called Arnaud de Tilh. Yet the incredible thing is that Bertrande and the rest of the family accepted him as the real Martin Guerre. It was only Martin's uncle, Pierre, who was in charge of administering the estate, who didn't believe him. And he took the case to court to prove that Arnaud was a fraud.
I: Why did Bertrande do that? She must have known it wasn't her husband.
C: We don't really know. Perhaps, having waited so long, she was just glad to have someone to support her again financially.
I: And what was the outcome of the case?
C: Well, Arnaud lost the first case but he appealed and the case went to a higher court. He thought he had succeeded in persuading the judges that he was Martin Guerre, until the real Martin Guerre, complete with wooden leg, appeared in the court and told his story. For Arnaud, the game was up and that was the end of his deception.

▶ 69

A: I've just read a fascinating book called *Fixing the Sky* about attempts by various people in history to control the weather.
B: What do you mean by 'control the weather'? Like stopping the rain?
A: Yes – or making it rain. It describes the kind of things people have traditionally done to get the weather they want – that's to say, things like praying for sunshine or doing rain dances when there's a drought and their crops are failing. But then it goes on to describe more recent experiments with artificial weather-changing technology and actually, it becomes quite scary.
B: What kind of experiments?
A: I'll give you an example. In the 1950s the government conducted a secret cloud-seeding experiment.
B: Sorry, what's that?
A: Cloud seeding? It means putting chemicals into clouds to make it rain. Silver iodide is one that's commonly used. But the point is that when people did these experiments, they didn't see it as interfering with nature – they seemed to have no idea that it might have unwanted consequences. So, what happened – though it's not actually proven, but it's very likely – their experiment caused the terrible floods that took place that year in the south-west of England.
B: Hang on, let me get this straight. Are you saying that the government experimented with making rain and it caused a natural disaster?
A: Pretty much, yes, though I doubt they meant to …
B: That's terrible. But actually, am I right in thinking that it could be quite useful technology now, you know, with climate change and all that?
A: Yes, and I guess that's the author's point: that we need to be looking at solutions like cloud-seeding, but that we should also be aware of the history of such techniques. In other words, we shouldn't just jump into things.

Unit 10
▶ 72

P = Presenter, A = Alejandra Sanchez
P: Did you know that Melbourne, Australia has the third biggest Greek population of any city after Athens and Thessaloniki? Or that London, England is now France's sixth biggest city? In Denver, Colorado, over a third of the population are Hispanic, mostly from Mexico. The majority of these ethnic groups – with the possible exception of the French in London – aren't made up of first-generation migrants, but second, third, fourth, even fifth generation. So what's it like to belong to a long-standing immigrant community? What are the implications for the individual and the community as a whole? I put this question to a resident of Denver, Alejandra Sanchez.
A: My grandparents came here from Mexico forty years ago as migrant workers, but I'm an American citizen and I participate fully in American life. I'm also Mexican-Hispanic and with that comes certain values, whether you are first or fourth generation. The most important thing for us is not the individual, it's the family. We grow up surrounded by our extended family: our brothers, our sisters, our cousins, our aunts and uncles. They're also our friends and without them, we're nothing. I think more than anything else, these deep-rooted values make us a very close-knit community. When we Hispanics come together at social gatherings, we celebrate this part of our heritage and treat each other as family. You can see this spirit of harmony at the Cinco de Mayo festivities, which is a wonderful celebration of our rich heritage.

▶ 74

Among all the serious business of life – the daily news, the work responsibilities, the forward planning, the everyday to-do list – we often forget to play. In fact, we seldom think of play as something necessary – it seems more like a luxury to indulge in when we have spare time. But actually play is an essential part of our well-being and our social interactions. I'll try to explain why.

When we take a break and participate in some light-hearted act of fun, we relieve feelings of tension and we begin to relax. And no sooner have we started to relax than our minds also begin to think differently – more creatively, more experimentally, more laterally, if you like. So, first of all, play is a brain stimulant: it increases our ability to solve problems and to think outside the box. Lots of tech companies like Google recognize this, providing play spaces for their workers to use at work.

Secondly, play is good for our health. Not only does it relieve tension, studies have also shown that laughter, which is a natural product of play, improves blood circulation and increases the body's resistance to disease.

Thirdly, play connects us. It's a way of socializing without pressure, because the focus is not the social relationship itself but the game. In most play – I'm not talking about organized, competitive sport here – there aren't high expectations on the players socially and there's hardly any formality either; just a shared feeling of enjoyment and of letting go. So play has the power to break down barriers between people, to encourage empathy and to improve communication.

Lastly, and this is particularly important, it keeps us in the present moment. The present is actually the only place where we can feel real happiness. But we don't spend enough time in the present. A lot of the time, our minds wander and we find ourselves thinking about things in the past, from which feelings of anger or regret can arise; or things in the future, from which feelings of anxiety can arise. But when we're engaged in play, we are usually so immersed in that activity that we lose ourselves in the present, which is the place where, as several psychologists have noted, true pleasure is found.

But what is the nature of this 'play' I've been talking about? Well, in many ways, it scarcely matters what kind of play it is. It could be an organized game – like football or a board game; it could be playing Frisbee casually in the park. But equally it could just be a playful conversation. Play doesn't have to be a specific activity; it's also a state of mind: sharing a joke, making a play on words, pointing out something absurd – generally just seeing the funny side of things.

▶ 78

Conversation 1
A: Hi, Reka! Fancy a game of tennis this afternoon?
B: Love to, but I can't, I'm afraid.
A: Why? What are you doing?
B: Working. I need to get an essay in by tomorrow afternoon.
A: Oh, that's a shame. What are you writing about?
B: Social change in the first half of the twentieth century. I'm really enjoying it, actually.
A: Are you?

Audioscripts

B: Yeah, I am, because the changes in that period were so huge, particularly for women. You can read it if you like when it's finished.
A: Yeah, I'd like to.

Conversation 2
C: Great party, last night.
D: It was, wasn't it? Trouble is, there's loads to clear up after it. The room we used is a real mess.
C: That's not your job, is it?
D: Yeah, I'm afraid so. Hey, you couldn't lend me a hand with it later, could you?
C: Mmm, I expect so. Oh, actually, no, sorry I can't. I just remembered that I've got to wait in this afternoon for a delivery.
D: Oh, have you? What kind of delivery?
C: Oh, I ordered one of those digital voice recorders online. It's to record lectures with, so I can listen back to them to check I haven't missed anything. I'm always missing things in lectures.
D: Yeah, me too. Sounds like a good idea. Was it expensive?
C: No, not expensive at all. I think I got it for around $18. I'll send you the link.
D: Yeah, please do. That'd be handy.

Unit 11

▶ 81

What makes a good photo? The composition and the colour are very important, but actually, it's the emotions it expresses or evokes that are key. Elijah Walker, a photo editor at *National Geographic*, calls it 'emotional gravity' – when a picture packs an emotional punch. Most often emotionally powerful photos are ones of people, when they reveal at one glance a moment of genuine joy or anger, sadness or surprise. It doesn't have to be an extreme emotion – like looking utterly miserable or ecstatically happy. More nuanced emotions can be almost more effective in a way: a shy smile or a look of calm pride.

Kids are great to photograph, because they tend not to hide their emotions in the way that adults sometimes do. I love this one. This little boy looks so proud and pleased with himself as he brings his catch back from a fishing trip. He's obviously delighted to have brought lunch home for his family. The appeal of the photo is that it reflects a simpler kind of life with simpler pleasures. That was certainly in the mind of the photographer who took it – he's nostalgic for this old India and concerned about increasing urbanization.

▶ 83

Part 1
Psychologist Daniel Kahneman's study of how we make certain judgements and decisions won him the Nobel Prize in Economics in 2002. What Kahneman found was that what seemed like rational decisions were often based on irrational thought processes. His research, which was based on asking people certain questions, is key to understanding how emotions can affect what should be otherwise logical decisions. If you just look at the screen, you'll see three examples of the type of questions that he asked. These were taken from his book *Thinking fast and slow*. I'd like you now to answer each one, but without thinking too hard about it. Should you get them wrong, you won't be alone: most people do, so please don't worry.

▶ 84

Part 2
So, what did you get? The answer to the first question is 53, but actually that's not what's interesting here. Kahneman says that what's psychologically interesting is that if for some reason you already had a high number in your mind, you would give a higher number as an answer. So, for example, if someone had just been talking with you about the weather and had said the temperature today was 82 degrees Fahrenheit, your answer to the Africa question would have been a higher number than if you had been told it was 28 degrees Celsius today. The answer to the second question is of course that neither is statistically more probable. However, the majority of people give the answer as 'b'. Were the same question presented as a logical formula, few would make this mistake. But we are influenced by the plausible details, preferring the human story to the hard logic. What about the last one? Well, if we look at both questions together, logically, you should choose the same option in both 3a and 3b – that is to say, you should either choose certainty or to take a risk. But it seems that most of us take fewer risks when there's a chance of winning something, so we choose the £500 for certain. However, if we are offered a chance to get out of a losing situation, most of us will take the gamble, i.e. we'll go for the fifty per cent chance of losing £1,000.

What Kahneman is trying to demonstrate is that our intuition can be unreliable and irrational. He describes our brain as having two systems: System One, where we form intuitive responses, and System Two, where more conscious, deliberate thought occurs.

The problem is that on many occasions, System One is always trying to help System Two, often with imperfect information. And so the result can be imperfect. Were it not for System One, in other words, if we were more aware of this influence, we would make better decisions, particularly financial decisions. Indeed, some people say that had the financial regulators been more aware of irrational thinking, the banking crisis of 2008 probably wouldn't have happened.

▶ 87

Conversation 1
J = Jennie, F = Felipe
J: Hi, Felipe. How are you?
F: Hi, Jennie. Yeah, I'm fine. You know …
J: You don't seem that fine. Are you sure everything's OK?
F: Sorry. I'm just a bit frustrated. Nothing seems to be working out today. I came in early to get some work done and I couldn't log into the system because they're doing some maintenance work. Now Fran has just rung and said she needs me to go to a meeting that I really don't want – or need – to go to. It's all lost time.
J: Is there anything I can do?
F: No, don't worry. I'll get over it! Thanks, though.

Conversation 2
L = Lewis, O = Ohoud
L: Hi, Ohoud, how are you doing? Mind if I join you?
O: Hi, Lewis. No, of course not.
L: How are you? You look a bit troubled.
O: No, I'm not troubled, really, I'm just a bit distracted. I'm trying to make a card for my brother. It's his thirtieth birthday. I can't seem to get it right.
L: Can I have a look?
O: Sure. But it's not finished yet. What do you think?
L: Er, what's it supposed to be?
O: It's a person skateboarding in a skateboard park – that's his hobby. Oh dear, I think I'd better start again. It's not very obvious, is it?
L: Oh, sorry. I didn't mean to offend you. I genuinely couldn't make out what it was. But that's probably just me being stupid. I can see it now you say it. Perhaps it'll be clearer when you add a bit of colour.

Conversation 3
P = Paola, M = Megumi
P: Hi Megumi. I haven't seen you for ages. How are you? Jen said you've got a new job with an American company in Tokyo.
M: Oh hi, Paola. Yes, that's right. With Disney. I'm going to be in charge of merchandise for Disney book characters, like Winnie the Pooh and Alice in Wonderland and Pinocchio. I'm really excited. Why are you smiling? Did I say something funny?
P: Oh, sorry. Don't get me wrong – I wasn't laughing at you. I'm really happy for you. It was just the idea of being in charge of all those cartoon characters – it conjured up a funny mental image. But it sounds amazing and a lot of fun. When do you start?

Unit 12

▶ 90

Speaker 1
I live in Azraq, east of Amman in Jordan. Officially the area is a desert, but not the desert of sand dunes and a blue, cloudless sky that most people think of. It's flat, rocky land with sparse vegetation. Some people think it's a bleak, monotonous landscape, but for me it's very beautiful. It is nature untouched by man. Azraq itself is the site of an oasis. So all around the water are tall grasses with some palm trees here and there and it attracts many birds.

Speaker 2
My village, Tyssedal, is in a valley between a fjord and the mountains. This part of Norway is famous for its dramatic scenery and we get a lot of hikers and tourists in the summer, particularly to Trolltunga. It means 'troll's tongue' and it's a piece of rock which juts out high over a lake. I love the contrasts

in the landscape here: glassy smooth lakes, wooded hillsides, snow-capped mountains. It's all on such a huge scale: as a person, it makes you feel kind of small, but it has a very calming effect too.

Speaker 3
People associate Wales with rich farmland and lush green valleys, but where I live in Blaenavon it's rugged, hilly terrain. Blaenavon is a UNESCO World Heritage Site, recognized for its importance in producing coal and iron in the nineteenth century, which is strange in a way, because in their time these industrial sites were considered a blot on the landscape. The industry's gone now and modern Blaenavon is nothing special, really. But what is special, at least for those of us brought up here, is that shared social history and sense of community. Those things are deeply connected to the land, because it was the coal and iron that gave people their livelihood.

▶ 92

Around five years ago, I took a trip to Madagascar to photograph the landscape. A guy I met at a party (he was a journalist or something) had told me that it had the most wonderful scenery. Normally I spend six months or so researching a place before I go there, but in this case I only spent about a week reading about it. Not long after, feeling kind of unprepared, I threw my stuff into a bag and left for Madagascar. During the trip I must have taken as many as 2,000 pictures, some of them a bit amateurish but a lot of high quality ones too. The landscape is incredibly varied. It's more or less like a different country in each region – desert, marshes, rainforest, sandy beaches. Incredible! And all of this is home to over 200,000 different species of plants and animals.

▶ 93

I = Interviewer, B = Biographer
I: Sophie Huxter, I think you're probably best known for writing travel guides, but I understand you've been writing recently about something rather different – a Japanese poet called Matsuo Basho. Could you tell us a bit more?
B: I'd love to, yes. Basically, I was on a trip to Japan, researching holidays there, and I came across this eight-day walk – the 'Basho Tour' – on the eastern side of the main island, Honshu. Basho was a poet who lived in seventeenth-century Japan. He was actually quite well known in his lifetime, but he wouldn't allow his celebrity to distract him from his real interests and so, quite late in life, he decided that he would escape in search of a simpler and more peaceful existence. And at the age of 46, he set off on a journey across the island of Honshu. That journey – which is what this tour is based on – was the background to his great collection of poems, *Narrow Road to a Far Province*.
I: But why didn't you just write about the tour? I'd imagine that's the sort of thing you normally write about. What was it about Basho that made you want to write about him and his poems?
B: Yes, that's a good question. The thing is, as a poet, one of Basho's preoccupations was observing nature. So, as he travelled on foot through this part of Honshu – about 1,100 miles in all he travelled – he kept a kind of diary of the things he saw. He would stop and observe what one writer called 'nature's modest dramas', in other words, little details or events in nature that pleased him: like the brilliant colour of a particular flower, or the way sunlight catches the spray from a waterfall and makes a rainbow, or the reflection of a floating leaf in a crystal clear stream, the splash of a frog as it jumps into the water … And then it struck me. There I was writing about holidays and tours and hotels and so on, and I wasn't paying attention to all these beautiful little details around me – around all of us.
I: Nature's modest dramas.
B: Exactly. It wouldn't really have worked if I had made that the focus of a travel guide, so I decided to write about Basho and his poetry instead.
I: And would you give us an example of one of the poems?
B: Yes, of course. They're haikus – three-line poems of seventeen syllables, written in plain and simple language, but at the same time profound. Each haiku is like a polished stone. He wrote this one when he came across an old military fort, in ruins and overgrown with grass and it upset him rather. He wrote: 'Mound of summer grass / Are soldiers' heroic deeds / Only dreams that pass?'

▶ 95

A: OK, so we'd like to hear your views about two possible ways of relieving traffic congestion in the city centre. Craig is just going to summarize the two main proposals before we open up the discussion. Craig …
B: Thank you. The first proposal is a congestion charging scheme, that's to say creating a zone in the centre of the city which vehicles have to pay a fixed charge to enter. The exact limits of the zone haven't been defined yet, nor has the exact amount of the charge. The second proposal involves simply banning all private cars from the centre and providing a park and ride bus service from various points on the outskirts of the city into the centre.
A: Thanks, Craig. So now we'll open the discussion to the floor. Please try and keep your comments reasonably short so that everyone gets a chance to have their say.
C: Well, I don't see how we can really comment on the first proposal without knowing what the scope of the zone is and how much it's going to cost: those are really key issues. I mean if it's going to mean that local residents have to pay to get into the centre then that's not really fair, is it? I live in Charles Street which is …
D: Sorry, can I just say something in answer to that? We had a similar scheme where I used to live and people who lived within the zone were exempted from paying the charge.
B: Yes, I think that's absolutely right and you can also give a discount to people who need to come into the centre for their work so that it doesn't discriminate against them either. Otherwise you find that a lot of people who really need their cars …
C: No, hang on, hang on a minute. If you keep making exceptions for different groups of people, you're going to end up with a system that costs a lot of money and doesn't bring much benefit. I think you have to be strict about this …
D: Yes, but how much is the charge going to be? No one's given us any …
C: Sorry, can I just finish what I was saying? The point *is* that unless you're strict about it, the scheme won't bring in enough revenue to pay for itself, and so those who do pay will question the whole scheme.

Communication activities • Quiz answers

UNIT 2a Exercise 1, page 22

SEA FACTS

1 **Over 70%** of the Earth's surface is covered by water.
2 About **50%** of the world's population live in coastal regions.
3 **90%** of the world's goods are transported by sea.
4 **90%** of the world's animals live in the sea.
5 The average consumption of fish per person per year is **20 kg**.
6 Fish is the main source of protein for **1 billion** people.
7 The average time someone can hold their breath underwater is **30–40 seconds**.

UNIT 2c Exercise 11, page 26

Answers to quiz

Mostly 'A's: You feel confident with new challenges and are happy to be in the spotlight. That's great, but be careful not to over-extend yourself.

Mostly 'B's: You are careful, but want to expand your comfort zone by doing things that challenge you.

Mostly 'C's: You are someone who likes to stay well within their comfort zone. That's OK, but remember that leaving your comfort zone now and then can be empowering.

UNIT 10e Exercise 5, page 125

Does it help students if parents pay for their university education?

A study from UC (University of California) Merced into children paying for their own university education versus parents paying.

Established view was that if children take jobs while studying, or build up debts, it distracts them from their studies.

Findings:

1 The more parents pay, the worse children's academic results are plus more time children spend on leisure activities.
2 If parents pay, fewer children leave university before graduating than if children pay for their own education.

UNIT 12a Exercise 1, page 142

Answers to Geography quiz

1 Pakistan
2 Monaco: Number 1 in the world (3 billionnaires, population 37,800)
  USA: Number 13 in the world (536 billionnaires, population 321 million)
  Kuwait: Number 14 in the world (5 billionnaires, population 3.2 million people)
3 Japan (110 active)
  Indonesia (76 active)
  Nicaragua (8 active)
4 1 nitrogen (N_2) 78.084%
  2 oxygen (O_2) 20.9476%
  3 argon (Ar) 0.934%
  4 carbon dioxide (CO_2) 0.0314%
5 Aleppo (at least 6000BC)
  Varanasi (1800BC)
  Beijing (1045BC)
6 grassland (around 50%)
  desert (25%)
  rainforest (less than 12%)

UNIT 12d Exercise 1, page 148

Answers

1 Buenos Aires
2 Beijing
3 Bucharest
4 Jakarta
5 Mexico City

Answers taken from a number of sources. Other sources may quote different figures or answers.

NATIONAL GEOGRAPHIC LEARNING

***Life Advanced Student's Book,* 2nd Edition**
**Paul Dummett, John Hughes,
Helen Stephenson**

Vice President, Editorial Director:
   John McHugh

Executive Editor: Sian Mavor

Publishing Consultant: Karen Spiller

Project Managers: Sarah Ratcliff,
   Laura Brant

Development Editor: Jess Rackham

Editorial Manager: Claire Merchant

Head of Strategic Marketing ELT:
   Charlotte Ellis

Senior Content Project Manager:
   Nick Ventullo

Manufacturing Buyer: Elaine Bevan

Senior IP Analyst: Michelle McKenna

Senior IP Project Manager:
   Carissa Poweleit

Cover: Lisa Trager

Text design: emc design ltd.

Compositor: emc design ltd.

Audio: Tom Dick and Debbie Productions Ltd
   and Prolingua Productions

Video: Tom Dick and Debbie Productions Ltd

Contributing writer: Graham Burton
   (Grammar summary)

© 2019 National Geographic Learning, a Cengage Learning Company

ALL RIGHTS RESERVED. No part of this work covered by the copyright herein may be reproduced or distributed in any form or by any means, except as permitted by U.S. copyright law, without the prior written permission of the copyright owner.

"National Geographic", "National Geographic Society" and the Yellow Border Design are registered trademarks of the National Geographic Society
® Marcas Registradas

For product information and technology assistance, contact us at
Cengage Learning Customer & Sales Support, cengage.com/contact

For permission to use material from this text or product,
submit all requests online at **cengage.com/permissions**
Further permissions questions can be emailed to
permissionrequest@cengage.com

ISBN: 978-1-337-28633-6

National Geographic Learning
Cheriton House, North Way,
Andover, Hampshire, SP10 5BE
United Kingdom

National Geographic Learning, a Cengage Learning Company, has a mission to bring the world to the classroom and the classroom to life. With our English language programs, students learn about their world by experiencing it. Through our partnerships with National Geographic and TED Talks, they develop the language and skills they need to be successful global citizens and leaders.

Locate your local office at **international.cengage.com/region**

Visit National Geographic Learning online at **NGL.Cengage.com/ELT**
Visit our corporate website at **www.cengage.com**

CREDITS

Text: p106 'Brown is as pretty as white', Letters of note, March 04, 2014. http://www.lettersofnote.com/; p118 Source: Quote from Antz (1998); p132 'Daniel Kahneman: "We're beautiful devices"', by Oliver Burkeman, The Guardian, November 14, 2011. https://www.theguardian.com/; p132 Source: Quotes from 'Thinking, Fast and Slow' by Daniel Kahneman, Copyright © 2011; p15 'Shakespeare's Coined Words Now Common Currency', by Jennifer Vernon, National Geographic, April 22, 2004. http://news.nationalgeographic.com/; p22 'Moken: Sea Gypsies of Myanmar', by Jacques Ivanoff, National Geographic, April 2005. ngm.nationalgeographic.com/; p24 'Women Smokejumpers: Fighting Fires, Stereotypes', by Hillary Mayell, National Geographic, August 08, 2003. http://news.nationalgeographic.com/; p27 'Yosemite Climbing', by Mark Jenkins, National Geographic, May 2011. http://ngm.nationalgeographic.com/; p75 'The Enigma of Beauty', by Cathy Newman, National Geographic. http://science.nationalgeographic.com/; p82 'The Science of Selfies: A Five-City Comparison', by Cathy Newman, National Geographic, February 26, 2014. http://news.nationalgeographic.com/; p87 'The hackers life – my weekend at Defcon', by Lou Lesko, National Geographic. http://ngablog.com/; p111 'Diamond Shipwreck', by Roff Smith, National Geographic, October 2009. http://ngm.nationalgeographic.com/; p118 'Army Ants: Inside the Ranks', by Mark W. Moffett, National Geographic, August 2006. http://ngm.nationalgeographic.com/; p123 'The Hadza', by Michael Finkel, National Geographic, December 2009. http://ngm.nationalgeographic.com/; p135 'My Battle to Prove I Write Better Than an AI Robot Called "Emma"', by Sarah O'Connor, National Geographic, May 05, 2016. http://news.nationalgeographic.com/; p142 'What is Geo-literacy?', National Geographic. https://www.nationalgeographic.org/; p144 'On the Poet's Trail', by Howard Norman, National Geographic, February 2008. http://ngm.nationalgeographic.com/; p147 'How Wild Animals Are Hacking Life in the City', by Christine Dell'Amore, National Geographic, April 18, 2016. http://news.nationalgeographic.com/.
Cover: © Subir Basak/Getty Images.

Photos: 6 (tl) © Carl Court/Getty Images; 6 (tr) © Norbert Rosing/National Geographic Creative; 6 (bl) © American Institute of Architects; 6 (br) © Mauricio Abreu/Getty Images; 7 (tl) © Sebastian Wahlhuetter; 7 (tr) © Lynn Johnson/National Geographic Creative; 7 (mt) © David Edwards/National Geographic Creative; 7 (mb) © O. Louis Mazzatenta/National Geographic Creative; 7 (b) Jake Lyell/Alamy Stock Photo; 8 (tl) © Bobby Model/National Geographic Creative; 8 (tm) © Sasha Leahovcenco; 8 (tr) © Albert Dros; 8 (mtl) © Peter Dazeley/Getty Images; 8 (mtm) © TOUR EIFFEL – Illuminations PIERRE BIDEAU, Photo: © Fred Derwal/Getty Images; 8 (mtr) PCN Photography/Alamy Stock Photo; 8 (mbl) © Raul Touzon/National Geographic Creative; 8 (mbm) © W. Laui; 8 (mbr) © Jim Richardson/National Geographic Creative; 8 (bl) © John McEvoy; 8 (bm) © Shaaz Jung; 8 (br) © David Epperson/Getty Images; 9 © Bobby Model/National Geographic Creative; 10 (l) © XiXinXing/Shutterstock.com; 10 (r) © Chris Johns/National Geographic Creative; 12 © Bruno Schlumberger/Ottawa Citizen;

Printed in China by RR Donnelley
Print Number: 02   Print Year: 2019

15 © Damir Spanic/Getty Images; 16 Christopher Vallis/Alamy Stock Photo; 18 © Norbert Rosing/National Geographic Creative; 20 Irene Abdou/Alamy Stock Photo; 21 © Sasha Leahovcenco; 22 Hemis/Alamy Stock Photo; 24 © Tim Matsui/Liaison/Getty Images; 25 © Bates Littlehales/National Geographic Creative; 27 © Jimmy Chin/National Geographic Creative; 28 © Antonio Guillem/Shutterstock.com; 30 © Jimmy Chin/National Geographic Creative; 32 © Pete McBride/National Geographic Creative; 33 © Albert Dros; 34 (l) © Mlenny/Getty Images; 34 (r) Robin Weaver/Alamy Stock Photo; 36 (t) © Borge Ousland/National Geographic Creative; 36 (b) © Mike Clarke/AFP/Getty Images; 39 (t) VIEW Pictures Ltd/Alamy Stock Photo; 39 (b) © Hufton and Crow/Getty Images; 40 © Annie Griffiths/National Geographic Creative; 41 JLImages/Alamy Stock Photo; 42 © American Institute of Architects; 44 (left col) VIEW Pictures Ltd/Alamy Stock Photo; 44 (right col: l) © Albert Dros; 44 (right col: m) © Mlenny/Getty Images; 44 (right col: r) © Borge Ousland/National Geographic Creative; 45 © Peter Dazeley/Getty Images; 46 (t) Haiyin Wang/Alamy Stock Photo; 46 (b) © The Asahi Shimbun/Getty Images; 48 © Bettmann/Getty Images; 51 © Noel Vasquez/Getty Images; 52 ZUMA Press, Inc./Alamy Stock Photo; 54 Jake Lyell/Alamy Stock Photo; 56 Igor Stevanovic/Alamy Stock Photo; 57 © TOUR EIFFEL – Illuminations PIERRE BIDEAU, Photo: © Fred Derwal/Getty Images; 58 © Pablo Corral Vega/National Geographic Creative; 60 Loop Images Ltd/Alamy Stock Photo; 63 Michael DeFreitas South America/Alamy Stock Photo; 64 © Design Pics Inc/National Geographic Creative; 65 GlowImages/Alamy Stock Photo; 66 © Mauricio Abreu/Getty Images; 68 © Mark Cosslett/National Geographic Creative; 69 PCN Photography/Alamy Stock Photo; 70 (t) Marcus Spedding/Alamy Stock Photo; 70 (m) © Christopher Furlong/Getty Images; 70 (b) © Emanuele Ciccomartino/robertharding/Getty Images; 72 Fry Vanessa/Alamy Stock Photo; 74 (l) Catchlight Visual Services/Alamy Stock Photo; 74 (ml) Fancy/Alamy Stock Photo; 74 (mml) © O. Louis Mazzatenta/National Geographic Creative; 74 (mmr) Bill Bachmann/Alamy Stock Photo; 74 (mr) Photo Japan/Alamy Stock Photo; 74 (r) LJSphotography/Alamy Stock Photo; 75 © Frans Lemmens/Getty Images; 76 Werli Francois/Alamy Stock Photo; 78 © Sebastian Wahlhuetter; 80 © Lynn Johnson/National Geographic Creative; 81 © Raul Touzon/National Geographic Creative; 82 © http://selfiecity.net, Dr. Lev Manovich, Noritz Stefaner, Dr. Mehrdad Yazdani, Dr. Dominikus Baur, Jay Chow, Daniel Goddemeyer, Alise Tifentale, Nadav Hochman, 2014; 84 © Jon Feingersh/Blend Images/Corbis; 87 © Lou Lesko; 88 © Doug Perrine/naturepl.com; 89 © AP Photo/AP Images; 90 © Lynn Johnson/National Geographic Creative; 92 © Harald Slauschek/Getty Images; 93 © W. Laui; 94 WENN Ltd/Alamy Stock Photo; 96 © Nisian Hughes/Getty Images; 98 Trinity Mirror/Mirrorpix/Alamy Stock Photo; 99 © Tino Soriano/National Geographic Creative; 100 Mayday/Alamy Stock Photo; 101 Mark Eveleigh/Alamy Stock Photo; 102 © Alex Abbott; 104 © Mel Finkelstein/NY Daily News/Getty Images; 105 © Jim Richardson/National Geographic Creative; 106 Science History Images/Alamy Stock Photo; 108 © Jules Gervais Courtellemont/National Geographic Creative; 110 © OSOMEDIA/Age Fotostock; 111 (t, b) © Amy Toensing/National Geographic Creative; 112 © Rich Reid/National Geographic Creative; 113 © Lawrence Smith/National Geographic Creative; 114 © O. Louis Mazzatenta/National Geographic Creative; 116 Mark Richardson/Alamy Stock Photo; 117 © John McEvoy; 118 (t) Photo 12/Alamy Stock Photo; 118 (b) © Jason Edwards/National Geographic Creative; 120 © B. Yen; 123 I6C © Matthieu Paley/National Geographic Creative; 124 chuck/Alamy Stock Photo; 125 © Alex Treadway/National Geographic Creative; 126 © COLLART Hervé/Getty Images; 128 © James Forte/National Geographic Creative; 129 © Shaaz Jung; 130 (all) © Joel Sartore/National Geographic Creative; 132 © Tom Barrick, Chris Clark, SGHMS/Science Photo Library/Getty Images; 135 Xinhua/Alamy Stock Photo; 136 © PhotoAlto/Eric Audras/Getty Images; 138 © Carl Court/Getty Images; 139 (l) AF archive/Alamy Stock Photo; 139 (r) © Zak Hussein/Getty Images; 140 Ice Tea Media/Alamy Stock Photo; 141 © David Epperson/Getty Images; 142 © Purvash Jha; 144 ASO FUJITA/a.collectionRF/amana images inc./Alamy Stock Photo; 145 © wragg/Getty Images; 146 (tl) © Matt Knoth/Shutterstock.com; 146 (tm) © Joel Sartore/National Geographic Creative; 146 (tr) © Martin Prochazkacz/Shutterstock.com; 146 (bl) © Maciej Olszewski/Shutterstock.com; 146 (br) © Design Pics Inc/National Geographic Creative; 147 © Steve Winter/National Geographic Creative; 148 © Randy Olson/National Geographic Creative; 149 © Eric Kruszewski/National Geographic Creative; 150 © David Edwards/National Geographic Creative; 152 © Mint Images - Frans Lanting/Getty Images.

Illustrations: 18, 76, 122 David Russell; 154 Laszlo Veres/Beehive Illustration.

ACKNOWLEDGEMENTS

The *Life* publishing team would like to thank the following teachers and students who provided invaluable and detailed feedback on the first edition:
Armik Adamians, Colombo Americano, Cali; Carlos Alberto Aguirre, Universidad Madero, Puebla; Anabel Aikin, La Escuela Oficial de Idiomas de Coslada, Madrid; Pamela Alvarez, Colegio Eccleston, Lanús; Manuel Antonio, CEL – Unicamp, São Paulo; Bob Ashcroft, Shonan Koka University; Linda Azzopardi, Clubclass; Éricka Bauchwitz, Universidad Madero, Puebla; Paola Biancolini, Università Cattolica del Sacro Cuore, Milan; Laura Bottiglieri, Universidad Nacional de Salta; Richard Brookes, Brookes Talen, Aalsmeer; Maria Cante, Universidad Madero, Puebla; Carmín Castillo, Universidad Madero, Puebla; Ana Laura Chacón, Universidad Madero, Puebla; Somchao Chatnaridom, Suratthani Rajabhat University, Surat Thani; Adrian Cini, British Study Centres, London; Andrew Clarke, Centre of English Studies, Dublin; Mariano Cordoni, Centro Universitario de Idiomas, Buenos Aries; Monica Cuellar, Universidad La Gran Colombia; Jacqui Davis-Bowen, St Giles International; Nuria Mendoza Dominguez, Universidad Nebrija, Madrid; Robin Duncan, ITC London; Christine Eade, Libera Università Internazionale degli Studi Sociali Guido Carli, Rome; Leopoldo Pinzon Escobar, Universidad Catolica; Joanne Evans, Linguarama, Berlin; Juan David Figueroa, Colombo Americano, Cali; Emmanuel Flores, Universidad del Valle de Puebla; Sally Fryer, University of Sheffield, Sheffield; Antonio David Berbel García, Escuela Oficial de Idiomas de Almería; Lia Gargioni, Feltrinelli Secondary School, Milan; Roberta Giugni, Galileo Galilei Secondary School, Legnano; Monica Gomez, Universidad Pontificia Bolivariana; Doctor Erwin Gonzales, Centro de Idiomas Universidad Nacional San Agustin; Ivonne Gonzalez, Universidad de La Sabana; J Gouman, Pieter Zandt Scholengemeenschap, Kampen; Cherryll Harrison, UNINT, Rome; Lottie Harrison, International House Recoleta; Marjo Heij, CSG Prins Maurits, Middelharnis; María del Pilar Hernández, Universidad Madero, Puebla; Luz Stella Hernandez, Universidad de La Sabana; Rogelio Herrera, Colombo Americano, Cali; Amy Huang, Language Canada Taipei; Huang Huei-Jiun, Pu Tai Senior High School; Nelson Jaramillo, Colombo Americano, Cali; Jacek Kaczmarek, Xiehe YouDe High School, Taipei; Thurgadevi Kalay, Kaplan, Singapore; Noreen Kane, Centre of English Studies, Dublin; Billy Kao, Jinwen University of Science and Technology; Shih-Fan Kao, Jinwen University of Science and Technology, Taipei; Youmay Kao, Mackay Junior College of Medicine, Nursing, and Management, Taipei; Fleur Kelder, Vechtstede College, Weesp; Dr Sarinya Khattiya, Chiang Mai University; Lucy Khoo, Kaplan, Singapore; Karen Koh, Kaplan, Singapore; Susan Langerfeld, Liceo Scientifico Statale Augusto Righi, Rome; Hilary Lawler, Centre of English Studies, Dublin; Eva Lendi, Kantonsschule Zürich Nord, Zürich; Evon Lo, Jinwen University of Science and Technology; Peter Loftus, Centre of English Studies, Dublin; José Luiz, Inglês com Tecnologia, Cruzeiro; Christopher MacGuire, UC Language Center; Eric Maher, Centre of English Studies, Dublin; Nick Malewski, ITC London; Claudia Maribell Loo, Universidad Madero, Puebla; Malcolm Marr, ITC London; Graciela Martin, ICANA (Belgrano); Erik Meek, CS Vincent van Gogh, Assen,; Marlene Merkt, Kantonsschule Zürich Nord, Zürich; David Moran, Qatar University, Doha; Rosella Morini, Feltrinelli Secondary School, Milan; Judith Mundell, Quarenghi Adult Learning Centre, Milan; Cinthya Nestor, Universidad Madero, Puebla; Peter O'Connor, Musashino University, Tokyo; Cliona O'Neill, Trinity School, Rome; María José Colón Orellana, Escola Oficial d'Idiomes de Terrassa, Barcelona; Viviana Ortega, Universidad Mayor, Santiago; Luc Peeters, Kyoto Sangyo University, Kyoto; Sanja Brekalo Pelin, La Escuela Oficial de Idiomas de Coslada, Madrid; Itzel Carolina Pérez, Universidad Madero, Puebla; Sutthima Peung, Rajamangala University of Technology Rattanakosin; Marina Pezzuoli, Liceo Scientifico Amedeo Avogadro, Rome; Andrew Pharis, Aichi Gakuin University, Nagoya; Hugh Podmore, St Giles International; Carolina Porras, Universidad de La Sabana; Brigit Portilla, Colombo Americano, Cali; Soudaben Pradeep, Kaplan; Judith Puertas, Colombo Americano, Cali; Takako Ramsden, Kyoto Sangyo University, Kyoto; Sophie Rebel-Dijkstra, Aeres Hogeschool; Zita Reszler, Nottingham Language Academy, Nottingham; Sophia Rizzo, St Giles International; Gloria Stella Quintero Riveros, Universidad Catolica; Cecilia Rosas, Euroidiomas; Eleonora Salas, IICANA Centro, Córdoba; Victoria Samaniego, La Escuela Oficial de Idiomas de Pozuelo de Alarcón, Madrid; Jeanette Sandre, Universidad Madero, Puebla; Bruno Scafati, ARICANA; Anya Shaw, International House Belgrano; Anne Smith, UNINT, Rome & University of Rome Tor Vergata; Suzannah Spencer-George, British Study Centres, Bournemouth; Students of Cultura Inglesa, São Paulo; Makiko Takeda, Aichi Gakuin University, Nagoya; Jilly Taylor, British Study Centres, London; Juliana Trisno, Kaplan, Singapore; Ruey Miin Tsao, National Cheng Kung University, Tainan City; Michelle Uitterhoeve, Vechtstede College, Weesp; Anna Maria Usai, Liceo Spallanzani, Rome; Carolina Valdiri, Colombo Americano, Cali; Gina Vasquez, Colombo Americano, Cali; Andreas Vikran, NET School of English, Milan; Mimi Watts, Università Cattolica del Sacro Cuore, Milan; Helen Ward, Oxford; Yvonne Wee, Kaplan Higher Education Academy, Singapore; Christopher Wood, Meijo University; Yanina Zagarrio, ARICANA